Managing Quality in Young Children's
Programs: The Leader's Role
MARY L. CULKIN, Ed.

Telling a Different Story: Teaching and
Literacy in an Urban Preschool
CATHERINE WILSON

Young Children Reinvent Arithmetic:
Implications of Piaget's Theory, 2nd Edition
CONSTANCE KAMII

Supervision in Early Childhood Education
2nd Ed.: A Developmental Perspective
JOSEPH J. CARUSO & M. TEMPLE FAWCETT

The Early Childhood Curriculum: A Review
of Current Research, 3rd Edition
CAROL SEEFELDT, Ed.

Leadership in Early Childhood 2nd Ed.:
The Pathway to Professionalism
JILLIAN RODD

Inside a Head Start Center:
Developing Policies from Practice
DEBORAH CEGLOWSKI

Uncommon Caring:
Learning from Men Who Teach
Young Children
JAMES R. KING

Teaching and Learning in a Diverse World:
Multicultural Education for Young Children,
2nd Ed.
PATRICIA G. RAMSEY

Windows on Learning:
Documenting Young Children's Work
JUDY HARRIS HELM, SALLEE BENEKE,
& KATHY STEINHEIMER

Bringing Reggio Emilia Home:
An Innovative Approach to
Early Childhood Education
LOUISE BOYD CADWELL

Major Trends and Issues in Early
Childhood Education: Challenges
Controversies, and Insights
JOAN P. ISENBERG &
MARY RENCK JALONGO, Eds.

Master Players:
Learning from Children at Play
GRETCHEN REYNOLDS & ELIZABETH JONES

Understanding Young Children's Behavior:
A Guide for Early Childhood Professionals
JILLIAN RODD

Understanding Quantitative and Qualitative
Research in Early Childhood Education
WILLIAM L. GOODWIN & LAURA D. GOODWIN

Diversity in the Classroom:
New Approaches to the Education
of Young Children, 2nd Ed.
FRANCES E. KENDALL

Developmentally Appropriate Practice
in "Real Life"
CAROL ANNE WIEN

Quality in Family Child Care
and Relative Care
SUSAN KONTOS, CAROLLEE HOWES,
MARYBETH SHINN, & ELLEN GALINSKY

Using the Supportive Play Model:
Individualized Intervention in Early
Childhood Practice
MARGARET K. SHERIDAN,
GILBERT M. FOLEY, & SARA H. RADLINSKI

The Full-Day Kindergarten:
A Dynamic Themes Curriculum, 2nd Ed.
DORIS PRONIN FROMBERG

Experimenting with the World: John Dewey
and the Early Childhood Classroom
HARRIET K. CUFFARO

New Perspectives in Early Childhood
Teacher Education: Bringing
Practitioners into the Debate
STACIE G. GOFFIN & DAVID E. DAY, Eds.

Assessment Methods for Infants and
Toddlers: Transdisciplinary Team
Approaches
DORIS BERGEN

The Emotional Development of Young
Children: Building an Emotion-Centered
Curriculum
MARION C. HYSON

(Continued)

Managing Quality in Young Children's Programs

THE LEADER'S ROLE

Mary L. Culkin
Editor

FOREWORD BY SHARON LYNN KAGAN

Teachers College, Columbia University
New York and London

Published by Teachers College Press, 1234 Amsterdam Avenue, New York, NY 10027

Library of Congress Cataloging-in-Publication Data

Managing quality in young children's programs : the leader's role / edited by Mary L. Culkin ; foreword by Sharon Lynn Kagan.
    p. cm. — (Early childhood education series)
    Includes bibliographical references and index.
    ISBN 0-8077-3916-2 (pbk. : alk. paper)
    Early childhood education—United States—Administration. 2. Educational leadership—United States   I. Culkin, Mary L.   II. Early childhood education series (Teachers College Press)
    LB2822.6.M36 2000
    372.12—dc21   99-047668

ISBN 0-8077-3916-2 (paper)

Printed on acid-free paper
Manufactured in the United States of America

07   06   05   04   03   02   01   8   7   6   5   4   3   2

To my mother and father:

Florence Culkin, who showed me the joy and challenge
of working with young children;

Hosmer Culkin, who demonstrated the value
of commitment to community

Contents

PART II: A Credential for Program Administrators

Foreword

That a fine, thoughtful volume on early care and education directors has arrived is cause for both wonder and applause. "Wonder" in that it is altogether remarkable that for decades, fields of organizational development, industrial psychology, and business management (to mention but a few) have focused on the importance of the leader. Indeed, scholars and practitioners have noted that the success of any institution is directly attributable to the caliber of the leader. Yet, early care and education, while acknowledging the importance of leadership implicitly, has been slow to act explicitly on it. "Applause" is due because the field has finally come to recognize and grapple with the importance of directorship and leadership. This volume, then, is not only welcome, but needs to be hall-marked as a pivotal contribution, a turning point in the reconceptualized and rapidly changing field of early care and education.

As prelude to this volume, it is important to ask why early childhood has been so slow to recognize the importance of leadership and director-ship. Why is it that information that has permeated and influenced other fields has been so remote from early care and education? In part, this question reflects the isolation that has long characterized the field. But that is only part of the answer; something more fundamental is at work. It may be that the field has always focused on the role of the teacher, assuming that the teacher is the person closest to the child and therefore simultaneously the prime arbiter and architect of quality. This suggests that early childhood has historically viewed quality as a characteristic of the more immediate surround (e.g., the home, the classroom) in which the child spends time. Pedagogical environments, though rhetorically deemed critical to healthy development, have actually been conceptual-ized in a somewhat circumscribed way. It may also be that focus on the teacher (in contrast to the system) was easier; we could justifiably talk about low levels of training and even lower levels of compensation. As early childhood pedagogues, there was most certainly greater comfort (and relatedly more interest) in addressing alterations in classroom practice. Further, for decades the early childhood research enterprise focused on classroom variables, including teachers as critical pedagogical factors.

Today, as the field widens its horizons, as it beckons fresh research, and as it investigates work in allied fields, there is a new awakening to the importance of other environmental variables that also affect quality. We are reminded of the importance of the early childhood workplace and its overall characteristics. We are reminded of the need to identify and support the infrastructure. And we are reminded that, ultimately, the classroom and program, while critical, are not the sole influences of quality and child outcomes. In other words, there is profound shift from the classrooms and programs as the primary locus of early childhood education to the entire early childhood organization and system as the focus for change.

Such dramatic changes, though not always immediately apparent, call for new kinds of leaders, individuals with diverse and rich training, individuals interested in the art and science of leadership, and individuals who are willing and able to think anew. These changes also occasion the need for the field to think about different kinds of leadership. Program directors are one important group. They are joined by early childhood leaders who emphasize policy in their work, early childhood leaders who work with communities, early childhood leaders who inspire us to new pedagogical heights, and early childhood leaders who envision an emerging system and the field as a whole. So that, while the focus on program directors is critical, demanding the field to think hard about the skills, knowledge, and habits of attitude and being this kind of leadership requires, the field must also consider if and how the development of directors' credentials will impact the advancement of leadership in these other areas. Will it narrow the definition of leadership? Will it forge the path for garnering increased attention to leadership in general? Will it evoke issues that apply to all types of leaders?

Indeed, the development of directors' credentials does raise serious policy and practice issues. I am indebted to my colleagues—the authors of this volume—who have not shied away from the challenges. It is to their credit and to that of Mary Culkin that we are able to have a rich discourse on the array of issues that impact the advancement of all types of leadership in early care and education. In many ways, then, those working on the development of a directors' credentials may be regarded as the advance team; the pioneers grappling with the difficult issues that must be addressed as we shape a leadership agenda where all forms of early care and education leadership can thrive.

Permit a word about the issues. Anyone who reads this volume in its entirety will be treated to a rich panorama of what is taking place in the field, and to the panoply of issues we face. Interestingly, the issues that challenge the development of a leadership agenda generally and a directors' credentials specifically address precisely the same themes that the field has wrestled with for decades: quality, equity, access, standardization, and definition—quintessential problems that characterize human services in a market-driven democracy.

Although many of these issues are discussed in this volume, a few warrant special emphasis at this juncture in the social trajectory of the field. First, the equity and access issue: As a field we need to decide the degree to which we are willing to create barriers (in the form of credentials) to key leadership roles in the field. When all is said and done, credentials, while leading to quality, may boomerang to lift the entry bar too high. We must be ever mindful of the fine line this exercise beckons us to walk, always recognizing that credentials don't automatically equate with quality. Second, on the allied issues of standardization and definition, we need to be mindful, particularly in an era of devolution of all sorts of authorities to the states, just how much state (and local) variation is tolerable in the establishment of directors' (or any leadership) credentials. If, indeed, the credentials are to set a new standard and to be an elixir of quality for the profession, then why should they be idiosyncratic from jurisdiction to jurisdiction? It seems we must be vigilant in examining the desirability and feasibility of advancing *a* Directors' credentials or *many* Directors' credentials. What is expedient may not always be excellent. Finally, if nothing else, contemporary events demand that early educators be strategists. Additional thought must be vested in creating the infrastructure—the licensing, training, regulatory, accountability systems—that will foster the implementation and sustenance of directors' credentials. The creation job is only the beginning of the task. To that end, those involved in considering the development of directors' credentials must vigorously join forces with others in the field who are advancing the early childhood agenda writ large. Without more support for early care and education generally, efforts to create and institute credentials, no matter how well conceived, will falter. As the field grows and we focus our interests and energies, we must remember—just like the Director in his or her center—success transcends the individual; it is a characteristic of our collective energies and investments. In focusing on directors' credentials, Mary Culkin and the contributors to this volume are paving the way to a new era of early childhood leadership. To them, we all owe much appreciation.

Sharon Lynn Kagan

Children's Program Administrators and the Advancement of an Administrative Credential

Mary L. Culkin

Until now the early care and education (ECE) field has considered one professional—the teacher—as the individual central to a child's developmental and learning experience. Working together, a group of teachers—the faculty—is the heart of the children's program or school. The quality of this teaching staff is an important criterion for parents in choosing an educational or care setting. In ECE the focus of professional development efforts, compensation improvements, higher education, and often advocacy efforts has been on supporting and training credentialed teachers as well as other care and education providers at work in a variety of settings.

Now, with the expansion of programs for young children over the last decade, the profession's view of the roles important in the provision of quality services has broadened. In addition to teachers, other positions—such as parent specialist, child care health specialist, inclusivity or diversity specialist, and administrators at various levels and in different types of organizations—are recognized as significant contributors to their organization's success. ECE practitioners recognize that the administrative leadership role is a crucial part of the production of quality services.

One result of this expanded view is the need to develop a director credential. This book recounts the current conversation about early care and education directors, continues the dialogue, and presents the case for a director credential. A credential may be the way to support directors in their initial administrative role as well as in their ongoing, expanding roles as managers and leaders.

Throughout this book the terms *director* and *administrator* are used to represent several titles that ECE programs use to designate the person in a management role. These include, but are not limited to, "program direc-tor," "program coordinator," "site supervisor," and "executive director." Jobs with these titles might be held by persons working in different types of programs, including child care for infants or preschool-age children, school-age child care, Head Start programs, family support programs, resource and referral agencies, and community-based early care and edu-cation initiatives. Such programs may be sponsored by different public, nonprofit, and for-profit organizations of different sizes.

A NEW APPRECIATION FOR THE WORK OF THE DIRECTOR

Studies of early care and education service quality, and of training for program directors, have emphasized the director's experience and train-ing as factors contributing to the provision of higher-quality service levels (Bloom, 1989, 1991; Bloom, Sheerer, & Britz, 1991; Bredekamp & Willer, 1996; Cost, Quality and Child Outcomes Study Team, 1995). Several ini-tiatives are examining the director's role and the possibility of a credential for the position. The American Business Collaboration for Quality Depen-dent Care (ABC Initiative) is investing in director training and creden-tialing through several projects at the state, local, and community agency level. Wheelock College's Center for Career Development in Early Care and Education is also examining and advancing leadership in the early childhood field by promoting the following:

- An increased understanding of how managers and leaders integrate their work with the work of their staff to provide high-quality services
- A recognition of the need to support new early care and education directors with training and professional preparation as they make what has been a *typical* transition from classroom to administrative responsibilities
- A commitment to promoting increased opportunities for diverse leadership in early care and education (Taking the Lead Initia-tive, 1997)

The business community is also interested in credentialing directors. Employers have a strong interest in strategies to improve the quality of child-care centers used by their employees. Working through the ABC Initiative, employers have supported numerous improvement initiatives across the country. To the business community, it should be self-evident that directors have a strong influence on producing and improving child care quality. Work/Family Directions, which administers the American Business Collaboration funds, hosted a symposium in 1995 designed to stimulate interest in director credentialing by bringing together leaders and local groups working on the issue. Out of that meeting an informal caucus emerged that initiated this book and also organized discussions of credentialing at national and state meetings and conferences.

In the fall of 1996, a dozen national foundations with strategic interests in early care and education joined in an effort to support an early care and education leadership initiative. The Center for Career Development in Early Care and Education at Wheelock College was selected to lead and manage the national 3-year initiative. Called "Taking the Lead," it aims to improve the quality of early childhood programs through strong, diverse, and effective leadership. This involves advancing the development of director credentialing and expanding the skills of new and existing leaders within the field to generate increased public and private investment in quality early care and education. Ten pilot projects are under way: four in director credentialing and six designed to test innovative approaches to developing emerging leaders.

The movement to develop new and improved professional preparation for administrators is occurring simultaneously with increased efforts to improve the quality of ECE services. (See Chapter 3 for a discussion of linking a credential and funding levels.) It also addresses the field's anticipation of a changing, more demanding and diversified business/service environment. (See Chapter 12 for a look at future market and industry trends.) We know that 80% of center child care is of low to mediocre quality and that low-quality child care settings lack the learning opportunities that promote children's healthy development (Cost, Quality and Child Outcomes Study Team, 1995).

Further, research findings regarding brain development stress the importance of nurturing a young child's capacity for learning (Shore, 1997). A longitudinal study of children in typical child care found that

> high quality child care is an important element in achieving the goal of having all children ready for school. . . . Children who attended higher quality child care centers performed better on measures of both cognitive skills (e.g., math and language abilities) and social skills (e.g., interactions with peers, problem behaviors) in child care and through the transition into school. (Peisner-Feinberg, Burchinal, Clifford, Culkin, Howes, Kagan, Yazejian, Byler, Rustici, & Zelazo, 1999, p. 1)

This greater understanding of how early nurturing and learning affect later school-based learning only emphasizes the importance of quality care and education services for infants and preschool-age children. As this connection becomes better understood and more accepted, informed consumers will demand higher-quality programs. Studies of quality services for children indicate that these programs will require that administrators have skills and knowledge in child development, teaching, and management and leadership.

WHY A DIRECTOR CREDENTIAL?

In a growing, changing ECE market, understanding the work of the director and providing for her or his professional preparation is essential. Directors are requesting more specialized training for their administrative work (Buckner, 1988; Culkin, 1994; Larkin, 1992; Morgan et al., 1993; Poster & Neugebauer, 1998). They also express the need for professional support through mentoring and coaching as well as opportunities for networking and training (Rafanello & Bloom, 1997). Directors' interest in increased professional preparation and continuing career development (see Chapter 11) coincides with both the field's efforts to increase quality and consumer concern about child care services. This convergence of ideas and needs in the ECE profession results in an opportunity to develop and test a variety of approaches to director credentialing and training. That variety provides a basis for developing credentials that reflect the complexity of the job and serve as the basis for awarding a certificate acknowledging a practitioner's professional capacity.

In past considerations of service quality, the ECE field has been focused on the teacher's contribution rather than on the director's. This book presents the view that the director is also central to the success of an ECE program and that a director credential will better equip directors with the necessary interdisciplinary and leadership knowledge and skills. A credential is not simply a stamp of approval, but rather a well-designed process that can frame and delineate a course of ongoing opportunities for career development. The creation of a credential with which to certify directors—at the start of, or at a later point in, their administrative careers—is an important step in the development of the ECE field.

In the early childhood field, our appreciation of the central relationship between children and teachers, combined with an appreciation of the democratic process, may have led us to minimize the central role of a director. Directors or other administrators play a leadership role in managing organizations toward attaining the vision of quality service. Taking a look at administrators means considering the interplay of authority, management, practice, communication, and leadership in day-to-day practice in ECE organizations.

Expanding the Focus

Taking a fresh look at the role of the director can re-form and shape the way we understand the work of an early childhood service organization. An expanded view keeps the focus on the child and teacher (or other caregiver) while broadening the frame to include families as well as organizational features authorized as responsibilities of the director.

Let's imagine it by thinking of a video camera scanning a classroom at a child care center, preschool, or Head Start program. The camera focuses on a teacher greeting a 4-year-old girl and her dad and inviting the child to put her coat and tote bag into her cubby. The child's dad signs her into the program for the day, gives a goodbye hug, bids his daughter and the teacher goodbye, and is off to work.

The camera pulls back from the closeup to a shot of a group of kindergarten boys and girls working together to build a city out of wooden blocks. Then the camera's lens opens to include additional classrooms and focuses on parents talking with teachers as they drop their children off for the day. Next we see a teacher, tapped by the administrator for her expertise in science activities, taking the lead in planning a training session for her fellow teachers and the administrator (Senge, 1990). Then the frame expands to include other activities. We see (1) the director and the teaching team in a curriculum planning meeting. They are struggling to resolve a conflict between two teachers about the most appropriate way to plan a developmentally appropriate and challenging curriculum for their increasingly diverse groups of children. The camera continues tracking (2) children engaged with teachers, and with each other, in learning activities; (3) two board members, a parent, and corporate volunteers planning a fund-raiser; and (4) an auditor at work in the director's office. At the periphery of the picture's frame, the focus blurs and expands to include the offices, shops, homes, and other buildings in the local neighborhood and larger community.

The camera's pan of the program involves an integrative process. This image of the program, established in a community, presents a more complete view of the interrelated parts and activities within an early care and education organization and culture (Schein, 1991). In this picture and in the planning for the future, there is no division between value of the teacher–child relationship and the worth of administrative or organizational structures that support classrooms and child, family, and staff learning and development.

An Organizational View

Rather than shifting emphasis from the critical importance of child–teacher relationships, this wide-angle approach puts a clearer organizational frame around the classrooms where children and teachers learn together. It circumscribes a more complete organizational view that includes the varied functions that serve children, families, staff, and community. Within this broader frame, the administrator, generally called director, is in a central role, managing and facilitating staff development, program resource development, and communication with external organizations. By shifting perspective to an organizational view and including the functions of a stronger director role, one looks toward promoting comprehensive organizational strength, adequate human and financial resources, and program stability and longevity. The broader perspective acknowledges the solid foundation of human and community resources—really the relationships—necessary to sustain early care and education organizations. The administrator is in the center of that network of relationships, often acting as leader but sometimes acting as follower, thereby providing the opportunity for other staff, parents, or community members to lead (Kelley, 1992). Figure 1.1 maps the primary stakeholders who interact with ECE administrators. Children, their families, and staff are the key stakeholders, but, as the diagram illustrates, an administrator interacts with a wide range of stakeholders more or less frequently, depending on their role in the children's program. While the number of stakeholders appears daunting, an able, skilled director can manage these relationships, using reflection to improve practice (Schön, 1983) and interacting effectively with the wide variety of individuals and groups. As one former director said, "Almost all management is by negotiation. Further a lot of tasks that you have to carry out are with people who are not within your organization . . . . The border between what is the organization and what is the place where it meets the environment keeps changing" (Culkin, 1994, p. 162). Emphasis on understanding a director's role, and a director credential, can reframe ECE administration as a central figure in this often complex organizational environment.

As the interest in director training and credentialing becomes more compelling, there is an opportunity to expand understanding of how an ECE organization operates. More emphasis on organizational issues serves to improve quality levels in child and family programs by building increased capacity in a cadre of credentialed administrators. Hopefully, training certified by a credential will provide administrators with the tools required to deal more effectively with their organization's internal and external constituents in the domains of service and policy. The goal of director development efforts—after considerable thought, planning,

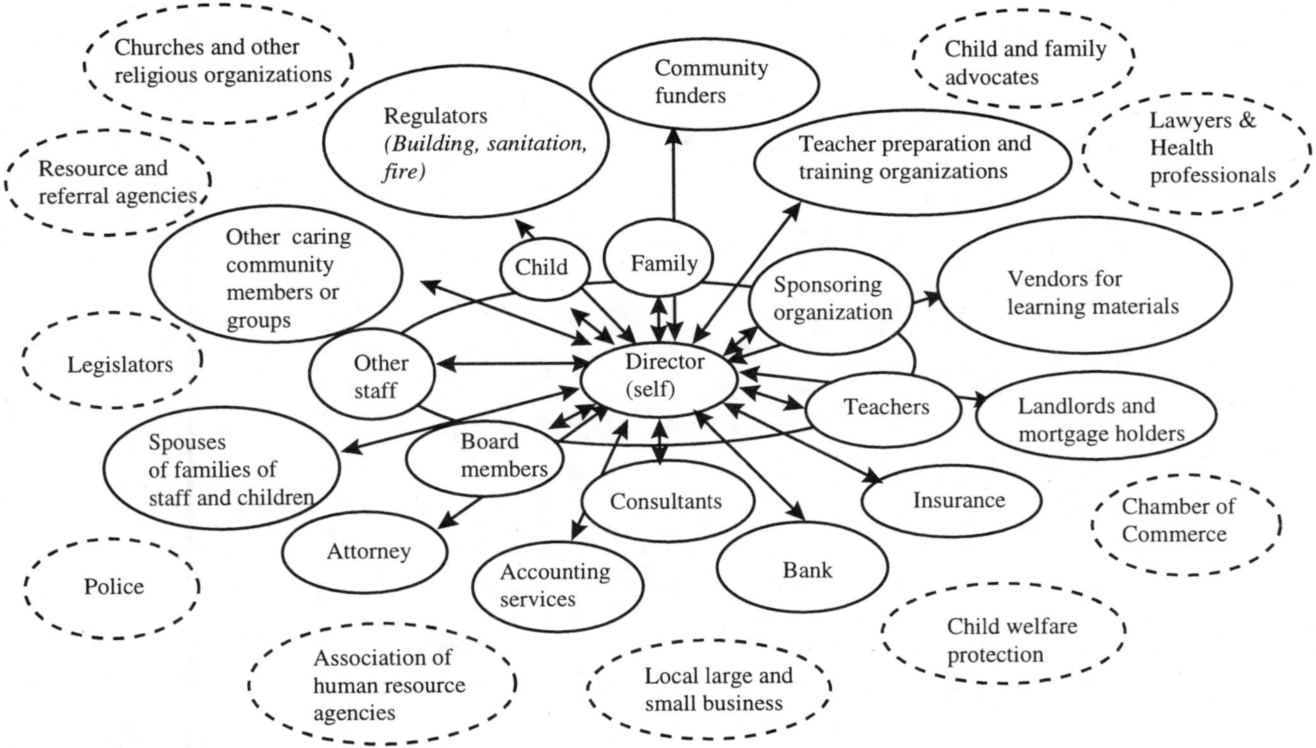

Figure 1.1. Stakeholder Map: Early Care and Education Administrator

and experimentation—is to improve the quality of early childhood settings and support the development of more complex and stable ECE organizations. ECE organizations serve children and their families. These consumers are the individuals who will benefit most from improved institutional know-how, organizational stability, and service quality improvements thought to be associated with more experienced, involved directors. With those consumers and improved service in mind, consider the current career development situation for directors. What professional preparation do directors have now, what is the focus of that training, and how might a credential change things?

CURRENT STATUS OF PROFESSIONAL PREPARATION

Because most directors are promoted from a teaching position, learning on the job remains the prime training ground for the majority of them (Rafanello & Bloom, 1997). New directors report that they face a difficult task as they struggle to learn the new and very different role of administrator (Culkin, 1994; Larkin, 1992). Often directors will strive to retain their old perspective as teachers, although they really must develop a different authoritative perspective to manage and lead their organization. Newly appointed directors have a new authority that they may not want or feel comfortable with. Generally, after much success in their program's service domain, they find themselves firmly situated in the policy domain dealing daily with matters of budget and organizational dynamics that they have little or no preparation for. It is not surprising that directors have expressed a desire for additional management training.

Current preservice and inservice director-focused training opportunities are varied and uneven in terms of scope of knowledge and design of learning activities. Some are embedded in higher education, others are based on practical experience, and some combine the theoretical with the practical, either in higher education settings or in programs designed for on-the-job learning. Around the country, although the formal requirements for a director's professional preparation are limited, directors report that they want more and varied opportunities for professional learning (Buckner, 1988; Culkin, 1994; Morgan et al., 1993; Rafanello & Bloom, 1997). As a result, more chances for learning are becoming available. In some parts of the country, director support groups are flourishing. At professional meetings there are increased opportunities for directors to study on separate conference tracks, and some higher education institutions offer newly designed coursework. But more typically, directors continue to learn to manage and lead through on-the-job experience (Burchinal & Culkin, 1995; Manning, 1998; Rafanello & Bloom, 1997).

While we know that management training is the most requested professional development experience in the ECE field today (Morgan et al., 1993), the typical administrator has had limited or no coursework on management before taking on the role of director (Burchinal & Culkin, 1995). State requirements for management professional preparation for early childhood directors range from those states that require no training to other states' expectation of several administrative and management courses. As we design a credential, an examination of the various types of knowledge required, and of the sets of competencies required for administrative work, is a crucial step. (See Chapter 5 for a review of core knowledge required by directors.)

Despite the lack of cohesion in professional preparation for administrators, there is a lively conversation under way about the components of a director's interdisciplinary knowledge base, role, and responsibilities. This book informs that conversation and gives voice to authors who have been at work articulating the issues, problems, and possibilities that surround expanded and explicit knowledge about both an administrator's role and a possible credential. The book brings together existing knowledge about the director, presents a discussion of the importance of the director's role from several views, and introduces the issues that need discussion and resolution as the movement for a director credential evolves within the early childhood profession.

WHAT ARE THE EARLY CARE AND EDUCATION DIRECTOR'S RESPONSIBILITIES?

The lack of broad, consistent attention to the role of a director means that one cannot yet point to a formal consensus concerning the role and work of the director. Nonetheless, there is overall agreement about a director's basic areas of responsibility (Decker & Decker, 1988; Hewes & Hartman, 1972; Hildebrand, 1984; Sciarra & Dorsey, 1990; Seaver & Cartwright, 1986). In the 1970s, a list of director responsibilities began circulating in the ECE field (Morgan, 1997). The list, provided as an Appendix to Chapter 3, describes a set of competencies required for the successful administration of early childhood programs.

A competent director possesses knowledge and skills in a variety of areas. The administrator's need to acquire this kind of comprehensive, interdisciplinary knowledge must be viewed in light of the facts that (1) most directors report limited support during the learning process and (2) salaries for directors vary widely. Directors' salaries were on average about $25,000 in the 1995 Cost, Quality and Child Outcomes Study and ranged from $20,000 to $78,000 in a 1996 study of salaries of campus child care center directors ("Results of the Child Care Directors Survey," 1996). Despite low salaries relative to management positions in other fields, work toward agreed-upon director competencies and knowledge is an important part of the director credentialing effort. Interest is high in developing directors as managers who can play an even more significant role in their early childhood organizations.

THE WORK OF MANAGERS ACROSS PROFESSIONS

Some administrators and managers in other fields have invested considerable financial and other resources in preparation for their position as corporate president, hospice director, managing attorney, foundation executive, school principal, or community church pastor. Certain concrete or symbolic indicators such as an elaborate office, special benefits as part of a compensation package, or professional awards may mark the administrator and his or her achievements. These accouterments of the office also connote the manager's authority.

An ECE administrator requires proficiency in human development, ECE programming, and management to effectively exercise her or his authority. Such administrative practitioners have often been called teaching directors. Other administrators, with other titles, may simultaneously work in their organizations as leaders, managers, and teachers of children. Despite the structure of the organization, or the design of the job, administrators work in a role that is central to the leadership of an effective school, for-profit business, or nonprofit organization (Culkin, 1994; Seplocha, 1998). In another field where women are in the majority—nursing—the leadership role is thought to be closely linked to caring relationships between the practitioner and the clients. The person in the leadership role is also thought to connect through caring relationships with the. staff at the health care facility. Fisher and Tronto (1990) describe caring as

> a species activity that includes everything that we do to maintain, continue, and repair our "world" so that we can live in it as well as possible. That world includes our bodies, our selves, and our environments, all of which we seek to interweave in a complex, life sustaining web. (p. 40)

Tronto (1998) continues:

> Caring is a process that can occur in a variety of institutions and settings. Care is found in the household, in services and goods sold in the market, in the workings of bureaucratic organizations in contemporary life. Care is not

restricted to the traditional realm of mother's work, to welfare agencies, or to hired domestic servants but is found in all of these realms. (p. 16)

The administrator who leads the organization is recognized as both the technical or skill leader in terms of professional ability and also as the caring leader in the organization—the individual who facilitates the weaving of a web of relationships between members of the community.

Within the last 25 years the topic of administration—and particularly of the role of the director as a manager and leader—has become one of general interest to the early childhood field. As researchers and educators find that the director's experience is a significant contribution to a program's quality and that training for the director can raise the quality of a center on specific measures of program quality, interest is growing in training and preparing administrators to do their job effectively. When you combine this research-based insight about a trained director's contribution with the fact that the ECE program director typically does not have specific preparation for the role, the development of a director credential is an opportunity. This process can enable the profession to use administrative knowledge and insight to train the directors and administrators of ECE programs to work toward raising the level of quality in ECE organizations and in the field as a whole.

Becoming an Administrator

If directors and administrative leaders are important to the ECE field's development, then steps to support the development of directors as leaders are important to the ECE profession. Asking how people become capable administrators in other fields is one way of thinking about director development. The manner in which business and service organizations develop a capacity for administration and management, create and monitor internal and external systems, and, ultimately, develop leadership is complex. Similarly, the ways in which the individual managers get their training and design systems of responsibility in organizations vary from one field to another. In the corporate world, a chief executive officer with an M.B.A. may lead an organization, and she or he may delegate to a group of managers in different parts of the company. In a factory setting, leaders and managers operate individually and in teams at many levels, from the boardroom to the assembly line. In schools, some principals develop the capacity to work to support teachers' development of expertise in curriculum and pedagogy through coaching and mentoring.

Management in Early Care and Education Programs

In early childhood programs the patterns for the development of management and leadership are less clear (Kagan & Bowman, 1997). The rewards and prestige accorded to administrators and leaders may have more in common with those in other service and educational professions than they do with the corporate world. Directors in children's programs work in settings that reflect widely varied organizational models, but there are some typical management realities.

In fact, ECE programs, like other organizations, may have one or many layers of administration. Consider these examples. In the cooperative nursery school model, the director generally focuses on program development, curriculum, teaching, and enrichment work with families. Administrative work is assigned to committees of the board, which are generally committees of parents of children attending the school. Another common administrative design for a single-site organization is one in which a director reports to a nonprofit board or owner. In a public or corporate setting, lines of authority are generally more complex, particularly in larger organizations, where directors may serve as part of the human resources division of their corporation or on the line of service provision in a hospital, college, or factory.

In slightly larger systems of two or more centers, administrators of nonprofit and for-profit centers often work with an owner, executive director, or district manager who supervises several site directors within a system of services. In the public school system, a preschool program director might work hand-in-hand with a principal in operating a public school–based early childhood project. An executive director of a large center in a public university or health facility likely reports to a public facilities or human services board within the larger institution's administrative structure. Competent directors can play an important role in these organizations.

Administrators Set the Tone

Whether in a simple, single-layer organization or in a more complex setting where there are multiple management levels, there is generally an identifiable head person, a director. That person takes the lead on a day-to-day basis. In all of these settings, directors have an opportunity to set the tone for successfully addressing the program's goals. Generally the administrator has a college degree and some tenure as a practitioner in the ECE field (Burchinal & Culkin, 1995; Rafanello & Bloom, 1997). What most directors lack, and are increasingly asking for, is the chance to learn administrative skills related to management, leadership, and the nurturing of the learning environment for children, families, and staff at their center. Directors want to acquire these skills through director support groups, classes, or other learning activities focused on their role, and administrative training can support directors in their work toward career and program goals.

A TIME FOR DIALOGUE

As the early care and education field determines the appropriateness and shape of an administrative credential, questions about issues such as jurisdiction and regulation, and how to design learning activities related to the credential, must be kept in mind. These topics are discussed in the following chapters. Ultimately the answers will be developed in professional groups and communities that are dedicated to investigating this issue as a way of supporting high-quality learning experiences for children and families.

Before we examine those questions, let us consider the work of the credentialing efforts now in operation. Wheelock College has completed a scan of the current director credentialing efforts in the United States (Taking the Lead, 1999). The scan separates the credentials into state credentials and national credentials. State credentials are available on a state level under a variety of sponsors, while national credentials are offered across the country under the sponsorship of national organizations.

A review of the scan reveals the range of credentialing initiatives at a state level. Alabama, Arizona, California, the District of Columbia, Florida, Illinois, Minnesota, Mississippi, New Jersey, New York, North Carolina, Oklahoma, South Carolina, Texas, and Wisconsin have credential programs in operation. Of these 15 programs, 10 are voluntary. Two (California and North Carolina) are required, while Florida's will be the minimum standard for licensure in 2003. In Wisconsin and Illinois the credential is voluntary. California's site supervisor permit is required for directors in state-funded programs and voluntary for private programs. The state legislature of North Carolina made an administrative credential requirement in the 1997–1998 session. Twelve credentials include college credit with the number of credit hours required ranging from 3 to 36, and some credentials are available at more than one level of competency. In Florida the credential is available at two levels, foundational and advanced, and North Carolina's credential is at level I, II, and III, with different requirements at each level.

While some programs have been in operation for several years

(Texas, 1988; Wisconsin, 1996; Minnesota and Mississippi, 1995; Alabama, 1993; Arizona, 1994), others have only just begun operations (California, 1997; New Jersey, New York, North Carolina, and Oklahoma, 1998; Florida, 1999). The Illinois program began full operation in the fall of 1999 and awards credentials at different levels. Texas has awarded the most credentials to date (500). Mississippi has over 400 awarded or in process. Wisconsin has awarded 38 credentials and 280 candidates are in process. In the other states where programs are underway, numbers of candidates vary and some states have not yet awarded any credentials. The number of credentials awarded, or students enrolled, are as follows: Alabama, 150; Arizona, 60 awarded or in progress; California, 1266; Minnesota, 12; and North Carolina, 60 with the number growing daily.

The three national credentials now available are the National Administrative Credential (NAC), sponsored by the National Child Care Association; the Christian Director's Child Development Education Credential, sponsored by the National Association for Child Development Education; and the Professional Administrator National Credentialing, sponsored by the National Association of Professional Administrators. The national credentials, like the state credentials, differ in requirements and structure.

The NAC fulfills a regulatory requirement in some states and is voluntary in others: 800 have been awarded. Eleven credentials have been awarded by the Christian Directors organization since 1994. College credits may be a part of the formal training. Professional Administrator Credentialing was established in 1985 and 40,000 credentials have been awarded. College course credit of 3 to 15 hours is required in some states. This credential can be a voluntary undertaking, is a licensing option in some states, or is a part of a career lattice in others.

Six states require administrative or management training for all center directors. While only North Carolina requires a credential, it is an alternative to experience and education qualifications for ECE administrators in a few other states. At this time, the majority of states do not specifically mandate management training as a requirement for directing an ECE program. Requirements are focused on child development, teaching, and other professional experiences. Thus, with few exceptions, the credentialing programs now underway are voluntary. One might think initially of a mandated credential as more logical and possible, but there are many reasons why voluntary credentialing efforts are of interest to administrators, their ECE programs, and to policymakers.

The following are some of the reasons administrators decide to acquire this credential, even when it is not required of them:

- A credential has value in the job market and might help them get a better-paying job.
- High-quality centers, such as employer-sponsored ones, might give preference to credentialed applicants for director.
- The content of the training would help directors succeed and find more satisfaction in the work.
- The credential is recognition of the status and importance of directors.
- A credentialed director can help centers in their marketing.
- A funding source might encourage or require a credential in the future, or at least prefer to fund programs with credentialed directors.
- There is a trend in states to pay more for higher quality.
- Credentialing would lead to more linkages among directors, and between directors and other community agencies, to do together what no one can do alone.

There are also reasons why centers might support a credential for directors. They include the following:

- Competent directors would reduce costly failure.
- Directors who can select and support good staff, and help them work well together, will improve the center's quality.
- A credentialed director would make a center more marketable to parents.
- Resource and referral agencies could list centers that have credentialed directors, as consumer information for parents.
- A credentialed director would increase a center's ability to get bank loans, corporate support, foundation support, and government subsidies.

Policy makers' reasons for supporting a credential for directors include the following.

- The credential offers access to leadership roles and to college credit for underrepresented groups.
- Competent directors protect the investment of dollars in child care by reducing failure and assuring operating at an effective level of quality.
- Director competence correlates with quality outcomes for children

and would increase the percentage of U.S. child care that is good to excellent.

• Competence of directors supports the effectiveness of staff and protects the investment in staff training and scholarships.

Although there are clear reasons for supporting a voluntary credential, ongoing efforts by practitioners, administrators, academics, and others will be required to develop appropriate criteria, curricula, and policies for specific credentials.

It is time for advancing new career development opportunities for administrators in ECE programs. Research supports this effort, and practitioners and planners alike view the effort favorably. There is the possibility of change here—change for individuals as well as groups. This change holds the promise both of improving the quality of services we deliver to young children and their families, and of improving the professional experiences of the individuals and organizations providing those services.

In the following chapters the contributors provide a thoughtful look at varied parts of the process. As the dialogue about the director and director credentialing continues, the profession needs a beginning place for this discussion—a kind of database, a resource collection or library of previous and current experience, ideas, and concerns. This book's collection of thoughts and ideas will inform the discussion and provide a common starting place concerning our history and shared thinking about the work of the administrator.

In this way, thoughtful, field-based responses and tested approaches to developing better-quality services will be in the foreground of the director credentialing effort. As new knowledge evolves and matures, administrators and their organizations will have the opportunity to utilize relevant interdisciplinary concepts and strategies in their practice– learning communities. Throughout the process, there are five questions to keep in mind:

1. How, if at all, do the administrative needs of ECE programs differ from those of other organizations?
2. What financial and other resources can be made available to support a diverse group of individuals in reaching their goal of advancing as directors on their professional career track?
3. What do we need to learn about the current professional paths of administrators? What opportunities would enhance and facilitate the professional development of administrators, and what are the critical elements needed for a successful transition from classroom practitioner to administrator?

4. How will we measure and evaluate the impact of improved administrative competence?
5. What can we anticipate about how an administrative credential will affect current and projected needs for ongoing career development options in ECE practice and in the related leadership areas of resource and referral services, public policy, youth and related services, and research?

Investigating administrative credentialing options will require the attention of practitioners working collaboratively with researchers as the ECE profession creates this new professional opportunity.

In this book the authors in Part I—Chapters 2 through 7—write about aspects of the administrator's roles and responsibilities. This first part is focused on the historical role of the director as a leader for quality services. It also presents a view of the interdisciplinary knowledge and management ability required for success in the job and includes an examination of a broader view of career opportunities in the early childhood field. In Part II—Chapters 8 through 12—the authors explore challenges, opportunities, and questions related to developing a credential for center directors and other administrators. We hope that the insights, analyses, and questions expressed in this book may serve as a foundation piece for the dialogue, thought, and decision making that is beginning. The dialogue is necessary to understand the work of the director and to develop a credential that supports and strengthens a variety of career development opportunities for ECE administrators.

REFERENCES

Bloom, P. J. (1989). *The Illinois director's study: A report to the Illinois Department of Children and Family Services.* Evanston, IL: Early Childhood Professional Development Project, National College of Education.

Bloom, P. J. (1991). Child care centers as organizations: A social systems perspective. *Child and Youth Care Forum, 20*(5), 313–333.

Bloom, P. J., Sheerer, M., & Britz, J. (1991). *Blueprint for action: Achieving center-based change through staff development.* Lake Forest, IL: New Horizons.

Bredekamp, S., & Willer, B. (Eds.). (1996). *NAEYC accreditation: A decade of learning and the years ahead.* Washington, DC: National Association for the Education of Young Children.

Buckner, L. M. (1988). *Supervising with communicative competence in early childhood centers: Sociopolitical implications of the legitimation deficit in administrator preparation.* Unpublished doctoral dissertation, San Francisco University, San Francisco. (UMI Abstracts International, No. 8820727)

Burchinal, M., & Culkin, M. (1995). Center structure. In S. Helburn (Ed.), *Cost, quality, and child outcomes in child care centers study: Technical report* (pp. 67–89). Denver: University of Colorado at Denver, Economics Department.

Cost, Quality and Child Outcomes Study Team. (1995). *Cost, quality, and child outcomes in child care centers study: Public report.* Denver: University of Colorado at Denver, Economics Department.

Culkin, M. (1994). *The administrator/leader in early care and education settings: A qualitative study with implications for theory and practice.* Unpublished doctoral dissertation, The Union Institute, Cincinnati, OH. (UMI Abstracts International, No. 9502953)

Decker, C. A., & Decker, J. R. (1988). *Planning and administering early childhood programs* (4th ed.). Columbus, OH: Merrill.

Fisher, B., & Tronto, J. (1990). Towards a feminist theory of care. In E. Abel & M. Nelson (Eds.), *Circles of care: Work and identity in women's lives* (p. 40). Albany: State University of New York Press.

Hewes, D. W., & Hartman, B. (1972). *Early childhood education: A workbook for administrators.* San Jose, CA: R & E Research Associates.

Hildebrand, V. (1984). *Management of child development centers.* New York: Macmillan.

Kagan, S. L., & Bowman, B. T. (Eds.). (1997). *Leadership in early care and education.* Washington, DC: National Association for the Education of Young Children.

Kelley, R. (1992). *The power of followership.* New York: Doubleday.

Larkin, L. (1992). *The preschool administrator: Perspectives in early childhood education.* Unpublished doctoral dissertation, Harvard University, Cambridge, MA. (UMI Abstracts International, No. 9219109)

Manning, J. (1998). *The relationship of directors to quality within child care programs in Massachusetts: An exploration into some contributing characteristics.* Unpublished doctoral dissertation, University of Massachusetts, Amherst. (UMI Abstracts International, No. 9841894)

Morgan, G. (1997). *Competencies of early care and education administrators.* Boston: Taking the Lead Initiative, Wheelock College.

Morgan, G., Azer, S. L., Costley, J. B., Genser, A., Goodman, I. F., Lombardi, J., & McGinsey, B. (1993). *Making a career of it: The state of the states report on career development in early care and education.* Boston: Center for Career Development in Early Care and Education, Wheelock College.

Peisner-Feinberg, E., Burchinal, M., Clifford, R., Culkin, M., Howes,.C., Kagan, S. L., Yazejian, N., Byler, P., Rustici, J., & Zelazo, J. (1999). *The children of the cost, quality, and outcomes study go to school: Executive summary.* Chapel Hill: University of North Carolina at Chapel Hill, Frank Porter Graham Child Study Center.

Poster, M., & Neugebauer, R. (1998). How experienced directors have developed their skills. *Child Care Information Exchange, 121,* 90–93.

Rafanello, D., & Bloom, P. J. (1997). *1997 Illinois Directors' Study.* Wheeling, IL: Center for Early Childhood Leadership, National–Louis University.

Results of the child care directors survey. (1996, May). *Campus child care news, 2*(2), 1.

Schein, E. H. (1991). What is culture? In P. J. Frost, L. F. Moore, M. R. Louis, & J. Martin (Eds.), *Reframing organizational culture* (pp. 243–253). Newbury Park, CA: Sage.

Schön, D. A. (1983). *The reflective practitioner: How professionals think in action.* New York: Basic Books.

Sciarra, D. J., & Dorsey, A. G. (1990). *Developing and administering a child care center* (2nd ed.). Albany, NY: Delmar.

Seaver, J. W., & Cartwright, C. A. (1986). *Child care administration.* Belmont, CA: Wadsworth.

Senge, P. (1990). *The learning organization.* New York: Doubleday.

Seplocha, H. (1998). *The good preschool: Profiles in leadership.* Unpublished doctoral dissertation, Rutgers, The State University of New Jersey, New Brunswick. (UMI Abstracts International, No. 9834121)

Shore, R. (1997). *Rethinking the brain: New insights into early development.* New York: Families and Work Institute.

Taking the Lead Initiative. (1997). *Initiative goal statement.* Boston: Taking the Lead Initiative, Center for Career Development in Education, Wheelock College.

Taking the Lead Initiative. (1999). *An overview of director credentialing initiatives: State credentials (as of May 1998).* Boston: Taking the Lead Initiative, Center for Career Development in Education, Wheelock College.

Tronto, J. C. (1998, Fall). An ethic of care. In *Ethics & Aging: Bringing the Issues Home,* pp. 15–20.

I

The Roles, Responsibilities, and Development of Program Directors

In Part I the chapter authors explore the work of the director as well as its history, significance, and value to the field. Dorothy W. Hewes traces the history of training for child care administration in Chapter 2. She discusses the contrast that existed in the late 19th century between the principles of efficient scientific management and the humanistic beliefs of early childhood practitioners. She points out that in the last century, there has been a shifting of these philosophies. Major parts of business administration have become more humanistic; and at the same time, early childhood program directors are recognizing that they must manage accurate and accountable systems, budgetary projections, and human resources.

In Chapter 3 Gwen G. Morgan presents the perspective that since the administrator role has been shown to be critical to achieving quality, creation of a director credential may be one way to improve the early care and education (ECE) field's capacity to provide higher levels of service quality. Morgan approaches the role by analyzing and listing the tasks performed by directors, examining why the different competencies included in the director role are so important to a program of good or excellent quality. She also presents an analysis of steps needed in order to use improved administrative capacity to move centers from unacceptable to good enough to good, and from good to excellent. To do so, Morgan points out, practitioners, led by administrators, will need to realistically appraise current program quality and set realistic goals for change.

Paula Jorde Bloom explores the developmental stages of directors in Chapter 4. Bloom presents directors' investigations of issues of role clarity, power and influence, communication, and perspective taking. She examines and analyzes metaphorical images created and utilized by practicing early care and education directors and other administrators. The directors used these metaphors to describe their jobs and organizations. Directors work from a variety of metaphors, including an orchestra conductor, a masterful director of a Broadway play, a family, a strong tree with roots in the community, and a pizza where each of the ingredients contributes to the delicious taste of the whole. The chapter also gives insights into the culture of ECE organizations.

Wherever they work, directors must draw on knowledge from several disciplines, including the study of child development and teaching, organizational psychology, management, human relations, business, law, finance, marketing, leadership, and outreach strategies. In Chapter 5 Nancy H. Brown and John P. Manning address the question of what interdisciplinary knowledge an ECE administrator needs, specifying the knowledge areas and global skills that they consider essential to effective program leadership in an ECE program setting. Brown and Manning use the concept of "core knowledge" as a metaphor for all the interrelated facts, data, reflection, and experiences administrators draw on in their day-to-day work.

Roger Neugebauer's premise in Chapter 6 is that directorship is more than the sum of its parts. Management is central to the director's work in an ECE program, and like child development or teaching, it can be learned. According to Neugebauer, an effective director is like a conductor, knowing when and where to channel efforts and attention to move the organization forward. Neugebauer presents the management side of the administrator's skills and reviews his personal selection of critical management literature for administrators of children's programs.

Karen VanderVen views children's programs broadly, including youth, school-age, residential, and other educational settings as well as typical ECE programs such as child care and preschool programs. In Chapter 7 she develops a systems view of early childhood programs. According to Vander-Ven, while ability to complete tasks such as supervision, budgeting, and personnel management is essential to running a program, a higher level of cognitive skill—the ability to think systemically and to deal with complexity—is also required for optimal leadership of a children's program. She describes a model of ongoing development for ECE leaders, including the implications for career development and for making the transition from a managerial to a leadership role.

In these chapters the authors lay a rich foundation of understanding of the director's role, knowledge, work, and value to the profession, as well as to the children and families they serve. The chapters in Part I are a ground for the conversation about administrators and credentials now under way in the ECE field. They also provide a stimulus for deepening understanding of the past, present, and future role of the administrator in children's programs.

2

Looking Back: How the Role of Director Has Been Understood, Studied, and Utilized in ECE Programs, Policy, and Practice

Dorothy W. Hewes

The dilemma commonly encountered by early childhood program directors was neatly summarized in the first issue of *Child Care Management*. An article entitled "Taking Charge ... When All You Want to Do Is Take Care of Children" reviewed the problems of "these former educators with little or no business management experience" who are "too nice" while trying to run a successful business (Keenan, 1990, p. 26). It provided no immediate solutions. In the next issue, "The Director's Dilemma: Crossing Over to Business" warned in smaller type that "If directors do not run their centers as money-making operations, the alternative may be disaster" (Smith, 1990, p. 31). If we accept the classic definition of administration as the "process of defining and attaining the objectives of an organization through a system of coordinated and cooperative effort" (Stein, 1965, p. 58), it is obvious that an early childhood program director must be prepared to handle "both horns" of this dilemma—to be *both* caring *and* businesslike.

While the origins of out-of-home care and education for young children have been dealt with in recent books by Youcha (1995) and Beatty (1995), in articles such as that by Prochner (1996), and by research reports at professional conferences, their focus has primarily been on philosophies and politics of caring and curriculum, not on management styles. An exception is the *Encyclopedia of Early Childhood Education*; in addition to contexts within which child care and curriculum variations have been developed, Williams and Fromberg (1992) stated that "supervision and administration of early childhood programs refer to general oversight and management." They predicted that "the development of uniform

standards for preparation and licensure . . . is a next step in professionalization in the field" (pp. 491–492). The constantly changing management
styles that have characterized early care and education (ECE) programs
over the past two centuries are the focus of this chapter.

THE CARING CURRICULUM

The "caring" emphasis of the early childhood curriculum is usually credited to a Swiss educator, Johann Pestalozzi (1746–1827), although his es-
tablishments were for older children. Like Piaget in the mid-20th century,
he stressed active learning, with children's sensory impressions becoming
internalized to form concepts. The greatest lesson he taught, according
to Seeley (1904), "is embodied in the word *love*. He loved little children,
he loved the distressed and lowly, and he loved all his fellow-men" (p.
271). However, Pestalozzi's life was a succession of financial failures. His
famed Yverdon boarding school, opened in 1804, closed ignominiously
after a 20-year struggle. Although Pestalozzi readily admitted that he
could not keep accounts, he was also unable to manage staff dissension
and to satisfy fee-paying parents that their sons were actually learning
something.

It is ironic that an "infant school" in New Lanarky, Scotland, led to
a radically different interpretation of Pestalozzian ideas. Based on mill
owner Robert Owen's observations at Yverdon, it opened in 1816 to care
for children aged 2 to 6. When a philanthropic infant asylum was established in London 2 years later, Owen sent his New Lanark teacher, James
Buchanan, to take charge. Buchanan was described as such "a queer fish"
that most of the sponsors withdrew, but he introduced the infant school
idea to Samuel Wilderspin. Like Buchanan, Wilderspin lacked any professional preparation. A shrewd entrepreneur, according to Raymont (1937),
he demonstrated that the route to success is to develop and market a cost-
effective system, publish widely, claim that the ideas of others are your
own, and pose as the only expert. He popularized galleries where a hundred seated pupils were supervised by a single teacher. Wilderspin represents a type of businesslike administrator who is anathema to the typical
early childhood educator.

In contrast to the authoritarian infant schools inspired by Wilderspin,
a "caring" Pestalozzian system in the United States was initiated in 1825,
when Robert Owen established the utopian community of New Harmony,
Indiana. Its educational program was directed by William Maclure, a
wealthy Philadelphia businessman who had sponsored the immigration
of Pestalozzi-trained teachers. Two of them, Marie Duclos Frettageot and

Elise Neef, were in charge of the infant school, where children as young as age 2 had a creative and active program. Although the New Harmony community had dissolved because of poor management and dissension by 1830, it had aroused public interest and its staff members continued to spread this system as they moved to other locations.

Pestalozzi's emphasis on "caring" influenced Friedrich Froebel (1782–1852), whose German kindergarten became the foundation for today's preschools. "Like Pestalozzi, Froebel was wholly incapable of financial management" (Seeley, 1904, p. 276). He ran out the back door to hide when creditors approached at the front. It was only through the devotion of a few dedicated disciples that his ideas were disseminated throughout the world. However, he was far ahead of his time in the field of personnel management. Froebel's expectations of children working together to jointly solve problems were extended to staff relationships, as in his 1847 proposal for a teacher training school. He explained that "I would never presume to interfere with anything decided by the faculty" (quoted in Heinemann, 1893, p. 90).

CONTRASTING APPROACHES IN AMERICAN KINDERGARTENS

After the Froebelian kindergartens were imported into the United States during the 1850s, two distinct approaches became apparent. Baylor (1965) and other biographers have rightfully credited a Bostonian, Elizabeth Peabody (1804–1894), with the "crusade" that popularized these schools for children from toddlerhood to primary grades. Although she opened the first English-language kindergarten in 1860 and edited the *Kindergarten Messenger* from 1873 to 1877, they were among the many poorly managed endeavors of her long life. Caring for children was Peabody's (1886) greatest concern, and she extolled prospective teachers to be "above mere pecuniary motive" as they worked with God "on the paradisaical ground of childhood" (pp. 18–19).

In contrast to Peabody, William and Eudora Hailmann (1836–1920, 1835–1904) combined the humanistic philosophy of Froebel with organizational and administrative capabilities. William's elementary education had been under a Pestalozzian schoolmaster in Zurich, where he worked in his family's textile business before emigrating to the United States at age 16. In 1865, when he became principal of a new German-American school in Louisville, Hailmann hired a German kindergarten teacher who received the same pay and status as teachers of higher grades. After Eudora was a parent volunteer in this class, she twice observed in European kindergartens. The two became an egalitarian team, promoting the Froebelian system through holding offices in professional associations, establishing teacher training institutions, and contributing a steady flow of publications. As leaders in the "New Education" movement, they maintained Froebel's basic beliefs about children learning through play and influenced turn-of-the-century "Progressive" educators such as John Dewey, psychologist G. Stanley Hall, and kindergarten director Patty Smith Hill.

As he moved upward in public school administrative positions, Hailmann favored the unionization of teachers and endorsed guaranteed retirement and other benefits. His career culminated in 1894 with his appointment as federal Superintendent of Indian Schools. He again instituted Froebelian methods, including kindergartens with community volunteers and teacher training programs for Native Americans. One long-range goal was to eliminate unqualified political appointees in supervisory positions. This might provide a clue for the investigation of early childhood director credentials, since he worked out a special merit selection plan with Theodore Roosevelt, the Civil Service Commissioner. "Scholastic requirements were less important than indications that applicants were aware of the physical and social hardships and could apply their knowledge to children's needs," he wrote. In Hailmann's frank opinion, the old examinations were useless because "the veteran and the genius were placed on a par with the neophyte and the parrot." New essay questions, related to the positions desired, were to be evaluated by nonpartisan representatives of Indian school sponsors (quoted in Hewes, 1981, p. 95).

PRECEDENTS FOR "BUSINESS" ASPECTS

By 1893, when about 4,000 kindergartens were operating in public schools and as independent private or philanthropic programs, the first health and safety regulations were developed. They were not for kindergartens, however. They came as an attempt to stem mortality rates in the foundling homes and orphanages that had existed since colonial times. Morgan (1972) provided participants at the 1971 Batelle conference with typical grim statistics. For example, in 1868, at Foundling's Hospital, near New York, "1,527 children were received in 11 months and all died within the first year but 80" (p. 131). Partly as a reaction to conditions in these institutions and partly to expand the Froebelian system, the late 1800s period of "sisterhood and sentimentality" was marked by philanthropic service that established attitudes against a mercenary (i.e., businesslike) approach to children's programs and community service for worthy parents (Hewes, 1995). Despite the complexity of the work and failing to recognize the innate value of women's work, sponsoring women's groups administered early childhood programs. As they merely utilized the skills that were needed to maintain a household, they helped set a precedent that "anyone can do it" in regard to child care management.

Although the philanthropic tradition heavily weighted the orientation of early childhood personnel toward caring for the children, rather than running a business, we must recognize that there were no specialized courses of study for *any* school administrators until the mid-1800s (Hewes, 1990). The 1861 founding of Sheldon's Pestalozzi-based normal school in Oswego, New York, marks the transition to professional teacher training. In a biographical sketch, Rogers (1961) noted that Sheldon lacked administrative training and that his previous schools had been failures. Sheldon was autocratic until he recognized that regimented teachers led to children's rote memorization. His discovery of Pestalozzian materials in a Toronto museum led to child-centered teaching in the United States. Despite Oswego's lack of specific coursework in management, Hollis (1898) documented that a large proportion of the public school administrators during the late 1800s were its graduates. Many were women who became successful principals and county superintendents.

But what about the "management" aspect? Although business transactions have been recorded since before arithmetic was developed, through knotted ropes or slashes on a slab of clay, modern business strategies and fiscal accounting originated during the Industrial Revolution. The title of "The Father of Modern Management" was bestowed upon Frederick W. Taylor, who established the discipline as a profession early in the 20th century. Wren (1987) wrote that he "gave a push and provided credibility to the idea of management. . . . Taylor provided a voice, a spirit which captured the imagination of the public, business leaders, and academics" (p. 130). Accounting education also grew rapidly at this time, with attention devoted primarily to the relative merits of alternative procedures and interpretations. By 1935, organizers of the American Accounting Association viewed standardization as their first major task. The resulting monograph provided a coherent, coordinated, consistent framework into which subsequent methods and standards could be integrated (Paton & Littleton, 1940).

There were other business perspectives stemming from the Industrial Revolution as well. As work began to be organized in assembly-line structures, business was studying the effects of those modern procedures on workers. Research findings of these early studies at Tavistock and the Hawthorne plant were critical of the assembly-line and narrowly rational accounting approaches, creating a new discipline of organizational psychology and a stream of thinking within business that has been continually more humanistic than the Taylor approach.

THE EVOLVING PROFESSION OF
ECE PROGRAM MANAGEMENT

Froebel-based nursery schools, introduced from England during the 1920s, mark the beginning of today's early childhood education. The kindergartens, originally for children as young as 2 years, were restricting enrollment in the public schools to those who were 4 and 5. Lawrence Frank (1962) pointed out that in 1920 there were only three nursery schools in the United States and no child research centers with laboratory preschools. Even the terms *preschool* and *child development* were not coined until mid-decade. As administrator of the Laura Spellman Rockefeller Memorial Fund, Frank helped child development become a multidisciplinary and family-supportive field of study through start-up monies to establish laboratory nursery schools within college home economics departments and for similar projects.

The interdisciplinary National Committee on Nursery Schools was organized in 1925. In 1931, it became the National Association for Nursery Education (NANE), precursor of the National Association for the Education of Young Children (NAEYC). One of the first projects of the Committee was to publish a pamphlet, *Minimum Essentials of Nursery School Education* (Eliot, 1929). It described appropriate equipment and physical facilities, but merely suggested that someone might assume the role of administrator. At their 1927 and 1929 conferences, panelists discussed admission criteria, the widely varied backgrounds of students, and the appropriate academic level for coursework. Despite the fact that most of those attending were administrators of laboratory schools or research centers, no recommendation was made for specific management training. A new element was introduced at the 1933 conference when administrators for schools with the "peculiar feature" of being completely dependent on tuition formed a discussion group. They requested that a system be devised for the endorsement of private schools organized and operated under standards determined by the association and that a system be developed for inspection and supervision (Hewes, 1976/1996). These proposals were not officially implemented until the NAEYC accreditation process was developed in 1985.

CHALLENGES OF FEDERAL FINANCING

During the Depression of the 1930s, funds to establish WPA (Workers Progress Administration) nursery schools brought a different challenge. At the 1933 Toronto NANE conference, it was announced that a federal preschool program had just been approved. After an all-night session, a mimeographed committee report was ready for distribution. It included recommendations that a network of educational institutions should immediately be organized to prepare nursery school workers and that instructional booklets should be prepared for distribution (Hewes, 1976/1996).

In a scholarly account of this period, Schwartz (1984) recognized that the successful outcome for WPA schools was due to the vigilance of NANE and other professional associations as they developed and guarded standards. With funding from an anonymous private source, the National Council of Parent Education set up an advisory committee to provide free materials and training. One result, the *Handbook for Leaders in Emergency Education Programs* (White, 1934), was a pioneering publication for nursery school directors. It still sounds remarkably up to date in dealing with role clarification for leaders (directors) and advisory board members, relationships with other community organizations, and responding to parental concerns through a feedback process.

By the time the nation had moved into the wartime mode of the late 1930s, a cadre of experienced staff had been prepared for the federally funded Lanham Act children's centers and other out-of-home care needed when fathers went to war and mothers went to work. Official concern for the problems posed by war mobilization was expressed at the 1941 Conference on Day Care of Children of Working Mothers, sponsored by the federal Children's Bureau. One result was the 1942 Rosenberg Foundation grant for an "Intensive Training Course for Directors of Wartime Child Care Centers" at Mills College in Oakland, California, where classes for Lanham Act directors continued through 1945.

PRESCHOOLS FOR THE BOOMER GENERATION

In an overview of the diverse early childhood programs existing by 1942, Landreth (1943) pointed out that "some met standards . . . and some operated as they saw fit, without even public health supervision. . . . The services these institutions offered were either free or at a fee so high that only a small percentage of parents could afford to pay it" (pp. 3–4). Almost half a century later, Host (1984) reminisced about those simpler times:

> Administrators were hired in the '50s primarily because of their program knowledge. Their need for knowledge of administration was a minor requirement. You really didn't need to know a great deal about finance; all

you needed to know was whether your balance sheet was positive or negative. (p. 21)

Nobody anticipated the proliferation of affordable parent-initiated nursery schools during those post–World War II years, when the baby-boom generation and Dr. Spock arrived on the scene. There had been a few cooperative nursery schools in the 1920s, and there were about a hundred by 1950. Soon, even the U.S. Office of Education was intrigued by the "mushroom growth of cooperative nursery schools, now so prevalent in our large cities" (Gabbard, 1957). By 1960, there were probably a thousand. Twenty years later, Taylor (1981) estimated that there were 5,000 in the United States and Canada. As Stevenson (1990) described them, co-ops are

> self-determined groups in which the members are the owners of the service. . . . Once the co-op assumes the role of owner/operator, it must conduct the operation in a businesslike manner. In replacing the intermediary, co-ops have assumed incorporation, asserting their goals through policies and procedures stated in by-laws. Insurance, audits, fund-raising and decision-making at executive, general, and annual meetings have all become part and parcel of running a co-op. Of necessity, teachers and parents (particularly board members) have had to acquire skills to handle each of these tasks. Sometimes these skills are developed through experience, but more often through planned workshop sessions with co-learners and with the advice of experts. (p. 228)

Participating mothers in the cooperatives, often with college degrees in fields not related to early education, learned informal management strategies that prepared them to become competent teachers and directors. The Silver Spring Nursery School in Maryland, organized in 1941, was the first to publish a widely distributed guidebook with financial management strategies, detailed job descriptions for professional staff and parent board members, and just about everything anybody needed to know to operate a successful morning preschool. As individual schools joined together to become councils, management strategies were shared. Conferences and publications provided balanced training in both caring and business, but requirements for directors continued to be expressed as general statements such as a "wide background in professional activity" or "some understanding of children's needs."

During this period, the Los Angeles Council of Cooperative Nursery Schools took a different approach to developing competent administrators. Directors and teachers formed a division of the local AFL-CIO and then joined the American Federation of Teachers (AFT) in 1964. It was seen as essential that specific management courses be developed at the community college and university levels. The first was taught at the University of California in Los Angeles in 1951. By 1960, University of California extension classes in Administration and Supervision became available throughout the state. Despite this, when Taylor (1981) used the California Co-op Council's "Criteria for Selection of a Director" as a model to be emulated, a degree in the humanities with nursery school training was considered optimal. She did not mention specific administration classes.

In Michigan, another state with a strong cooperative nursery school movement, Merrill-Palmer College began providing workshops for co-op directors in 1952. Beginning in 1971, an extension class in Preschool and Child Care Administration was given by the School of Education at the University of Michigan. A loose-leaf notebook "training kit" compiled by Pearl Axelrod emphasized the managerial aspects of the director's job. Since it was difficult for directors to get to Ann Arbor once a week, a Mobile Training Project for five other cities was developed with federal funding (Hewes, 1998).

Other than those of the cooperative nursery schools, few management-oriented publications existed before the 1970s. Instructors taught from personal experience, with ditto handouts to supplement the WPA and Lanham Act booklets. Hinitz (1990), in summarizing the development of administration textbooks, wrote that "when one contemplates the growing wealth of resources for the administrator of an early education program, it is difficult to conceive of the fact that prior to 1971, few such materials existed" (p. 49). As co-author of the first textbook designed to introduce business administration principles to prospective directors of a wide variety of programs (Hewes & Hartman, 1972), I found that major publishers were unwilling to even consider it. Within the next few years, most of them had recognized the potential of this new area within education and were eager to garner its benefits. Another indication of the professional growth of preschool management can be seen in the evolution of *Child Care Information Exchange,* appropriately described on its cover as "The Director's Magazine Since 1978." Its current sophisticated format bears little resemblance to the 1978 original version, but its contents have consistently balanced the elements of caring and business.

LICENSING AND REGULATIONS

Although 1953 census listed 35 million women as "housewives" and did not indicate maternal employment until 1958, family members and small day nurseries provided out-of-home care for increasing numbers of young children. Care centers were often unregistered, unlicensed, and undetected by authorities—if a state *had* authorities. Judith Cauman reported at the 1957 NANE Conference that a survey just completed by the Child Welfare League of America showed that 21 states had enacted licensing laws for child care programs since 1950, bringing the total to 43 of the 48 states. The League's study had been done because of the "deluge" of requests for information. Cauman expressed the conviction that "Licensing of day care protects children, families, communities and society. Community responsibility is reflected in licensing. In some communities it is easier to open up a day care center than a dog pound" (quoted in Mahler, 1957, p. 30). Confirming this, a mimeographed chart prepared by the Florida Children's Commission in 1953 showed "No Accreditation or Licensing" on record for 27 states. A California survey indicated that in 1959 the "educational attainment" level for 19% of the directors and 35% of the teachers was high school or less but that 40% of the directors and 20% of the teachers had college degrees. Another questionnaire, sent to 57 representative colleges across the nation, indicated that enrollments in nursery education were very low because a degree in kindergarten–primary teaching led to better salaries and working conditions (Burgess, 1961).

Anthony Celebreeze (1964), President John Kennedy's secretary of the Department of Health, Education and Welfare, estimated that in 1962 there had been only 18,000 licensed day-care facilities in the nation, with a capacity of 185,000 children. The welfare reform package, enacted that year as Public Law 87-543, provided federal funding conditional upon a preschool obtaining a state license. Critics were quick to notice that almost half of the appropriated $800,000 was spent on modernization of regulations, but 42 states immediately began planning to extend or expand their day-care services.

Another component of early education was added by the development of Head Start after 1965. Like the WPA schools of the 1930s, this was a situation without adequate advance planning. In a comprehensive review of federal day-care regulations, including those for Head Start, Nelson (1982) traced efforts to reconcile conflicting viewpoints about their goals and standards. Again, it is not mentioned that center directors should be required to complete a specific sequence of coursework—including administration.

Persons who were involved with the cooperative nursery schools during this time use words like *decimated* to describe the exodus of their directors, experienced both in program management and in working with parents, who moved into the federally subsidized centers. As in the co-ops, Head Start has provided a "career lattice" by which mothers can move upward through the system. In Colorado, where community colleges were authorized in 1970 to include an A. A. degree in child care and management, some Head Start parents received high school equivalency certificates so that they could enroll. In 1975, when the nation's first Child Development Associate (CDA) certificates were presented to 13 recipients, two were from Colorado (Graham, 1980). As has happened in other states, the taste of success was stimulating; many Head Start mothers continued to bachelor's or graduate degrees. While this has not been the usual route to executive power for other professional fields, participatory parenting has provided an experiential training program for early childhood directors.

RECOGNITION OF DAY CARE AS AN "INDUSTRY"

The changed situation by the 1970s was cogently summarized by Cornelia Goldsmith (1972):

> A greatly increased interest in federal legislation affecting children was evidenced. Of the 11 million women already in the labor force, 5 million were known to have preschool children. Of these, it was estimated, less than a third were enrolled in any kind of daytime program, whether good, bad or indifferent. Only by legislative action at the federal level could appropriate steps be taken to provide all states with the needed funds, guidelines and the skilled leadership that would assure protection and true benefits to all the children so critically in need of them. . . . In the fall of 1971, Congressional activity regarding child care legislation reached a crescendo. (p. 118)

That temporal marker of fall 1971 referred to the Mondale Bill, S. 626 and H. R. 2966, which had received bipartisan support from members of Congress, the cabinet, and federal agencies. Legislation had been structured with input from early childhood educators and multidisciplinary theorists across the nation, although its failure to require specific administrative coursework was of concern to many participants in the hearings. The legislation, described in the public press as the catalyst to create a federally funded network of publicly and privately operated child daycare centers, was to be based upon a sliding-scale subsidy so that families with higher incomes would pay full cost while low-income families would have an incentive to seek work and training.

President Nixon justified his veto of the Mondale Bill by asserting that it was a communistic scheme to destroy the American family. It is somewhat ironic that the anticipated enactment of federal support introduced a profitable new growth industry, with "business" more important than "caring." Critics coined terms like "Kentucky-Fried children" and questioned whether this was "hype or hope" when a modified bill was passed in 1972. All types of proprietary or for-profit child care centers proliferated. Although chains and franchise operations were best known, a preponderance of the proprietary centers were independently owned and managed, often by a husband–wife team. Even home day care became more professional, with Griffin (1973) explaining in his how-to-do-it book that the 1973 income tax credit "may well have done more to expand the use of day care services than all other federal, state, municipal and private agencies combined" (p. 1). Parents could take this deduction only if the center was registered or licensed. By 1987 a directory of "child care chains" in *Ms. Magazine* stated that "Child care is a $10 billion business. The number of children under six whose mothers work is expected to rise to 12.2 million by 1990. No wonder smart entrepreneurs are getting into this business now, while it's growing" (Rubin, 1987, p. 62).

In the hypothetical child care model described by Evans, Shub, and Weinstein (1971), comparatively high salaries were justified in the new for-profit centers because: "Ideally, the director will be both educated and experienced in early childhood education and day care administration, and the secretary-administrative assistant will have both bookkeeping and secretarial skills of the highest quality" (p. 26). Since most states required only high school education for directors, head teachers, or teachers, they suggested that the legal requirements could be met with an inexperienced and uneducated staff, if they were of good character.

As this expansion period began, the difficulties of assessing qualifications for day-care directors were expressed by Keyserling (1972) in the extensive study conducted by the National Council of Jewish Women. The educational background of directors was a small but vital portion of their investigation. Interviewers found that it was difficult to assess information about qualifications, since a college degree might be in a totally unrelated field. A director with "some early childhood training" might have had one short course or 2 years of intensive teacher preparation or merely a few discussion sessions. It was determined that directors of nonprofit centers were much more likely to have academic degrees than those in proprietary centers. The directors of about 90% of the Head Start and hospital centers visited had a college education, while nearly a quarter of those in proprietary centers were categorized as untrained.

Keyserling (1972) cited the Child Welfare League of America standards that the director should have professional education and experience in either the field of early childhood education, or child development, or the field of social work, and knowledge of the contribution to day care of the fields of health, education, and social work. (p. 52)

The League recommended that the director should be a person of administrative skills, with such personal qualifications as "stability, judgment, friendliness, sensitivity to the feelings of children and parents, a fundamental respect for the dignity and rights of human beings, flexibility, capacity for growth, integrity, and courage" (quoted in Keyserling, 1972, p. 53). Nothing was said about the "business" aspects of administration.

This League report found that 97% of the proprietary centers were licensed but considered that state and local requirements with respect to center directors' education and training were "low or conspicuous by their absence." Only a high school education was required in 22 states, and in 27 others directors were expected to have "some college or equivalent experience" (quoted in Keyserling, 1972, p. 53). Endorsement of college class work was implied by the detailed description of a community college course sequence providing an associate of science degree in nursery school education, operation, and management.

A committee established in 1976 by the National Academy of Sciences estimated that there were approximately 1.3 million children in licensed or approved centers (including Head Start) and another 1.7 million in informal day care. In addition, 4.7 million of those aged 3–5 were in preschools or private nurseries, with three-quarters of them part-day. It was impossible to estimate how many children were left with neighbors or family members. One recommendation was that each state should have an early childhood coordinator to encourage the professionalization of preschool directors. The National Association of State Directors of Child Development (NASDCD) and the Early Childhood Project of the Education Commission of the States were commended for efforts to develop joint guidelines that would facilitate the planning, management, and delivery of child and family services (Himelrick & Aitken, 1976).

Snow, Teleki, and Reguero-de-Atiles (1996) compared the regulations immediately following the 1962 and 1967 Social Security grants-in-aid with licensing standards in 1981 and 1995. Their survey showed that regulations are still complex, with wide variations on child–staff ratios, group size, and staff education/training. One of the few areas to show change was the requirement for increased inservice training, but this had merely been substituted for preservice education. Larger group sizes had been permitted by some states, with more children per adult, as a necessary cost reduction for welfare reform programs.

Also in 1996, 70 years after the Committee on Nursery Schools began to work on standards, the NAEYC Public Policy Report in *Young Children* stated:

> Despite some improvements in child–staff ratio, group size, and education of staff, licensing standards in most states still do not meet all of (our) recommended standards of good quality. . . . Variation among the states reflects differences in the public understanding and acceptance of children's needs. . . . We need to lobby for comprehensive regulations that improve the quality of child care for children of all ages. (p. 41)

CONCLUSION

"History buffs" like to quote a warning engraved on the portico of the National Archives Building—that "Those who cannot remember the past are condemned to repeat it." Recognition that there *is* a past is essential to establishment of a profession. As a 1947 historical review of early education expressed it:

> Now and then, in the complicated affairs of men, the factors in a situation arrange themselves in such a way as to accelerate the development of some service or institution so that it makes a generation's normal growth in a few short years. This has happened in the development of educational services for young children. (Goodykoontz, Davis, & Gabbard, p. 44)

As we look backward, we can detect some turning points. Changed patterns of family life and child rearing bring about innovative solutions. Political actions affecting the welfare of young children confirm the old adage that public money is spent for public gain. Technology has caused revolutionary changes, from desktop publishing and distance learning to computer programs that make recordkeeping and decision processing little more than hitting the right keyboard combinations.

However, in the "Final Words" of *Past Caring*, Cahan (1989) reminded readers:

> Historically, differences in quality of child care have been associated with differences in socioeconomic class. As we enter into an era in which child care has, for the first time, become a widely discussed political issue, we must remain mindful of the historical persistence of a tiered system of child care and education. (p. 50)

The dilemma of "caring" versus "business" reflects this stratification, with requirements for an administrator often determined by the potential salary. Few professionals in the early childhood field are willing to follow Peabody's injunction to be above pecuniary motive—although this remains an intangible factor of career choice.

Despite all of the changes, perhaps early childhood directors are *not* facing a dilemma. Perhaps they have been displaying appropriate "business" acumen while "caring" for entire family constellations and their community. Trend guru Faith Popcorn predicts that "no business will survive without Female-Think" and that to be successful it is necessary to combine F-T with the way men traditionally think (Popcorn & Marigold, 1996, p. 167). My *Exchange* article about total quality management (TQM) pointed out that nursery school directors have a long precedent for participative management systems like those recently extolled by American industry (Hewes, 1994). Early in the Industrial Revolution, while employers were treating their workers as inferior dependents, Froebel advocated self-government for schools. His motto, for persons of all ages, was "What one tries to represent or do is what one understands." By the 1890s, when scientific management meant maximum productivity at minimum cost without regard for the workers, William Hailmann was telling kindergarten teachers that "self-direction of the participants . . . imparts the deeper intensity and dignity that comes through feelings of autonomy" (quoted in Hewes, 1994, p. 24). Not only have traditional directors been employing TQM strategies in managing their centers, but this ineffable quality in their professional lives has sustained them through the years.

Perhaps the greatest lesson from history is a question. How can certification of administrators be designed to balance caring and management, and how will we determine when that necessary equilibrium between *caring* and *business* has been achieved?

REFERENCES

Baylor, R. M. (1965). *Elizabeth Palmer Peabody: Kindergarten pioneer.* Philadelphia: University of Pennsylvania Press.

Beatty, B. (1995). *Preschool education in America: The culture of young children from the colonial era to the present.* New Haven, CT: Yale University Press.

Burgess, E. (1961). Standards for teacher education—A challenge to NANE. *Journal of Nursery Education, 17,* 9–14.

Cahan, E. (1989). *Past caring—A history of U.S. preschool care and education for the poor, 1820–1965.* New York: National Center for Children in Poverty, Columbia University.

Celebreeze, A. J. (1964). Our responsibilities to children. In *Journal of Nursery Education, 19,* 169–173.

Eliot, A. (1929). *Minimum essentials of nursery school education.* Boston: National Committee on Nursery Schools.

Evans, E. B., Shub, B., & Weinstein, M. (1971). *Day care: How to plan, develop, and operate a day care center.* Boston: Beacon Press.

Frank, L. K. (1962). The beginnings of child development and family life education in the twentieth century. Edna Noble White Memorial Lecture. *Merrill-Palmer Quarterly, 8,* 1–28.

Gabbard, H. (1957). Legislative report. *Journal of Nursery Education, 9,* 25–26

Goldsmith, C. (1972). *Better day care for the young child.* Washington, DC: National Association for the Education of Young Children.

Goodykoontz, B., Davis, M. D., & Gabbard, H. F. (1947). Recent history and present status of education for young children. In G. Whipple (Ed.), *Forty-Sixth Yearbook, Vol. II* (pp. 44–69). Chicago: National Society for the Study of Education.

Graham, W. (1980). *History of early childhood education in Colorado.* Unpublished research study.

Griffin, A. (1973). *How to start and operate a day care home.* Chicago: Henry Regnery.

Heinemann, A. H. (1893). *Froebel's letters to his wife and others.* Boston: Lee & Shephard.

Hewes, D. W. (1981). Those first good years of Indian education: 1894 to 1898. *American Indian Culture and Research Journal, 5,* 63–82.

Hewes, D. W. (1990). Historical foundations of early childhood teacher training. In B. Spodek & O. N. Saracho (Eds.), *Yearbook in Early Childhood Education: Vol. 1. Early Childhood Teacher Preparation* (pp. 1–22). New York: Teachers College Press.

Hewes, D. W. (1994). TQ what? *Child Care Information Exchange, 98,* 20–24.

Hewes, D. W. (1995). Sisterhood and sentimentality—America's earliest child care centers. *Child Care Information Exchange, 106,* 24–26.

Hewes, D. W. (1996). NAEYC's *first half century—1926–1976.* Washington, DC: National Association for the Education of Young Children. (Original work published 1976).

Hewes, D. W. (1998). *It's the camaraderie: A history of parent cooperative preschools.* Davis: University of California, Center for Cooperatives.

Hewes, D. W., & Hartman, B. (1972). *Early childhood education: A workbook for administrators.* San Jose, CA: R & E Research Associates.

Himelrick, J. B., & Aitken, S. A. (1976). *An introduction to state capacity building.* Denver: Education Commission of the States.

Hinitz, B. F. (1990). Perspectives on administrative issues, 1960–1990. *Delaware Valley AEYC Conference Journal* [special issue].

Hollis, A. P. (1898). *The contribution of the Oswego Normal School to educational progress in the United States.* Boston: Heath.

Host, M. S. (1984). The changing world of the child care director: A 30-year perspective. *Child Care Information Exchange, 3,* 21–23.

Keenan, L. (1990). Taking charge . . . when all you want to do is take care of children. *Child Care, 1,* 26–28.

Keyserling, M. D. (1972). *Windows on day care.* Washington, DC: National Council of Jewish Women.

Landreth, C. (1943). *Education of the young child.* New York: Wiley.

Mahler, T. S. (1957). Let's talk legislation. *Journal of Nursery Education, 8,* 27–30.

Morgan, G. G. (1972). Regulation of early childhood programs. In D. N. McFadden (Ed.), *Early childhood development programs and services: Planning for action* (pp. 129–178). Washington, DC: National Association for the Education of Young Children reprint of Battelle Memorial Institute Report.

NAEYC public policy report. (1996). *Young Children, 51,* p. 41.

Nelson, J. R., Jr. (1982). The politics of federal day care regulation. In E. F. Zigler & E. W. Gordon, *Day care— Scientific and social policy issues* (pp. 267–306). Boston: Auburn House.

Paton, W. A., & Littleton, A. C. (1940). *An introduction to corporate accounting standards.* New York: American Accounting Association.

Peabody, E. P. (1886). *Lectures in the training school.* Boston: Heath.

Popcorn, F., & Marigold, L. (1996). *Clicking.* New York: HarperCollins.

Prochner, L. (1996). Quality of care in historical perspective. *Early Childhood Research Quarterly, 11,* 5–17.

Raymont, R. (1937). *A history of the education of young children.* New York: Longmans, Green.

Rogers, D. (1961). *Oswego: Fountainhead of teacher education.* New York: Appleton-Century-Croft.

Rubin, K. (1987, March). Whose job is child care? In *Ms Magazine,* pp. 32, 64.

Schwartz, B. F. (1984). *The Civil Works Administration, 1933–1934.* Princeton, NJ: Princeton University Press.

Seeley, L. (1904). *History of education.* New York: American Book Co.

Smith, B (1990). The director's dilemma: Crossing over to business. *Child Care Management, 1,* 31–37.

Snow, C. W., Teleki, J. K., & Reguero-de-Atiles, J. T. (1996). Child care licensing standards in the United States: 1981 to 1995. *Young Children, 51*(6), 36–41.

Stein, H. (1965). Administration. In *Encyclopedia of Social Work.* New York: National Association of Social Workers.

Stevenson, J. H. (1990). The cooperative preschool model in Canada. In I. M. Doxey (Ed.), *Child care and education: Canadian dimensions* (pp. 221–239). Scarsborough, Ontario: Nelson Canada.

Taylor, K. W. (1981). *Parents and children learn together* (2nd ed.). New York: Teachers College Press.

White, E. N. (1934). *Handbook for leaders in emergency education programs.* Washington, DC: Office of Education.

Williams, L. R., & Fromberg, D. P. (1992). *Encyclopedia of early childhood education.* New York: Garland.

Wren, D. A. (1987). *The evolution of management thought.* New York: Wiley.

Youcha, G. (1995). *Child care in America from colonial times to the present.* New York: Scribners.

3

The Director as a Key to Quality

Gwen G. Morgan

There are 120,000 children's centers in the United States, including nursery schools, preschools, child development centers, Head Start, and school-age programs, but not including small family child care homes. That is the number of directors (or managers, administrators, program directors, executives, or other titles) who are responsible for the quality, stability, and survival of center programs. Yet only a handful of colleges offer courses in early childhood administration, and only eight states even mention administrative training in their licensing requirements. In most states, the administrator is required to have knowledge about early childhood, but not about how to operate a children's program.

For parents in the United States, early care and education (ECE) programs are a necessity. In our economy, it takes at least a job and a half to make it to the median income. The Family and Medical Leave Act established the right of parents to return to their jobs after a brief leave. In 1995, 55% of new mothers returned to the labor force within 12 months of giving birth; in 1976, the number was 31%. Working parents must rely on public policy to protect their right to choose a quality arrangement to supplement their own care.

Half the children enrolled in nursery schools have working mothers and half have nonworking parents. Nonworking parents, too, view supplemental care and education as a necessity.

Only 14% of centers in the United States are good to excellent (Cost, Quality and Child Outcomes Study Team, 1995). For a country with an economy so dependent on women's labor, and so concerned about the quality of education, 14% is not nearly good enough. The assumption that early childhood professional preparation as a teacher is the only training that administrators need is one of the reasons the quality of children's programs in the United States is largely poor to mediocre. Our field needs to face the reality of children in programs that are just not good enough.

THE IMPORTANCE OF THE DIRECTOR

The role of the director, administrator, or executive in a center is a chal-lenging one. The Appendix lists in full the different aspects of the role and the tasks associated with each. The eight areas of competencies are:

1. The ability to plan and implement a developmentally appropriate care and education program for children and families
2. The ability to develop and maintain an effective organization
3. The ability to plan and implement administrative systems that effectively carry out the program's mission, goals, and objectives
4. The ability to administer effectively a program of personnel man-agement and staff development
5. The ability to foster good community relations and to influence the child care policy that affects the program
6. The ability to maintain and develop the physical facility
7. The legal knowledge necessary for effective management
8. The ability to apply financial management tools

A century ago, programs were small and the director was the key professional person, responsible for training all the other staff. As the field has evolved, emphasis is currently placed on professional prepa-ration of the teacher/caregiver, and little attention is being paid to the qualifications of the person accountable for the entire program or organ-ization.

Those of us who work closely with children's program organizations believe that the director is a key to quality. We know that even a highly trained staff is unlikely to provide quality if there is an unsupportive director.

A major child care policy study (Cost, Quality and Child Outcomes Study Team, 1995) found that the work experience of the director was a critical factor in quality. Directors with administrative experience were found in the small percentage of centers that were good or excellent. Ini-tially a little surprising, the lack of a finding on the effects of administra-tive training in that study probably reflects the obvious fact that almost no academic preparation exists for ECE directors.

Why is the director so important? What does the director do that enables a center to achieve good quality? The most common assumption in the field is that the director is the supervisor of the staff. It is true that we will not achieve quality unless the director has in-depth knowledge in child development, programming, family relations, and family culture and needs; is caring; and can lead the staff. A director who has no specialized understanding of the work will undermine and throw up roadblocks to good teaching. Even if all states required high levels of preparation for teachers, quality would still be largely defeated if the administrators were not competent and supportive.

Before making policy about the preparation and qualifications of directors, it is important to examine what directors actually do that is important to quality. This list might give us an agenda for future research, and it certainly gives us a framework for preparation for the role.

Program Planning and Program Leadership

The director is a part of the child development field/profession, not an outside manager brought in with a different set of skills. While directors need other skills and knowledge that teachers and caregivers may not need, the director must have the technical knowledge of child development theory and practice. Almost all the direct work with children, and much of the relationship with parents, is the responsibility of the staff. The director may have more direct responsibility for working with parents than she or he has for working with children. High-quality ECE programs affect the parent–child dyad positively—not just the children, and not just the parents. Trying to achieve the mission and the vision of the program through others is a frustrating task, one that requires more than supervision. It requires inspiration and leadership.

Supervision

Good directors have found a number of different ways of supervising the performance of staff—from peer supervision systems, to customized training plans, to frequent informal feedback, problem-solving assistance, and coaching.

Most of the college preparation that a director may receive in supervision focuses on the supervision of the personal and professional growth of teachers/caregivers/group leaders. However, the director must also supervise the cook, the office staff, and the maintenance person, whose assumptions about growth might be different and who might require a different set of supervisory skills. Directors must be skilled in giving feedback and in holding all staff to high expectations.

Quality depends on the relationships staff have with children and their parents. The director must achieve quality through the work of others, an often frustrating task and one that demands skills and knowledge.

Other Human Relations Functions

Directors have other equally important tasks that relate to staff. Probably the most important one is recruiting and selecting the right individuals and then integrating them into the organization in a way that results in the staff person's commitment to the organization's goals and mission. No amount of supervision can compensate for a poor choice in hiring.

Quality for children and parents requires directors to be able to diversify their staff. A culturally diverse staff enriches all children and helps to prepare them for the diverse world. One-third of all White children, one-third of all Black children, 17% of Hispanic children, and 28% of all other children are enrolled in centers (National Center for Education Statistics, 1995).

It is important for children from different cultural and language-usage groups to see members of their own culture in positions of leadership and status. Otherwise the program sends a powerful and negative message to children about their own hopes for the future. Once a director has succeeded in diversifying the staffing, staff members will all need help in learning to work together productively.

Directors must also build a healthy organization, creating a strong supportive internal community that supports the staff in their work and in which parents feel comfortable and respected. Building the climate of support entails a great deal of effort in team building and organizational process. Many of these skills fall in the domain of organizational theory and leadership.

An agonizingly large percentage of the director's time can be spent in resolving conflict with staff as well as conflict between staff and parents or between staff and staff. These issues are very difficult and painful, and they do not respond rapidly to rational problem solving. They involve emotions, values, and perspective, and they may take a long time to overcome. Meanwhile, they may seriously undermine quality. The director must balance the needs of children and families with the needs of the people in the organization.

The director's decisions on personnel policies, benefits, and work processes are all directly related to the supportive climate of the organization. It is the director who is usually responsible for establishing the salary scale for staff, benefits, and working conditions. Few directors are able to muster enough resources to pay their staff as well as they would like, but they can set fair salary schedules for each role based on amount of specialized education as well as length of employment.

Internal Policy Making

Many or even most directors play a strong role in centers' policy develop-ment. Center quality is closely related to its mission, its goals, its prin-ciples, and its philosophy. Sometimes the director is simply an agent carrying out policy established elsewhere. But since many children's pro-grams are small, free-standing organizations, the chances are great that most directors are not simply implementing policy but are also deeply involved in guiding policy development. In larger organizations, they may have a smaller role, but they will probably have a voice in policy making.

When the director is the entrepreneur, for-profit or not-for-profit, who started the program and is committed to its future, he or she is often the maker of policy. When there is a board of directors responsible for policy, it is the director who is the technically knowledgeable person who brings information to the board about the changing needs of the commu-nity, about the needs of children and families, and about policy that needs to be developed.

Whether largely alone or with others, the director is often respon-sible for the development and change of the mission, the goals, and the design of the program to meet needs of the community. The director rep-resents the program in networking and collaborating with other commu-nity agencies. The director is the most important antenna for sensing changes in the environment and the need for new policy in response.

The pattern of director involvement in policy looks somewhat differ-ent when the program is part of a larger organization, such as a chain or a school system, college, or Head Start. But there are so many directors involved in policy development that it is important to view policy knowl-edge and skills as within the competencies that directors need to have in the interest of quality. Those who are part of larger organizations need a set of skills in order to influence policy in their situation. They also need the ability to move to a different type of organization.

Internal Policy Implementation

Directors do carry out policy, in addition to some degree of policy mak-ing. Directors are responsible and accountable for the implementation of policy. Their major role is making policy happen.

Knowledge and planning skills are not enough; policy must be imple-mented. It is the director who is accountable for maintaining the baseline of quality required for licensing or the higher level of quality promised by accreditation. A director may know what quality is, and be committed to quality, without achieving it day to day. The director may say to himself or herself, "This was a bad day because the toilets overflowed, that parent expressed such strong feelings, and the licensing office made an unannounced visit." Yesterday, the director had three other reasons that quality wasn't achieved. Tomorrow there will be three others. The day-to-day crises of operation can derail the center from its quality objectives to such an extent that there is almost never a day when the center operates as the director intended.

Skills in creating operating systems are needed to assure that quality is achieved, such as scheduling staff, monitoring attendance and enrollment, communicating with everybody, purchasing, and maintaining the physical facility in good condition. The director makes decisions about the number of staff to hire based on knowledge of the research that makes ratio and group size key indicators of quality and based on his or her own experience of quality for children. The director needs to know what policies need to be hard-and-fast commitments and what policies can have some leeway in implementation.

Financial Management

The director's financial management role is essential to quality. Financial management is different from accounting. It requires more than tracking where the money went; it requires forecasting, using money soundly on the basis of priorities, making good predictions, and being alert to changes on one side of the budget that require changes on the other side. Often the director has skills in garnering new resources. Certainly the director must be able to allocate resources according to the program's priorities—the essence of quality.

All the director's dreams and aspirations for children and families are found in the budget in the language of money. If the director lacks skill in financial management, or if the director has delegated financial management to another board or staff member, someone else is going to be making all the decisions that determine policy and quality.

The full budget process is quite different from what the administrator in Head Start or in public school–run programs encounters. In these systems, the administrator may have few responsibilities for the income side of the budget, being responsible only for spending within limits set elsewhere. However, future reforms may focus on management at the program level, creating a demand for administrators with financial skills. If administrators are to move readily from one system to another, and if they are to be prepared for future changes and reforms, basic financial management skills—such as budgeting, break-even analysis, cost analysis, cash-flow projection, and budget projection—are desirable. If the director is participating in both budget policy and program policy, and understands how closely they are married, quality is more likely.

Community Collaboration and Public Policy

The director also has external roles and relationships that are important to quality.

The community role is one aspect of this side of the director's work. Tasks include gathering resources, networking, interprofessional collaboration, and negotiating with funding sources and regulators. They require interpersonal skills, an "eagle-eye view" of the community configuration of services, and the ability to conceptualize and strategize for the future. Working together with other community agencies that serve families will enable each program to respond more fully to the needs of children and their families.

The public policy role is a second aspect of the director's work that is focused outside the organization. As directors seek quality for their centers, they find some aspects that are within their control at their centers and other aspects that are constraints or opportunities coming from public policy outside the center. A good example is the critical issue of salaries of ECE staff. Within the resources of the center, the director may be limited to assuring that a salary scale is fair and offers incentives and rewards to those who increase their learning. But the administrator is also a community leader influencing public policy who will be alert to opportunities for bringing more public resources to bear on the issue of paying the cost of quality, including compensation. To be effective in public policy, the director must be knowledgeable about both the policy process per se and the background and policy history of each important issue in the field.

The description above of the director's various roles and tasks is intended to summarize the reasons that the director is the key to quality. We know that we need quality for positive effects on children and that low quality will have negative, harmful effects. All positive effects of child care and education correlate with the quality of the program; harmful effects correlate with poor quality. The next question is how best to assure that there are regulatory, funding, and educational policies in place that assure that directors have the knowledge and skill they need.

A CREDENTIAL FOR DIRECTORS

The term *director credentialing* is used here to refer to the awarding of a certificate, permit, or other document. The document certifies that an individual has mastered a specific set of defined skills and knowledge, and has demonstrated competencies to prepare for performance as a director in any ECE or school-age setting (e.g., Head Start, private nonprofit programs, for-profit programs, public and private schools). A credential may be awarded by a professional association, state agency, higher education consortium, or other organization with a legitimate interest in the qualifications of directors.

The process of credentialing begins in most places as an optional process. Directors are invited to seek the credential on a purely voluntary basis, and there may be help for them in paying for it. Since it is in early stages, it could evolve in a number of different directions. If required in licensing some day, it would become the necessary level of quality to prevent harm to children. If voluntary but required for funding or accreditation, it could be part of a higher level of quality or a part of a continuous pursuit of excellence.

LEVELS OF QUALITY

In order to think about how a credential can have maximum effect on quality in a particular state or locality, it is important to conceptualize different levels of quality. Different strategies are needed to address different levels of quality. Norris Class (1969) presented a conceptual framework for levels of standards for ECE at a National Association for the Education of Young Children (NAEYC) meeting in Seattle many years ago. Since then, the framework has been reworked and summarized a number of times in print. Conceptually it is useful to define four levels of quality:

1. Harmful, which is unacceptable
2. Good enough so that the program can be permitted to exist
3. Good quality
4. Pursuit of excellence

These different levels of quality are implemented in public policy by different strategies that can use levels of standards. The three most important are licensing standards, funding standards, and accreditation standards (Morgan, 1996).

Good Enough to Do No Harm

The most basic level of quality in licensing is good enough to do no harm. Licensing is a powerful state intervention into the right of citizens to earn a living caring for children, on behalf of children's right not to be harmed and parents' right to safe choices. Licensing laws have been in place in the states for many years, the first passed in Pennsylvania in the 1880s. The law usually begins by completely outlawing the service, because the legislative body has determined there is a risk of harm. Permission is then restored to certain individuals who have met standards and received an official license, or permit, from the state. The accountable individual responsible for meeting these basic standards is the director. In this way licensing affects all legally operating programs.

Strategies at the level of potential harm must address reducing the risk of harm—harm from developmental impairment just as much as the harm that comes from fire, unsafe buildings, disease, poisoning, or injury.

A first principle has to be "First, do no harm." There are many research findings that harm is more likely to come to children in programs with higher ratios of children cared for by untrained teachers, and under various other conditions that licensing rules seek to eliminate. It is the director who is responsible and accountable for maintaining the level of quality that reduces the risk of harm.

Penalties, and in some situations help, is ordered for programs that operate at a harmful level, to try to bring them to a level where harm will not be likely. Other incentives are needed to move programs from this "good enough to do no harm" level to higher levels of quality, since the state cannot require programs to achieve their ideals.

Misperceptions of Licensing. In general, advocates in the ECE field do not define levels of quality. We want only the best for America's children. We have given policy makers the impression that we are in favor of unnecessary expense, to benefit ourselves and our field. To quote an influential author in the present climate (Howard, 1994), "What they dream up, and then turn into law, is their view of the ideal facility. It is as if the illustrator Norman Rockwell had been made dictator and ordered everyone to do things his way" (p. 39).

Howard continues, "Less idealized rules would permit affordable day care for parents who can't possibly pay $4,000 for each child, while still providing a basic oversight function. This would require, however, accepting the idea that everything can't be perfect" (p. 41).

Currently, no state is requiring "ideal" quality, or "Cadillac child care," in its licensing, despite perceptions like these. The fact that there is a massive misperception of licensing may tell us that we as advocates have given the impression that we want licensing to mandate the ideal. In our pursuit of quality, we may have reinforced the views of the antiregulators.

Licensing must be feasible in the evolving field of practice. Licensing can eliminate intentionally harmful programs, reduce risks, educate new providers, and maintain a level of "good enough" care. But it cannot go beyond "good enough" until the citizens of a state raise the bar and redefine what is "good enough." However, the fact that 86% of all centers are mediocre to poor is an indication that some states, at least, have not set a reasonable level of "good enough" quality to prevent harmful care.

The level of "good enough" is agreed on when there are programs in a state able and willing to meet the rules. If a state sets its rules higher than the field of practice can meet—an unlikely possibility—it will not be able to enforce the rule, and widespread waivers will result.

However, the field of practice is continually learning and improving beyond what is required. Accreditation, training programs, professional meetings, publications, talented administrators, and expert advice affect the level of quality in a state. At fairly frequent intervals when the state is rewriting its rules, there will be more practitioners able to reach a higher level of quality and a redefinition of "good enough" based on new knowledge of how to prevent harm to children.

Licensing therefore tends to continue to raise its level of required "good enough" quality, over time, as more and more practitioners improve their programs and are able to meet new rules. A strategy that has been successfully used in many states in recent years (Georgia, North Carolina, and Texas) has been to adopt new rules and to postpone the effective date for implementing them. In that way, opposition to change can be defused by giving operators time to make the transition.

Administrative Requirements for Director Qualifications. As noted in Chapter 1, at the licensed level, there are currently very few states that even mention administrative training as necessary for directors, although they may require child development training.

Good Quality

Even though licensing alone cannot get us to good quality, there are other policy tools that states can use as incentives for higher quality. The next level up of standards would be funding standards. A funding source might specify that programs receiving its dollars should not only meet basic licensing requirements but also reach a higher level of quality. Funding standards apply to subsidized programs rather than to all programs. Programs not receiving these funds are not obligated to meet these standards, but the funding source can specify a level of quality it wishes to attain to achieve its goals. Head Start's performance standards are one example of funding standards.

Accreditation standards represent a level of quality that is voluntarily sought by programs that wish to be recognized for their higher quality. Accreditation is one of our best tools for stimulating programs to be "good" or to pursue excellence. The bottom line for accreditation cannot be "good enough"; it has to be "good." There are now accreditation systems for centers, family child care homes, and school-age programs from national organizations representing each of those types of programs. Programs with the will toward higher quality voluntarily apply for accreditation, which recognizes their will and their accomplishments, regardless of state subsidy policy. Accreditation in the long run affects all market care.

Pursuit of Excellence

Excellence is a pursuit that never ends, as most directors know. We should not be satisfied with "good" programs, even those that meet every accreditation standard. It is important to take a look at our excellent programs, and at excellence in other fields, to see what we can do to inspire and challenge the ECE field to pursue excellence.

Centers for young children often have a high degree of program autonomy, with a minimum of the red tape and bureaucracy that impedes school-based management as a school reform. Each small licensed program can be establishing its own unique place in the community and pursuing its own unique vision.

Knowing this, we might think of ways of writing accreditation standards that will expect continuous improvement and inspire excellence. We might consider whether we could ask programs to identify further improvement beyond accreditation standards that they intend to make, and then ask for a progress report at the time for reaccreditation.

DIRECTOR-BASED STRATEGIES TOWARD IMPROVING ALL LEVELS OF QUALITY

Promising avenues for improvement of ECE programs must include much more attention to an administrator's professional training, in both licensing requirements and accreditation standards. Much of our emphasis has been limited to assuring that directors or other administrators are qualified in child development. However, they need to understand how to manage, how to maintain policy in their operations, how to give feedback to their staff, and how to create a healthy organization—the competencies summarized in the Appendix. A complex set of competencies enables administrators to design their programs to meet the changing needs of the families and children who use them. A credential can support administrators and staff in working toward higher levels of quality. The following strategies can be adopted to move toward director credentialing.

Institute Licensing Requirements for Training in Administration

A credential for directors, to the extent that it is necessary to prevent harm, must become a part of the licensing strategy—or at the very least some administrative content should be part of the required training. Since directors are so important to quality, states should increase the amount of administrative training required over and above child development training, and eventually should require a credential.

If a program cannot or will not consistently meet the basic requirements a state has determined to be necessary, it may be that the director lacks necessary competence. A state could require additional training or a change in management as a further enforcement tool.

Some of the content of director credentialing training will be directly useful in further improvement of family child care, since the provider's role, too, requires both a knowledge of administration and a knowledge of service to children and their families. The administrative content should be accessible to providers as part of required training.

Require Administrative Training for Recognition at Higher Levels of Quality

A director credential that is above the basic level of licensing could be required as an accreditation standard. Initially it could be a funding requirement for directors of centers above a certain size, where a case can be made that the requirement would protect the investment of public dollars in the program.

Since director competence predicts success in achieving accreditation, it is justifiable to strengthen the qualifications of directors in the accreditation standards.

The credential required for licensing might not be as extensive as what the state will establish for its voluntary credential. For example, Wisconsin is developing a credential based on six courses. The first course is required for licensing. The other courses are initially voluntary, although the entire credential might be required by a private funding source or a board of directors seeking to employ a competent director.

Pay More for Higher-Quality Programs

Funding strategies can and should be tied to level of quality, and a qualified director should be included in the definition of rate structure. Starting at the lowest level, we certainly should not fund the programs that are low in compliance with licensing. Texas now has a system of numerically rating centers on their level of compliance, from 1 to 3. Centers with high compliance are visited less often by licensors. Those with lower compliance are visited more often. The state will not fund centers that are rated in the bottom tier.

Some states have defined a level between licensing and accreditation. A very interesting trend in the states has been a recent policy of paying a higher subsidy rate for higher-quality care. Some states have established three levels, the "good enough" level of licensing; a middle "good" level; and the high quality represented by accreditation. At least 17 states have adopted the policy of paying at least two levels of subsidy (Arkansas, Arizona, Colorado, Connecticut, Florida, Kentucky, Minnesota, Mississippi, New Jersey, New Mexico, North Carolina, Ohio, Oklahoma, Pennsylvania, South Carolina, Vermont, and Wisconsin), and of these, at least four have three tiers—low, medium, and high (Blank & Adams, 1997).

It is the middle tier where states are most likely to become creative, specifying in their reimbursement policy more stringent regulations for staffing than they can impose in licensing. Key standards at this level might include more qualified teachers, better ratios and group size, fair salary schedules, and diverse staffing. A credentialed director at this level could be expected to have a greater amount of training than the state would require of all directors through licensing. This credentialed director would be the accountable person for achieving the higher level of quality.

Improve Access to Training

The incentives to further training through scholarship programs such as the Teacher Education and Compensation Helps (T.E.A.C.H.®) Early Childhood Program in North Carolina can inspire the field of practice to move to another level. Teacher Education and Compensation Helps can be tailored to many different purposes, including a scholarship program for directors to help them finance a credential.

It may well be that at some future time we will develop some kind of awards for excellence that will go beyond accreditation to recognize the uniqueness of each vision of quality. Before that can happen, we will need a national supply of highly skilled and knowledgeable administrators, pursuing excellence and refining their visions. Strategies for excellence will be dependent on the excellence of the administrator's leadership.

APPENDIX: COMPETENCIES OF EARLY CARE AND EDUCATION PROGRAM ADMINISTRATORS

This list of director competencies was adapted from a list I prepared based on work by Joe Perrault and Nancy Travis at Save the Children, refined through class discussion and assignments by administrators from across the country who participate in administrators' courses at Wheelock College. The following competencies should be possessed by administrators:

1. The ability to plan and implement a developmentally appropriate care and education program for children and families.

A competent director has
- The ability to hire competent staff to work with children and contribute to their further development in a staff development plan that includes frequent feedback sessions between director and children.
- Knowledge of current research findings in child and human development theory and their applicability to children's programs. This includes knowledge of brain development.
- Knowledge of caring concepts, including their history and applicable theory, in relation to other child development findings.
- Familiarity with best practices in programming for children.
- Focus on the child in the family.
- Understanding of the potential of observation as a tool in programming, and support for observation and documentation as an important staff function.
- Ability to inspire and stimulate staff to continuous improvement of the program with attention to:
  —Pacing for a long day
  —Transitions
  —Family culture and values
  —Family-friendly service
  —Presentation skills and communicating to parents
  —Display of child work to give meaning to the activities of the program
  —Anti-bias curriculum
  —Developmentally appropriate practice for all children

For work with families, directors need competence in all the above, plus
- Helping relationships.
- Family development, parent development, education, leadership development, and interprofessional perspectives.
- Skills in feedback and communication.

- Empathy with parent perspectives.
- Skills to support family culture and language; ability to negotiate across differences.
- Respect for centrality of the parent role in a child's life.
- Ability to see the child care program as a support for parent's lives (family centric) rather than exclusively focusing on the parent as part of a supportive environment for the early care and education program (center centric).

2. The ability to develop and maintain an effective organization.

A competent director must

- Understand the legal form of the organization, its philosophical base, its history, and its goals.
- Be able to sense and respond to environmental influences and to stakeholders, both external and internal.
- Understand and comply with all applicable rules and regulations.
- Develop a management philosophy that includes a clear mission statement and clear objectives based on the organization's values and the needs expressed by parents in the community.
- Develop and implement strategies for management that build teamwork and participation of staff; make effective use of time and other resources; engage in short-term problem solving and long-term planning.
- Work with and contribute to board development in organizations that have boards; develop advisory groups where applicable.
- Be able to evaluate the program and all its components, and use this evaluation to change and improve the program.
- Know basic strategic planning processes.

3. The ability to plan and implement administrative systems that effectively carry out the program's mission, goals, and objectives.

A competent director is ultimately responsible for

- Systems for implementing curriculum, addressing all aspects of development for each child appropriate to their individual age, culture, and level of development.
- Regular communication with parents that respects their values and culture; involves them appropriately in the life of the program; supports their lives, including their home language; and focuses on contributing to the parent–child dyad and improving the quality of life for families.
- Nutrition and food service management.
- Recruitment and enrollment of children, as well as attention to separation issues for children and parents.
- Social services and health care, appropriate to the needs of the parent group.

- Organization of tasks and decision-making teamwork throughout the organization.
- Systems for maintaining all aspects of the physical facility in a safe and healthy condition, as well as in a creative design that contributes to learning and teaching.
- Knowledge of basic total quality management concepts.

4. The ability to administer effectively a program of personnel management and staff development.

In the organization as a whole, a competent director must effectively

- Give and receive feedback.
- Gather needed information through regular communication with all staff and parents.
- Facilitate the development of community among staff, among parents, among the board or advisory groups, and among children.
- Maintain personal stability and confidence, self-awareness, desire for growth, and the ability to change.
- Set the stage for recruiting, accepting, and retaining a diverse group of staff members.

For staff development and support, a competent director must

- Observe objectively and give positive and negative feedback in a way that helps individuals to change.
- Motivate and challenge people and set a high standard.
- Communicate clear expectations for performance and ensure that goals and objectives are met.
- Possess effective training skills and knowledge of training methods.
- Have the skills needed, including interviewing skills, to hire the right person.
- Supervise performance over time, with follow through, so that poor performance leads to termination and good performance is recognized.
- Have knowledge of different supervisory styles and methods that can meet individual needs of supervisees and be appropriate to classroom staff as well as the cook, maintenance staff, office staff, and other nonclassroom personnel.
- Model appropriate behavior.
- Understand different cultural styles of interacting, leading, and participating.

5. The ability to foster good community relations and to influence child care policy that affects the program.

A competent director must

- Have knowledge of community services and functions, including knowledge of:

—Child care resource and referral organizations and what they offer parents and providers

—Ending fees, charged and service options, and how to network to form professional collaborative relationships with other program administrators

—Health services, social services, and other vendors and providers of functions needed by the program and the parents using them

—Community-based organizations such as religious institutions that have influence on families' lives

—Child care policies and changes that are made in them, including regulatory policies, funding policies, and governmental structure

—Legislative processes and how to participate in them

—Media and other ways to develop public support

- Use this knowledge to build networks and coalitions as needed.
- Have effective skills in communication, including:

—Public speaking

—Writing letters

—Writing proposals, marketing plans, and business plans

—Communicating in languages other than English

—Giving media interviews and maintaining media contacts

—Supervising or producing brochures, flyers, parent handbooks, and other materials

—Maintaining regular communication with other advocates

—Maintaining a commitment to educate the community on issues affecting young children and their programs on a regular basis

6. The ability to maintain and develop the physical facility.

A competent director must have the knowledge and skills to

- Establish procedures to monitor and correct in order to maintain compliance with all applicable codes—fire, safety, health, sanitation, building, and zoning.
- Maintain all equipment to ensure safe working condition and have knowledge of procedures for maintenance and repair.
- Establish and maintain safe security practices and equipment at all times.
- Ensure appropriate room arrangement/space design and support the design and redesign of effective space, based on knowledge of environmental psychology and early childhood education.

7. The legal knowledge necessary for effective management.

The competent director must be able to work with legal counsel and will have general personal knowledge in the following areas

- Applicable regulatory standards and concepts, including the rights of licensees

- Custody issues that affect child care
- Confidentiality and child welfare laws that affect child care
- Labor laws that affect child care
- Antidiscrimination laws that affect child care and employee rights
- Working knowledge of liability issues
- Health rules
- Basics of contracts that affect the center

8. The ability to apply financial management tools.

The competent director will assume responsibility for financial management and will have the ability to direct the accountant or other financial staff on how to present figures on income, expenditures, enrollment, and other information in ways that inform decision making. This includes the ability and knowledge needed to

- Mobilize needed resources, including the use of fund-raising, marketing, unrelated business income, and governmental grants or third-party purchase-of-service agreements.
- Maintain accurate and complete financial expenditure records.
- Use financial tools in planning:
  —Effective budget planning and monitoring
      Establishing a staffing pattern for each room
      Setting an annual budget and projections
      Conducting deviation analysis
      Conducting functional cost analysis
  —Cash-flow projection
  —Break-even analysis
- Identify federal, state, and local funding sources, both public and private.
- Understand basic marketing concepts.
- Develop and implement fee policies that fit the needs of the organization.
- Develop a compensation structure that rewards retention and increased knowledge and skills of staff.

Note: The above competencies are needed by directors of centers who serve as executives, fully responsible for program operation. If the income side of the budget is someone else's responsibility, as is usually the case in public school–based programs or Head Start, the director may not need the full range of competencies. Directors of small programs and group child care home licensees need the competencies at a more generalist level than directors of large programs.

REFERENCES

Blank, H., & Adams, G. (1997). *State developments in child care and early education 1997*. Washington, DC: Children's Defense Fund.

Class, N. E. (1969, November). *Safeguarding day care through regulatory programs: The need for a multiple approach*. Paper presented at the National Association for the Education of Young Children annual conference, Seattle, WA.

Cost, Quality and Child Outcomes Study Team. (1995). *Cost, quality and child outcomes in child care study: Public report*. Denver: University of Colorado at Denver, Economics Department.

Howard, P. K. (1994). *The death of common sense: How law is suffocating America*. New York: Random House.

Morgan, G. (1996). Licensing and accreditation: How much quality is quality? In S. Bredekamp & B. Willer (Eds.), NAEYC *accreditation: A decade of learning and the years ahead* (pp. 129–138). Washington, DC: National Association for the Education of Young Children.

National Center for Education Statistics. (1995). *Child care and early education program participation of infants, toddlers, and preschoolers* (NCES 95-824). Washington, DC: U.S. Department of Educational Research and Improvement.

Travis, N. E., & Perrault, J. (1981). *The effective day care director: A discussion of the role and its responsibilities*. Atlanta: Save the Children Child Care Support Center.

4

Images from the Field: How Directors View Their Organizations, Their Roles, and Their Jobs

Paula Jorde Bloom

My interest in directors' role perceptions was prompted by an incident several years ago when I was the director of a preschool. I had just finished giving a new parent a tour of my school. While she completed her enrollment forms, I offered to entertain her son in my office. Jonathan inspected the photographs and plaques on my wall, surveyed the books and knick-knacks on my shelf, and carefully eyed the stack of papers on my desk. He then turned to me and with the unabashed candor so characteristic of a 4-year-old said, "You must be the queen of this school." Deciding that a 4-year-old wasn't quite ready for lecture on how "queen" didn't exactly square with my management philosophy, I simply turned to Jonathan and said, "Yes, I guess a director is a lot like a queen."

Jonathan has since graduated from college, but his innocent remark has remained etched in my memory. During these intervening 20 years I've thought a lot about how individuals view their roles and the power that personal perceptions have in shaping one's professional identity.

Different roles in any organization carry with them associated expectations; both self-expectations and the expectations of others. These role perceptions evolve from a set of beliefs about the workplace and the status and worth of chosen careers. They also tend to reflect an individual's experiences and preferences, culture, level of education, and personal philosophy.

While research has been conducted on the role perceptions of administrators at the elementary and secondary educational level (Duke, 1988; Wax & Hale, 1984), little systematic research has been conducted on how early care and education (ECE) program directors perceive their roles. This chapter is designed to fill that gap.

A WORD ABOUT METHODOLOGY

During the past 5 years I have been collecting data from directors regarding their view of their organizations, their perception of their administrative roles, and their evaluation of their specific jobs. Some of the data have been qualitative in nature, gathered from in-depth interviews and reflective narrative journals. Interviews have been particularly useful for gaining a deeper understanding of the idiosyncratic nature of directors' career decisions. I have found that directors' narratives provide a useful vehicle for probing their interpretations of the context in which they make professional decisions. The use of narratives is premised on the belief that practitioner-derived knowledge is both trustworthy and relevant (Schön, 1987; Smyth, 1989). As Witherell and Noddings (1991) state, "The stories we hear and the stories we tell shape the meaning and texture of our lives at every stage and juncture" (p. 1).

I have also gathered quantitative data from 257 directors who have completed the Directors' Role Perceptions Questionnaire. This questionnaire was designed to discern patterns in responses relating to role definition, job satisfaction, job commitment, role stress, and directors' growth and change over their career cycle.

I have found metaphorical analysis to be an important technique in this line of inquiry. A linguistic metaphor is a word picture whereby the individual creates an image with words, combining and integrating nonlinear/imaging communication with linear/verbal communication (Kopp, 1995). Different types of metaphors include: anecdotes and short stories aimed at achieving specific, limited goals; similes and analogies that emphasize a specific point; and artistic productions such as drawings or models that symbolize other things (Barker, 1985).

Using a metaphor to describe the nature of metaphors, Kopp (1995) states, "Metaphors are mirrors reflecting our inner images of self, life, and others" (p. xiii). The word *metaphor* comes from the Greek *meta*, meaning "above or over," and *phorein*, which means "to carry or bear from one place to another." A metaphor carries meaning from one domain to another. Metaphors are powerful because they engage the mind in making translations from a literal mental language to the analogic, from word thinking to picture thinking, from left brain to right brain thought (Lakoff & Johnson, 1980).

I have found the use of metaphors to be a powerful tool in promoting the personal and professional growth of early childhood directors. This is because the metaphors directors use often carry with them implicit natural solutions to the personal concerns they may be dealing with. As Schön (1979) points out, metaphors provide both a perspective or frame (a certain way of looking at things) and the process by which new per-spectives on the world come into existence. Individuals tend to seek out personal metaphors to highlight and make coherent their own pasts, their present activities, and their goals for the future. Thus, the metaphorical images directors use can be a useful method for clarifying dominant issues relating to their personal and professional roles and for shaping their future behavior.

HOW DIRECTORS VIEW THEIR ORGANIZATIONS

Early childhood organizations are complex social systems. They embody ambiguous and often paradoxical phenomena that can be understood in many ways. The challenge for early childhood directors is to make sense of and deal with this complexity. Examining the metaphors that directors use to describe their centers is one way to gain insight into the assumptions, beliefs, and personal visions they have about their organizations. Metaphors form the heart of the conceptualizations people have about what things mean and how things work. If we can help directors tap into these understandings, a bridge can be built between vision and practice.

Metaphorical Themes

In an analysis of the organizational metaphors of 257 directors, several themes surfaced. *Caring and nurturing* is the theme of 22% of the directors' metaphors when referring to their centers. The specific metaphor most characteristic of this category is family. One director states:

> In a family each person is loved unconditionally in an emotionally secure and stable environment. At our center, we not only nurture the children, we nurture one another. We celebrate every teacher's birthday and the anniversary date of their employment. The things I do also communicate this spirit. I try to give lots of hugs to the children and emotional support to the staff.

The family metaphor is not unique to early childhood educational settings (Baker, 1991; Morgan, 1986; Schlechty & Joslin, 1984; Wincek, 1995). Other educational settings often promote mission statements that use terminology like "family of learners" or "family atmosphere" and are built on the core beliefs of loyalty, trust, compassion, and a commitment to shared values. In their study of 47 elementary and secondary schools, Steinhoff and Owens (1988) found that one-third of their respon-

Figure 4.1. Visual Representation—Caring and Nurturing Metaphorical Theme

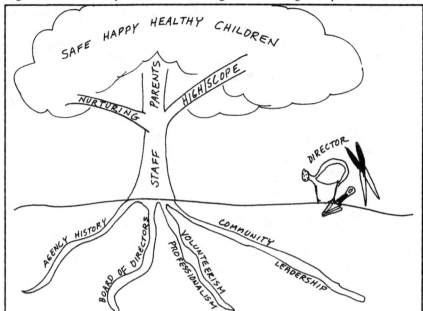

dents identified with the family metaphor. They state, "Not unlike a 'real' family, food rituals appear to be a significant glue which binds these faculty members to one another and provides a major avenue for socializing, commiserating, and bonding" (p. 5).

Other metaphors expressed by directors that fall into the category of caring and nurturing include haven and garden. Figure 4.1 is a visual representation of one director's metaphor that captures this theme.

Change, growth, and surprise are important elements in a cluster of metaphors used by 18% of directors. These directors see their centers as ever-changing and growing organizations. Flux, transformation, change, and growth are generally viewed in positive terms in the metaphors selected by these directors (e.g., climbing a ladder, lens coming into focus). Even the occurrence of surprise is cast in positive terms (surprise party, a box of chocolates). Directors whose dominant metaphors fall into this category see their organizations as living, dynamic systems, not static or stagnant entities. Figure 4.2 is one director's metaphorical representation that could be classified in this category.

Making connections as a metaphorical theme characterized another 16% of directors' responses. Here the emphasis is on the relationship be-

Figure 4.2. Visual Representation—Change, Growth, and Surprise Metaphorical Theme

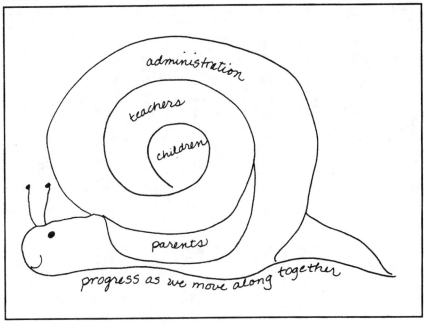

tween the parts to the whole (as in jigsaw puzzle or quilt) and working together (as in Broadway play). Figure 4.3 is an example of a visual representation of this metaphorical category. In describing her choice of a jigsaw puzzle, Karen elaborates:

> In operating a center there are a lot of different pieces. Every piece has a place, and it fits to make a whole. Typically, the director is the only one who sees the picture on the top of the puzzle box and is capable of fitting those pieces together, but she can't do it alone.

The *centrality of relationships* is seen in the metaphors in this category. As a management philosophy, many of these directors believe that sustaining positive productive relationships is at the core of effective program administration. Themes of empowerment, responsibility to others, interdependence, collaboration, and collegiality are basic values underlying their philosophy and practice.

In describing the leadership style of women, Helgesen (1990) uses the metaphor of a web, with the leader in the middle connected to its

Figure 4.3. Visual Representation—Making Connections Metaphorical Theme

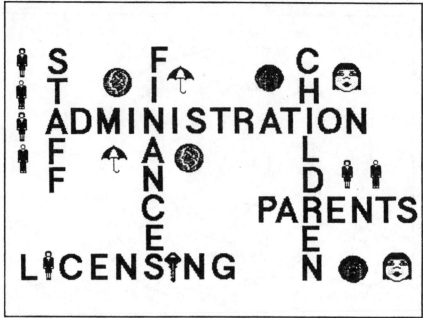

many strands. Implicit in the management philosophy of women leaders embracing this theme is the importance of affiliation, inclusion, and group versus individual achievement.

> Webs and nets . . . suggest a complexity of relationships and the delicate interrelatedness of all so that tension and movement in one part of the system will grow to be felt in all parts of the whole. In the complexity of a web, no one position dominates over the rest. Each person—no matter how small—has some potential for power; each is always subject to the actions of others. (Belenky, Clinchy, Goldberger, & Tarule, 1986, p. 178)

Uniqueness and diversity are viewed as positive organizational characteristics in the metaphors of 14% of the directors. This metaphorical theme probably reflects the general emphasis in the field on celebrating individual differences as well as directors' heightened awareness of diversity issues in the wider culture. Lisa, the director of a community college child care center, used the metaphor of a box of gourmet cookies to capture the essence of her center (see Figure 4.4). She states, "Each staff member is unique in his/her own way and brings certain talents which contribute to the entire package."

Figure 4.4. Visual Representation—Uniqueness and Diversity Metaphorical Theme

Organizational stress, tension, and obstacles are evident in the metaphors that 12% of directors use to describe the dysfunctional elements of their centers. Some of these relate to negative surprise (volcano—you never know when it's going to erupt); others relate to a breakdown in communication systems or operations (frozen pond with a crack down the center separating staff and management). Some of the examples under this rubric capture the stress and tension that directors experience when they encounter obstacles or roadblocks in achieving their goals. The visual metaphoric representation depicted in Figure 4.5, for example, expresses one director's frustration at the obstacles she has encountered while pursuing her goal of National Association for the Education of Young Children (NAEYC) accreditation.

Activity and entertainment metaphors characterize a cluster of organizational descriptors used by 10% of directors. These metaphors exude energy and vitality; they capture the variety and pace of activity of everyday life in programs. Circus and beehive are the most popular metaphors used in this category. Many of the metaphors in this category also capture the structural elements of organizational life—people are assigned many

Figure 4.5. Visual Representation—Organizational Stress, Tension, and
Obstacles Metaphorical Theme

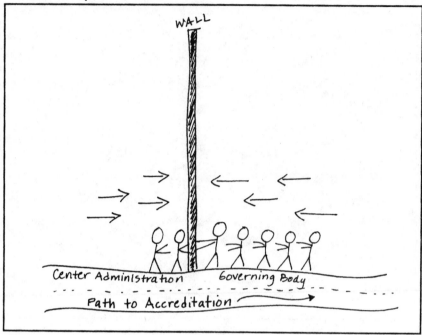

different tasks and these tasks must be coordinated. Figure 4.6 is one director's visual representation of her center that conveys this activity theme.

  Steadfast, resilient, and dependable are the defining characteristics of a
small group of the metaphors that directors use to describe their centers.
Much of the organizational management literature from business and industry refers to organizations as machines, operating with efficiency and
precision (Morgan, 1986). This theme is not embraced widely by early
childhood directors. Only 5% of directors referred to the constancy and
dependability of their centers. When they did, their metaphors had a de-
cidedly early childhood ring to them (e.g., Energizer bunny—it keeps
going and going—or a well-oiled gerbil wheel—it functions constantly).

The Discrepancy Between Current and Ideal

The metaphors directors use to describe their organizations can serve
as a prism for understanding their management philosophies and their
perceptions of the culture of their centers. They can also serve to illumi-

Figure 4.6. Visual Representation—Activity and Entertainment Metaphorical Theme

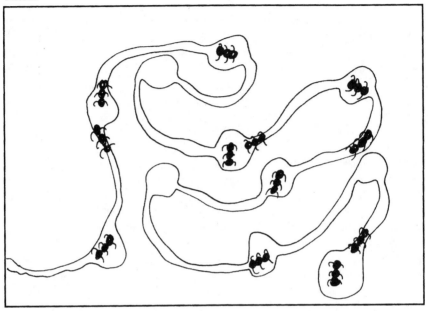

nate issues that need to be resolved and inconsistencies between the director's beliefs and assumptions and his or her actual behavior. The following case study provides an example of this type of analysis.

Linda is the director of a Head Start program who used the metaphor family to describe her center. Upon reflection, however, she came to realize that embracing this metaphor might actually be impeding her desire to promote professionalism among her staff. A management philosophy built around the family metaphor was promoting dependence on her (the parent figure) rather than promoting the development of autonomous professionals—teachers who could make decisions on their own. She also came to realize how her own role stress was tied to her internal conceptualizations of her program and her personal belief that she had somehow failed if a valued teacher left her center or if staff didn't get along. In reflecting out loud, Linda says:

> For years, I've felt like a failure every time one of my teachers left the center. I saw each departing teacher as either a death or a divorce, depending on the circumstances of that teacher's departure. I also see now that I've taken minor disagreements among my staff (nor-

mal sibling rivalry) way too personally. I guess, like a parent, I wanted my children to live in total harmony.

In conceptualizing a new metaphor for her ideal organization, Linda came up with the metaphor of a Broadway play. For her, the play metaphor retains the notion of trust and caring but also has elements of independence and autonomy. In creating a play production, the director deals with a multifaceted set of tasks. Among the director's tasks are auditions, staging, and improving the production through rehearsals. Each role in the play has a specific set of lines, stage directions, and character development. In a larger view of the production company, each individual has a specific set of tasks: The actor interprets and performs a role, the set designer creates the scenery, the musician adds music, and the producer manages finances and other support for the play. Each individual performs specific tasks and—as important—also has a set of relationships with co-workers. Hopefully—as all are committed to the successful production of the play—through their working relationships they complete the tasks that are a part of their roles. When you add up all these tasks— and roles are successfully performed—the result is a Broadway production. Linda felt putting this metaphor into practice mentally and behaviorally would help her achieve the affective neutrality that she needed in order to reduce the role stress in her life.

HOW DIRECTORS PERCEIVE THEIR ROLES AND THEIR JOBS

The sociological literature on work organizations defines *role* in terms of expectations—the normative rights and duties of a role incumbent. "Role expectations can range from required to prohibited, from specific to diffuse, and from impersonal to personal" (Lipham, 1988, p. 174). Role theory assumes that for any particular role there is a set of expected tasks and responsibilities that lead to certain behaviors. In some settings, such as the military, role expectations are highly prescribed. In a play, such as the one described above, role definitions will depend to some extent on the director. However, the success of the endeavor depends on each person, actors and others, working at his or her role in the relationships that create a production. In other situations, such as many early childhood work environments, the expectations may be loosely structured and defined by the individual's interests and preferences.

Role perception is defined as an individual's unique and private perception of his or her phenomenological world in terms of expectations, motivation, accomplishment, relationships, psychophysical state, and time orientation (Wax & Hale, 1984). Every individual represents a range of interests, values, abilities, priorities, and expectations; and each functions as a unique, unified combination of these characteristics. The metaphors that directors use to describe their administrative role and their specific jobs are illustrative because they provide a glimpse into the director's inner world of expectations, concerns, hopes, and dreams.

When asked to think of a metaphor for their administrative role ("A director is a . . ."), individuals tend to select somewhat different images than they do for their own specific jobs ("My job is a . . ."). Metaphors regarding their overall administrative role often reflect a set of idealized expectations about their position, their beliefs about the importance of the role, and their summary judgment about the nature of the position. The metaphors directors use to describe their specific jobs are richly descriptive of the demands they experience every day.

Role

As shown in the metaphor examples in Figure 4.7, the most dominant theme that surfaces when directors refer to their administrative role is the multifaceted nature of the position that requires the balancing of multiple tasks and responsibilities. In my sample of 257 directors, 40% gave responses that fit into one of three related categories: balancing, multiple tasks and responsibilities, or balancing multiple tasks and responsibilities. The most frequently mentioned metaphor used was juggler.

Anyone who has chased the shadow of a director for even a brief time will appreciate the accuracy of this metaphor. Being an effective administrator means keeping many balls in the air—budget analysis, nutrition, nursing, fund-raising, to name a few. The list is long and varied. While administering an early childhood program has never been easy, the director's job has gotten increasingly complex and more difficult in recent years; the number of balls to keep up in the air at any one time has multiplied. Listen to Tom, a director for 20 years, as he describes the personal relevance of the juggler metaphor to his professional experience.

> The director needs to keep his eye on many things at once and hopefully not let too many of them drop, at least not the important things. It's a daily choice which things you're going to deal with. You need to be comfortable with the understanding that you're never going to be able to do everything you need to. There is simply no rest from it—there is always something coming at you.

Metaphors that describe the leading and guiding functions of the director's role were used by 29% of the directors. These metaphors were more varied, however. Individuals used metaphorical references both to

Figure 4.7. Metaphorical Categories for Role (A director is a . . .) $N = 257$

Balancing (5%)[*]
- Seesaw—everything has to balance and little things can throw it off
- Scale—constantly balancing all aspects of the environment
- Tightrope walker—balancing the demands of the parents and the staff

Multiple Tasks and Responsibilities (7%)
- Actor/actress—we must create and become many roles
- Rack full of hats—I assume different roles through the day

Balancing + Multiple tasks and responsibilities (28%)
- Juggler—she has to keep her eyes on many things at once and try not to let them drop
- Circus clown—I am juggling so many balls
- Plate spinner—I work frantically to keep all the plates spinning
- Octopus—I'm expected to do 20 things all at once

Leading and Guiding (29%)
- Coach—she needs a game plan and has to choose the right team members
- Quarterback—her job is to lead, but she often gets too much credit and too much blame
- Captain of a space craft—gets input from other people in order to navigate the ship on course
- Orchestra conductor—knows how to achieve harmony out of different (and sometimes competing) sounds
- Lighthouse—guides teachers, parents, and children

Nurturing and Protecting (15%)
- Tree—she branches out to reach and support others
- Umbrella—she protects and shields staff from outside forces
- Gardener—she nurtures her seedlings by tending, caring, and fertilizing
- Mom—she nurtures everyone but herself

Making Connections (8%)
- Wheel hub—central connection point through which other things flow
- DNA double-helix strand—all the interconnected, interrelated work supports the lives of children
- Puzzle solver—putting together the pieces of an intricate puzzle

Dealing with the Unexpected (4%)
- Firefighter—you never know when or where the next fire will be
- Meteorologist—I forecast one thing, Mother Nature delivers another

Miscellaneous (4%)

[*] Percentage of responses falling into this category.

leadership roles in other fields (e.g., orchestra conductor, football coach, safari guide) as well as things that symbolize leadership attributes (e.g., lighthouse).

Interestingly, absent from directors' metaphorical references is the theme of exerting power and influence. Leadership is virtually always viewed as guiding, coordinating, inspiring, and motivating; never cajoling, forcing, or imposing. The lack of metaphors connoting power and influence is consistent with previous research that has found that early childhood directors (most of whom are female) have a preference for participatory, nonhierarchical management styles. Many directors even express discomfort when thinking about their role as involving a position of authority (Culkin, 1994).

Two additional metaphorical categories—nurturing/protecting and making connections—merit discussion because they are central to the field of early childhood and to feminist literature. Several scholars identify the themes of connection and caring as central to women's psychological development and learning (Belenky et al., 1986; Caffarella, 1992; Chodorow, 1987; Gilligan, 1982; Noddings, 1984). Together, these two categories were mentioned by 23% of directors. These are important themes because they provide an explanatory framework for understanding the management philosophy of many early childhood directors as well as many of the role-related stress issues that confront directors.

Job

When directors are asked to use a metaphor to describe their specific jobs, there is a clear and consistent pattern to their responses (see Figure 4.8). One-half of all responses relate to pace and dealing with the unexpected. The most frequently cited metaphor combining these two elements is roller coaster. Karen, a seasoned director of a large nonprofit center, describes her use of this metaphor:

> The roller coaster typically has the longest line in the amusement park. Pretend that those waiting in line have never been to an amusement park, much less been on the roller coaster. They look up and say, "Why can't those people get control of that ride? Why don't they just slow it down?" How surprised they are to find out that when they get on the ride, they can't do any better. That's why it's such a wild ride. It is a never-ending ride up and down. With maturity you can learn to handle the fast downs. But a director in the survival stage is in the last car getting whipped around. You don't really get off until you leave your program.

Figure 4.8. Metaphorical Categories for Job (My job is a . . .) $N = 257$

Pace (15%)[*]

- Cartoon roadrunner—I'm animated and moving fast constantly
- Whirlwind—I'm always spinning and twirling
- Rolling stone—I don't stop long enough to gather moss
- Treadmill—I'm always running to catch up

Dealing with the Unexpected (16%)

- A freeway—it goes in different directions and you make all kinds of detours
- Maze—there is always a new twist or turn to deal with
- Temperature—because it has its ups and downs
- Hot-air balloon—it has its ups and downs in good and bad weather

Pace + Dealing with the Unexpected (19%)

- Roller coaster—it's fast/slow, up/down, smooth/bumpy, fun/scary
- White-water rafting—riding the rapids
- Riding a surfboard—sometimes I ride the big wave, but mostly I just try to keep from falling off

Caring and Nurturing (17%)

- Mother Teresa—I'm always giving so much to so many
- Gardener—I till the soil, fertilize, and weed when necessary to keep the plants healthy and growing
- Big ear—I listen, empathize, and support staff, children, and parents
- ATM machine—I'm always ready to give different amounts of time, energy, care to different people at a moment's notice

Challenge and Problem Solving (11%)

- Climbing a mountain—the challenges are awesome, the views are breathtaking, even though momentary
- Plumber—I stop the leaks and keep the communication flowing smoothly
- Magician—I'm supposed to make money appear out of nowhere

Stress (8%)

- Like walking on eggshells—I'm afraid I'll upset certain people
- Rubber band—I'm being stretched beyond my limits; I'm ready to snap
- Doormat—everyone walks all over me

Making Connections (6%)

- Tapestry—every day it's a new stitch in creating a masterpiece
- Charlotte the spider—I spin a web of connections bringing staff, parents, and children together

Multiple Tasks and Responsibilities (3%)

- Like a broken mirror—my job is so fragmented
- Hat rack—I wear so many hats during the day

Miscellaneous (5%)

[*] Percentage of responses falling into this category

Additional metaphorical categories relating to directors' specific jobs include caring and nurturing (17%), challenge and problem solving (11%), stress (8%), making connections (6%), multiple tasks and responsibilities (3%), and miscellaneous (5%).

The Discrepancy Between Current and Ideal

When directors reflect on the subtext and personal meanings associated with specific metaphor choices, such analysis often surfaces a discrepancy between current and ideal perceptions of their role. If directors have expectations, for example, that they should be like a captain of a jumbo jet or the head coach for a Super Bowl team and yet the reality of their everyday life is more like a ferris wheel spinning out of control or a doormat that everyone walks all over, that discrepancy can lead to role stress and feelings of inadequacy.

The in-depth interviews I conducted with directors revealed that most experience conflicting emotions about their jobs. On the one hand, they derive enormous satisfaction and personal rewards from serving children and families. They appreciate the diversity of tasks, the opportunity to solve complex problems, and the chance to learn more about their own abilities and beliefs. At the same time, however, they also experience enormous frustration about not being able to meet everyone's needs and not having enough time and energy to achieve their dream of operating a smoothly functioning, crisis-free program. Metaphorical analysis can be a useful technique for assisting directors in identifying the discrepancy between their current and ideal situation.

Marlene, the director of a small for-profit center, is typical of many directors with whom I have worked over the years. She states: "My greatest satisfaction is the smile on parents' faces when their children tell them all the wonderful things they did during the course of the day." When asked to describe her frustrations on the job, she pours out a litany of complaints about parents who don't comply with the center's policies, parents who don't follow through with their commitments, and parents who are neglectful of their basic parenting responsibilities. Parents are the source of her greatest satisfaction, yet also the source of her deepest frustrations.

When asked to describe the role of the director in metaphorical terms, Marlene used the metaphor of an orchestra conductor: "The good conductor is 'in charge' and knows how to achieve real harmony out of very different (and sometimes competing) sounds." This metaphor captured Marlene's idealized expectations for herself as a director—that she should be able to achieve perfect harmony out of all the competing needs at her center. In sharp contrast was the metaphor she used to describe her specific job: "I'm like a marionette. Everyone pulls my strings. They can make me jump, hop, and dance, even when I don't want to."

In discussions about role stress, a common theme expressed by many directors is that they are expected to be all things to all people. Certainly Marlene's metaphor about her job captures elements of this theme. Several scholars (Belenky et al., 1986; Gilligan, 1982; Noddings, 1984) emphasize that a primary organizing principle for women's lives is "doing for others." This means that women often respond to the initiatives and directives of others before attending to their own needs. Women define themselves as moral agents in terms of their capacity to care. Thus their sense of self-worth is often tied to how much they give to others. The result of this orientation is that many women often put their own needs at the bottom of the list after children, staff, and family members—even to the point of depletion.

In my work with directors I point out some of the ways that metaphorical analysis can provide insights into how they can modify their current situation (both their behavior and their expectations) to reduce job-related stress. I begin with a metaphor like the one Diane, the director of a half-day preschool program, shared with me: "I'm an ATM machine—I'm always ready to give different amounts of time, energy, and care to different people at a moment's notice."

Diane's ATM metaphor captures the essence of the caring/nurturing role perception expressed by many directors. After sharing this metaphor with a group of directors, I ask them to come up with creative strategies that a director could use to reduce role stress. They are quick to offer advice. "The ATM machine could give out smaller bills." "How about putting an 'out of order' sign up and directing people to another ATM machine." "I'd increase the service charge for using the ATM machine." "I think the bank needs to let its customers know that they also need to give deposits to the ATM machine, not only take withdrawals."

After generating a dozen or so creative ideas, we then take time as a group to translate each of these metaphorical solutions to concrete practical strategies that directors can use to put the ever-pressing emotional demands of their jobs in perspective. This kind of group exercise, I have found, is a nonthreatening way for directors to deal with the real, and often painful, decisions they need to make about modifying their expectations and their behavior to ensure they will remain a *thriver* in the field of early childhood.

CONCLUSION

The evocative metaphorical images that directors use to capture the essence of their administrative experience paint a portrait of real people in real situations, struggling with real problems. They also provide a glimpse into the future—the possibilities for reshaping roles, solving problems, and redirecting energies to achieve greater personal and professional fulfillment.

In her book *Composing a Life,* Bateson (1989) states that the act of composing our lives is oftentimes improvisation, "discovering the shape of our creation along the way, rather than pursuing a vision already defined" (p. 1). Self-awareness, reflection, and self-assessment are integral tools that facilitate this process. A fulfilling job has balance and diversity, coherence and fit. It is as much crafted as it is the result of a series of serendipitous decisions that we come upon. Whitmyer (1994) stresses the importance of finding meaningful work and the Buddhist tradition of "right livelihood." He states that, "Work is no less necessary for our emotional and physical health than food or shelter" (p. 19). He believes that reflecting on what we do, how we do it, and why we do it will help expand and enhance our ability to find meaningful work.

Understanding directors rests upon our ability to pay close attention to the complexities of their individual lives. Because all people make their own meanings, it is essential that we perceive what they say, how they think, how they feel, and how they understand (Levine, 1989). In listening to directors, one hears both similarities and differences. The similarities often relate to their career stage or the context of their work situation; the differences underscore the many ways in which their experiences impact them uniquely. As the movement to credential directors grows, it will be important to continue examining administrative metaphors. New and deeper levels of training and education as well as increased clarity about the multiplicity of roles of the director may deepen our understanding of ECE administrators and programs. Possibly, more complex metaphors may develop to express the administrator's ability to blend the technical, financial, and policy roles with education, human relations and development, and caring.

Requiring directors to look inward at themselves—their fears, anxieties, and disappointments as well as those things that make them happy or satisfied—can be uncomfortable, but as Bowman (1989) underscores, it is essential for professional growth and development. When directors are aware of their own strengths and weaknesses and how their expectations shape their behavior, they will be better able to understand, monitor, and modify their personal and professional interactions.

The developmental constructs described in this chapter help to explain common and individual differences among directors in how they view their organizations, their roles, and their specific jobs. Additional research is needed, however, to help us understand how changes in growth and development in these various dimensions occur as a function of experience, education, and specific training. This information should help in the design of effective credentialing programs for directors.

REFERENCES

Baker, P. J. (1991). Metaphors of mindful engagement and a vision of better schools. *Educational Leadership, 48,* 32–35.

Barker, P. (1985). *Using metaphors in psychotherapy.* New York: Brunner/Mazel.

Bateson, M. C. (1989). *Composing a life.* New York: Atlantic Monthly Press.

Belenky, M., Clinchy, M., Goldberger, N., & Tarule, J. (1986). *Women's ways of knowing.* New York: Basic Books.

Bowman, B. (1989). Self-reflection as an element of professionalism. *Teachers College Record, 90*(3), 444–451.

Caffarella, R. S. (1992). *Psychosocial development of women: Linkages to teaching and leadership in adult education.* Washington, DC: Office of Educational Research and Improvement. (ERIC Document Reproduction Services No. ED 354 386)

Chodorow, N. (1987). Feminism and difference: Gender, relation, and difference in psychoanalytic perspective. In M. R. Walsh (Ed.), *The psychology of women* (pp. 249–264). New Haven, CT: Yale University Press.

Culkin, M. (1994). *The administrator/leader in early care and education settings: A qualitative study with implications for theory and practice.* Unpublished doctoral dissertation, The Union Institute, Cincinnati, OH. (UMI Abstracts International, No. 39502053)

Duke, D. (1988). Why principals consider quitting. *Phi Delta Kappan, 70*(4), 308–312.

Gilligan, C. (1982). *In a different voice: Psychological theory and women's development.* Cambridge, MA: Harvard University Press.

Helgesen, S. (1990). *The female advantage.* New York: Doubleday.

Kopp, R. R. (1995). *Metaphor therapy.* New York: Brunner/Mazel.

Lakoff, G., & Johnson, M. (1980). *Metaphors we live by.* Chicago: University of Chicago Press.

Levine, S. (1989). *Promoting adult growth in schools.* Boston: Allyn & Bacon.

Lipham, J. M. (1988). Getzel's models in educational administration. In N. Boyan (Ed.), *Handbook of research on educational administration* (pp. 171–184). New York: Longman.

Morgan, G. (1986). *Images of organizations.* Beverly Hills, CA: Sage.

Noddings, N. (1984). *Caring: A feminine approach to ethics and moral education.* Berkeley: University of California Press.

Schlechty, P., & Joslin, A. W. (1984). Images of schools. *Teachers College Record, 86*(1), 156–170.

Schön, D. (1979). Generative metaphor: A perspective on problem-setting in social policy. In A. Ortony (Ed.), *Metaphor and thought* (pp. 254–283). London: Cambridge University Press.

Schön, D. (1987). *Educating the reflective practitioner.* San Francisco: Jossey-Bass.

Smyth, J. (1989, March/April). Developing and sustaining critical reflection in teacher education. *Journal of Teacher Education, 40*(2), 2–9.

Steinhoff, C., & Owens, R. (1988, May). *The organizational culture assessment inventory: A metaphorical analysis of organizational culture in educational settings.* Paper presented at the annual meeting of the American Educational Research Association, New Orleans.

Wax, A. S., & Hale, L. (1984, April). *The development of an instrument for measuring burnout in public school administrators.* Paper presented at the annual meeting of the American Educational Research Association, New Orleans.

Whitmyer, C. (1994). *Mindfulness and meaningful work: Exploration in right livelihood.* Berkeley, CA: Parallax Press.

Wincek, J. (1995). *Negotiating the maze of school reform: How metaphor shapes culture in a new magnet school.* New York: Teachers College Press.

Witherell, C., & Noddings, N. (1991). *Stories lives tell: Narrative and dialogue in education.* New York: Teachers College Press.

5

Core Knowledge for Directors

Nancy H. Brown and John P. Manning

What do directors of early care and education (ECE) programs need to know in order to succeed? This question is complex. As practitioners and policy makers focus on the administrative role in the provision of services for children, a dialogue is underway: What is appropriate and necessary in an administrator's education and training? What must directors know to do their job? In this chapter we investigate what basic or core knowledge an administrator must acquire to function comfortably and successfully in leading a children's program. We present four knowledge areas as the ground upon which a director or other administrator builds increasing skill, knowledge, and expertise in her or his work of managing and leading an ECE program:

- Knowledge of *others*—the stakeholders and groups of stakeholders involved with the program
- Knowledge about *organizations*
- Knowledge about the *external world* that surrounds the children's program and is, in effect, its community
- Knowledge of *self*—referred to as reflective knowledge

When ECE practitioners discuss the administrator's knowledge base, issues of management, budget, and business must be linked with (among others) child development and guidance, curriculum development, and staff training. A dialogue about director knowledge may also focus on the topic of how program sponsorship (nonprofit, for-profit, public, church-related) affects what an administrator needs to know.

In learning to be effective, an administrator integrates his or her learning from these four areas into a base of ideas, attitudes, feelings, and values. This conceptual system guides administrators in their work. (See Chapter 7 for a discussion of how administrators expand their "mental models.") In this chapter, the learning that administrators integrate into their conceptual system is described at this "core knowledge" level. (See Chapter 3 for basic administrative competencies.)

Currently, as we consider a credential for ECE administrators, a newly appointed director typically has professional knowledge, experience, and possibly a degree or other credential in the area of child development or teaching. As noted in other chapters, it is generally the successful practitioner who is promoted to an administrative role. A newly appointed director may be gifted in the area of human relations, working well with colleagues and families as well as with children. Nonetheless, typically a new director has no training in management, leadership, or human relations.

Over time in their work, ECE directors integrate knowledge from at least the disciplines of child development and teaching, human relations, organizational management, communication (including conflict resolution), law and finance, adult learning, and family support. Even the talented, intuitive director with a commitment to ECE benefits from both academic preparation and professional experience. These two sources, along with personal life experience and reflective practice, provide the base on which a director can build a foundation of formal and informal knowledge.

Through ongoing reflective practice and continuing professional development, directors create their knowledge base—the core knowledge from which they practice. In this ongoing learning process, new experiences occur supporting the administrator's development and offering challenges and opportunities for new understanding. A director who has been an excellent teacher will need to learn something about at least adult education, effective communication, and human relations to successfully provide career development opportunities for his or her teaching staff. A director with no previous business experience will need to learn to work with legal and financial staff or consultants. New knowledge about communication may support a novice administrator in learning to write effective grant proposals. Core knowledge is integrated in a director's professional and personal development both consciously and unconsciously. It serves as a backdrop of understanding while a director hones skills, masters competencies, and integrates knowledge into a personal style.

ACQUISITION OF KNOWLEDGE ENGAGES
THE WHOLE PERSON

A director acquires the four types of core knowledge in formal (or official) and informal (or unofficial) ways. Knowledge gained formally includes interdisciplinary academic preparation, as well as participation in professional organizations, conferences, and other training opportunities. Personal experiences in family, community, and other professional or social contexts are informal means of learning.

As a director's knowledge deepens in these four areas, the knowledge areas are interdependent and complementary. A director, for instance, works with a family and teacher to create inclusive learning activities for a young child with a disability. Through this experience, the director may learn about a stakeholder group that is new to her or him—the parents of children with special needs. As she or he works with teachers to adapt a classroom to the needs of the child, the director reflects, learning more about her or his own values, communication skills, and training abilities. In this situation, a director might approach a local corporation to raise funds for renovating the classroom to support the child's learning. Throughout this process, the administrator gains knowledge of the external world and the resources and supports available through connection to the larger community. Integrating professional knowledge means that a director brings together learning from several areas as she or he makes decisions. At the heart of the process of knowing, working, and decision making is self-knowledge, sometimes called reflective knowledge.

Before discussing the core knowledge that we consider fundamental areas of knowing (and learning) for ECE administrators, we believe a review of the ECE literature on the four topic areas would be informative.

EARLY CARE AND EDUCATION LITERATURE
ON CORE KNOWLEDGE

In this chapter the review of the literature on core knowledge is, overall, limited to early childhood literature. There is a wealth of other literature available in business, management, organizational development, and human relations on these topics (see Chapter 6). As the dialogue on director development continues, an understanding of the core knowledge base will require continued examination of that literature as well as the development of new ECE resources. In this way, developing knowledge will be integrated into administrator training, curricula, and other learning experiences. This review is divided into the four knowledge areas.

Others—Stakeholders

Some researchers highlight the importance of a director's communication ability. In a study of the traits of directors of five excellent child care centers, Reckmeyer (1990) found that strong leaders valued one-to-one relationships between and among three groups—children, parents, and teachers. Personal involvement and communication with each group significantly contributed to overall program quality.

In another study of the directors of ECE programs, Buckner (1988) found communicative competence to be the most important director ability. A director's ability to communicate effectively was valued highly by staff and parents. Community members with a stake in ECE programs, such as state legislators and ECE trainers, also considered communication the most important skill. Buckner found that most administrators were well intentioned toward clarity and understanding in their communications. However, they did not know how to handle breakdowns in communication. Buckner recommended training for administrators on negotiation and conflict resolution.

Bloom (1988, 1996) has researched the administrator's role with one of the most immediate stakeholder groups—teachers and other program personnel. She emphasizes that directors need to know how to promote a positive professional climate at their program. Identifying dimensions such as collegiality, supervisor support, and decision making, Bloom's research illustrates the director's need to be knowledgeable about the perspectives, aspirations, and personal needs of the people at all levels of the organization.

The key stakeholders in the ECE program are the children, families, and staff, but the literature about working with families and children is primarily focused on teachers. There may be an assumption that teaching experience prepares the director for communicating with families about administrative issues. In fact, while the roles are complementary, a director's role in work with families is quite different from a teacher's role. It differs both in terms of the dynamics of authority and areas of responsibility. Recognizing this gap in responsibility and the resultant ECE program director's need for specific administrative knowledge, Neugebauer's *Child Care Information Exchange* offers comprehensive professional guidance specifically for directors, including ideas focused on working with families and other customers. Another ECE journal for administrators, *Leadership Quest*, reports on information and research on management topics, including specific stakeholder groups. ECE administrative texts address issues of supervision and the importance of good communication with parents, personnel, and other groups (Caruso & Fawcett, 1999;

Decker & Decker, 1988; Hewes & Hartman, 1972; Hildebrand, 1984; Poster, 1986). Specific texts also focus on the teacher's work with families but may not address the unique opportunities and challenges for the administrator in forming working relationships with families (Springate & Steglin, 1999).

While attention to the director's need for knowledge about relationships with key stakeholders (children, parents, and personnel) is still somewhat sparse, literature about stakeholders outside those key groups is even more limited. *Child Care Information Exchange* and *Leadership Quest* provide useful articles on communicating with and managing a larger circle of stakeholder groups. Information about stakeholders may be included in publications on specific topics, such as budget or collaboration. For example a book such as *Managing the Day Care Dollars* (Morgan, 1982) provides information and strategies for managing budgetary policy. Information about expanded stakeholder groups and the budget is a valuable part of the discussion. However, in general, a director must turn to nonprofit organizational and business literature for in-depth guidance about working with a larger network of stakeholders toward the program's mission. Literature on nonprofits is available on topics such as board development, volunteer management, leadership development, and grant writing.

Organizations

Bloom (1988, 1996) focuses on the work environment, particularly the organizational climate, and the director's role in organizational change. *Child Care Information Exchange* and *Leadership Quest* also respond to directors' knowledge and technical assistance needs on organizational topics. Also, material produced by the Center for Career Development in Early Care and Education at Wheelock College and by centers such as the National Louis University Leadership Center promises to continue to be an important source of published information on ECE leaders and organizations.

Business literature is a rich source of knowledge on organizations, and ECE administrators can go directly to that literature to enhance their understanding of organizational management. A review (Morgan, 1997) of the business literature relevant to ECE leaders includes topics of leadership, systems theory, marketing, stakeholder management, authority, and continuous improvement.

Some business management literature may seem particularly appropriate to ECE practitioners. Covey (1992) addresses the human side of management—that is, issues such as balancing pressures of personal and professional life, teaching and learning (Jones, 1986), empowering others while maintaining focus on the organizational mission, character and leadership, and how attitudes and perceptions have an impact on organizational health. Continuous improvement and total quality management (TQM) strategies have particular appeal and may seem compatible with early childhood professional values. Deming (1986), the father of the TQM concept, was instrumental in promoting the value of involving all employees in training for leadership, self-improvement, and team building. This approach is reflected in some of the ECE professional development models reported in Chapter 11.

There is an abundance of literature from other disciplines about organizations and leadership that is relevant to ECE administrators. However, much more research and scholarly focus needs to be directed toward analysis of how ECE programs function as organizations. Organizational issues are a routine part of the administrative role, and as such they are a part of core knowledge.

The External World—Community

This body of literature has generally focused on the ECE field at large, although the work of collaboration and program development generally falls to the administrator. Several key resources are important for administrators interested in learning about the communities that interact with children's programs. Kagan (1991) offered a historical and social perspective on the external world that affects early childhood programs, including public agencies such as schools and child welfare agencies, health practitioners, funders, and policy makers. A 1988 publication (Goffin & Lombardi) is a primer for new advocates focused on work at the state and federal level. The book offers practitioners (including directors) guidance regarding basic local policy and advocacy for children and families. In a study of the directors of accredited centers in Massachusetts, Manning (1998) found that involvement with community activities was related to quality services.

Publications on accreditation (Bredekamp & Willer, 1996) and regulation (Gormley, 1995; Bredekamp, 1989) offer administrators insights into issues that are central to a director's job and to the public debate on improving service quality. Several other current publications provide insight and guidance to individuals and groups working toward new policies, service, and increased investment in children's programs (Dombro, O'Donnell, Galinsky, Melcher, & Farber, 1996; Kagan & Cohen, 1997). Professional journals and other professional publications will continue to be valuable resources on public policy and other community issues. Web sites sponsored by professional organizations and developmental or advocacy initiatives offer many learning resources. Increasingly, as administrators utilize e-mail and the Internet, they will gain easy access to a wide variety of resources. Directors will need to develop the skills and judgment of the informed consumer to effectively use Internet resources.

Self—Reflective Knowledge

As in other areas, ECE references on self-knowledge and practice are generally focused on teacher practitioners. They highlight reflective practice, self-discovery, and professional development (Bowman, 1989; Katz, 1977; Katz & Goffin, 1990; Schön, 1987; Tertell, Klein, & Jewett, 1998; VanderVen, 1988). Also, as director development continues, research and analysis is needed concerning the administrator as reflective practitioner. Stressing the importance of reflective practice, Kagan and Bowman (1997) encourage ECE practitioners to define self-knowledge as a leadership skill.

Larkin (1992) suggested that it is not the technical aspects of administration that create stumbling blocks for new directors:

> The more difficult hurdles are internal: the tension between being an authority and providing support; the psychological isolation of being at the top; and being able to conceptualize and articulate a clear philosophy to parents and teachers (p. 125)

In a review of the attributes of directors in good quality programs, Culkin (1994) identified several behaviors that are related to the director's need for self-knowledge. Directors who valued human relationships, developed communication systems, and used participatory planning appeared to have developed confidence in their professional judgment as they grew in self-knowledge.

Review of the literature in other disciplines provides resources for reflective practice. The study of leadership has included consideration of self-knowledge, reflection, service, and caring. Greenleaf (1977) initiated the concept of "servant leader" as a descriptor of a fundamental attribute available to managers interested in awareness, leadership, community, and responsibility. He indicated that the leader's interests lay in serving the needs of those being led. Similarly, Kelley (1992) talks about the importance of followership in an organization where the leader is sensitive to the multiple leadership needs and roles required for the organization to meet its goals. A reflective administrator knows when to lead and when to follow in her or his organization. Covey (1992) associates the habit of being proactive with self-knowledge. Covey defines self-knowledge as an ability to choose your response. He also talks about the relationship of trust in the leadership role and encourages leaders to "seek first to understand, then to be understood" (p. 272).

While knowledge of self is fundamental to success in the other three core knowledge areas, we begin our discussion with knowledge of others—that is, stakeholders—because interactions with others form a majority of an administrator's responsibilities.

KNOWLEDGE OF OTHERS

There are multiple individuals and sets of other people with whom a director interacts. Role theory would tell us that they come in sets—sets of "stakeholders" or "others." Stakeholders for ECE programs are the children, staff, families of the children in care, ECE colleagues in other programs, board members, sometimes a higher level of administration (or program sponsors), volunteers, funding agents, vendors who supply the program, and regulators. Stakeholder groups also include other individuals and groups with whom the director has frequent contact (refer to Figure 1.1). Some stakeholders share common interests in the program, but their perspectives and level of investment in and importance to the program vary significantly. On a given day, a parent wants to understand the fee structure, a colleague needs help to access the state fee-subsidy program, a plumber completing a repair needs a copy of the building's original plans, and a federal proposal for funds for staff training is due. Those who have seen an administrator in action know the variety of tasks that engage a director daily.

It is critically important for a director to develop the communication and interpersonal skills necessary to relate effectively to all these individuals and groups. A director who values and works to understand the individual perspectives and needs of their program's stakeholders, is creating a foundation for informed problem solving. Recognizing the importance of knowing and empathizing with the actual people in the environment—"the stakeholders"—is analogous to planning activities for children by keeping the needs of individual children in mind. The director generally functions as the primary day-to-day leader in the group. When he or she respects individual skills, listens well, and appreciates diversity, "others" (families, staff, clients, and colleagues in the larger community) are encouraged to feel safe and valued. In this way a director's knowledge promotes an environment in which teachers and other staff are encouraged to develop positive working relationships and empathy with the stakeholders they serve—children and families.

Knowledge to Work with Stakeholders

Understanding the dynamics of relationships among various stakeholders is central to a director's role. Relating effectively with others involves supporting them in learning, problem solving, negotiating within the program community, and resolving conflict (Seplocha, 1998). This knowledge includes development of communication skills and caring, as described in Chapter 1. Caring leadership is characterized by attention to the complex needs of clients and to the ethical issues involved in making decisions about stakeholders and organizational processes (Tronto, 1998). The work of caring practitioners reflects a knowledge of the importance of each stakeholder to organizational success.

Directors' day-to-day communication can set a tone for communication throughout their programs (Buckner, 1988; Culkin, 1994). Personnel, customers, children, and other stakeholders observe, interact with, and follow the communication example provided by the director. An effective director knows how to communicate with consistency and grammatical accuracy in writing as well as in speech.

A successful director knows, understands, and is open to the varying perspectives of the different stakeholders in her or his program. By seeking to clarify and respond to stakeholder group interests, a director sets in motion a process of communication that informs stakeholders about each other's needs and interests. Stakeholders have different interests.

- Teachers may focus on the need for an increase in compensation and funds to create appropriate activities for children.
- Parents may focus on their need for flexible scheduling to accommodate their family and work schedules and on outcomes.
- Corporate founders work to monitor how well the program reduces their employees' stress and supports productivity.
- Regulators may focus on ratios or the ground cover under the outdoor play equipment.
- Board members may focus on the reputation of the program in the community.

It is the director who must empathize with—or at least know about—all these perspectives and respond to them coherently. A skilled director helps the stakeholders learn something about each other's point of view while she or he balances individual stakeholder objectives. In essence, a director must know how to "champion the causes" of each of the stakeholder groups while leading toward consensus around the program's missions and goals (Gardner, 1990).

How Is Knowledge of Others Acquired?

Directors have a variety of sources for learning about how to work with "others." Informally, respecting and understanding the importance of knowing others as members of specific stakeholder groups, and as individuals, is a critical first step. However, general knowledge about the various needs and issues related to enrolled children, families, personnel, and external stakeholders is not enough. A director must be an active part of the program, taking time to observe, interact with, and take a personal interest in children, families, and teachers. Regular involvement enables a director to collect valuable experiences and knowledge for use in working with stakeholders to design a caring and thoughtful program to serve and support those who are a part of the organization and its external communities.

Formal or official academic learning expands and deepens the director's practical and informal knowledge of work with stakeholders. Formal sources include studies in management, human development, learning, developmentally appropriate practice, teacher development, adult education, communication, and working with families.

Successful directors take their obligation to know others and respond appropriately to the various stakeholder groups very seriously. Similarly, the director who values the contributions of others will seek their input in decision making about the program. The stakeholders—viewed collectively—are all part of the organization.

KNOWLEDGE OF ORGANIZATIONS

A successful director knows about organizational issues. At the start of a practitioner's administrative career, this knowledge may be intuitive rather than conceptual. In this section we address the organizational development issues that are a part of core knowledge.

Organizational Issues

The organizational systems designed by a director, sponsoring agency (such as a board), or owner working with the director define authority, culture, and responsibility in the organization. Culture encompasses the deeply held values and assumptions of the organization. Organizations such as ECE programs develop a unique, individualized culture that embodies the meaning of the organization and its activities. Schein (1991) says that the culture of the organization or group consists of the assumptions (frequently unconscious) that underlie the group behavior in regard to values. Assumptions are made regarding human nature and whether an authoritarian, democratic, or collegial approach is most effective in the organization. These assumptions, which are developed over time, provide meaning, stability, and predictability to the group.

As policies and practice need to be congruent with organizational values, culture, and mission in order for an organization to function well, a director needs to understand how organizational culture is established and preserved. A director must know how to either develop or work with established policies and procedures created to assist staff and stakeholders in working toward a shared vision for children and families.

How Is Knowledge of Organizations Acquired?

Few ECE administrators formally study organizational theory in academic settings. The initiation of director credential programs and other training efforts is changing this. (See the overview of director credentialing programs in Chapter 1.) Working with a mentor or other personal teacher has been a favored means of learning about organizations and management for new directors during the transition from teaching to administration (Larkin, 1992). There are other options for novices as well.

A look at conference programming indicates that the number of workshops and specialized management conference tracks designed for directors has increased. Professional organizations and training institutes for directors exist in some parts of the country. Attendance at these meetings is an excellent way to gain an organizational perspective. Many current leaders in program administration are people who had to "make their own path" (Mitchell, 1997). They learned from mentors, trial-and-error, and self-selected reading (Culkin, 1994). (See Chapter 11 for personal histories of director development.)

In summary, effective administrators recognize and know that an ECE program is an organization. They know how to monitor and manage obvious organizational elements, such as regulation, funding, personnel, and facilities. Sensitivity to the interplay of influences (represented by stakeholders) within the organization is essential to effective management and leadership. An effective manager also needs to know, understand, and affect the influences and conditions outside the organization.

KNOWLEDGE OF THE EXTERNAL WORLD

The early childhood program is a community within itself, but it is also a part of the larger community here called the external world. A children's program affects the immediate community in which it is located, and external communities affect the program. Clearly, a director interacts with a variety of stakeholders from the external community. These include vendors, regulators, other administrators, resource and referral specialists, and members of the medical and human service professions. Through work with individuals and groups of stakeholders outside the organization, an administrator may become involved in advocacy as well as in collaborative efforts within the profession focused on training, compensation, or other policy issues.

The External World—A Source of Practical Knowledge

The external world begins with the local community that the program serves—its cultures, economic base, and the resources it devotes to serving children and families. Knowledge about these features enables the director to formulate a personal response to community needs, including issues of diversity and inclusion. Going further, a director may become involved in state or local efforts regarding overarching issues, for example, to create training for inclusive practice, to reduce local teacher turnover, or to improve compensation. Such work may or may not be associated with a professional organization. Professional experience in the eternal world is a valuable source of learning for an administrator. When a director is a reflective practitioner, she or he can translate experience into a deeper understanding of the program's clients, ECE service needs, and of the self in the administrative role. In some instances, a director's deeper understanding of the local community and culture may translate to more empathic relationships with families. Or understanding of how local policy is made can translate to more effective outreach for resource development, marketing, and advocacy.

To gain knowledge of the program's community, a knowledgeable director gets acquainted with members of the public and private sectors of their immediate locale. In the public sector, a director may meet the town officials, city council and county government members, and public agency representatives. In the private sector, directors work on child or ECE issues with business leaders, church leaders, and nonprofit service agencies or organizations. Essentially, a director builds a knowledge base of relationships in the community. This base is enhanced by involvement in local professional associations and activities that build respect for the profession and by consensus about the value of children and families to the community. Learning about state and national communities can be a natural extension of knowledge of the local community.

Directors who are knowledgeable about current policy debates at the state and national levels are better equipped to lead both in their program and in the larger ECE community. Moreover, directors who are cognizant of the external world are more apt to seek and find creative funding solutions, to market their program effectively, and to interact more effectively with representatives of the corporate and philanthropic domain.

How Is Knowledge of the External World Acquired?

An administrator can learn a great deal about the external world by observation. For instance, as a center director meets families and enrolls their children into a children's program, the culture and economic resources of the population served become evident, as does the director's cultural response. Being reflective and knowledgeable about this aspect of the ECE program offers a director initial insight into the community where the center is based. Other directors and professional colleagues in the community, local media, school, and religious activities also serve as informal sources for acquiring knowledge about the local community— an important part of the external world.

When a children's program is established and running smoothly, some administrators become involved in outreach and advocacy for children and families. Directors in professional organizations, or in director support groups, can share information about resources, data collection, and strategies to improve services and the ECE profession. These directors may become more confident about the tasks of contacting local businesses, the city council, or state legislators. Directors' groups may also serve as study groups for advocacy and other professional development needs, and they sometimes connect with more formal opportunities for learning. Options for acquiring knowledge about work with external communities include professional conferences, director institutes, and academic courses in disciplines such as political science, public administration, community development, and business or educational leadership.

It may seem to some that only more experienced directors should be expected to expand their knowledge of the community. (See Chapter 7 for a discussion of stages of director development.) Writing proposals to expand resources and acting as an advocate can involve risks—especially for the novice. However, measured involvement with other directors and professional associations facilitates the novice director's growth and understanding of the role. A director's first priority is to uphold her or his program's service. Ongoing learning leads to new skills and greater competency. In fact, it may be only through learning, reflection, and the resultant self-discovery that directors can begin to encompass the multiple responsibilities of the role.

KNOWLEDGE OF SELF

The director's need to know and address stakeholder needs, to do so within the context of a well-defined organizational structure, and to develop understanding of the external community may seem overwhelming. Indeed, some readers may have concluded that it is unrealistic to expect any one person to acquire knowledge in these core knowledge areas and to manage an ECE program at the same time. An administrative role is challenging, and knowledge of self is the key to success in this role.

Successful directors, like others in leadership positions, need to be cognizant of their own abilities and limitations, strengths and weaknesses. This awareness requires a balanced understanding of their roles and responsibilities, not just as director, but as a member of the profession, organization, family, and community. Growth in self-knowledge builds self-esteem, confidence, and humility.

Self-Knowledge Guides Daily Practice

Accepting one's capabilities along with fallibilities supports reflective practice, which leads to ongoing learning. Through reflection on their decisions about program, staff, clients, and opportunities, a director can better understand the outcomes of decisions; their organization's strengths, weaknesses, and outcomes; and their own personal and professional goals. For example, directors who function in this manner use self-knowledge to recognize appropriate times and means for staff coaching and consulting, or when to seek assistance inside or outside the organization.

Self-knowledge supports an administrator in assessing options, selecting priorities, and allocating time. Support for the staff as reflective practitioners may lead a confident and experienced director to create a team reflection time. A reflection time is similar to a class-debriefing meeting and, led by a director, can serve as a foundation for careful team planning for children's educational activities.

The self-aware director may become more open to searching for better and more efficient ways to provide good services. This may include use of technology or pursuit of creative and appropriate ways of working within regulatory guidelines. Whether the issue is communication, time management, or developmentally appropriate practice, directors who know their organization's strengths and needs recognize the opportunities and limitations of the position, as well as their own personal strengths and weaknesses.

How Is Knowledge of Self Acquired?

Acquiring knowledge of self is heavily dependent on informal learning, but formal avenues for learning are also available. Personal experiences, on-the-job challenges, and interactions with colleagues in the profession all contribute to a director's developing knowledge of self. Individuals who seek to learn can find a plethora of learning opportunities to guide their growth in self-knowledge. Perhaps foremost is reflective practice (Bowman, 1989; Schön, 1987). Other sources of formal learning include business-sector training opportunities, the popular press, leadership development opportunities, and other self-development workshops and seminars. Academic courses and professional conferences in the disciplines of communication, leadership, time management, and professionalism are helpful. Formal learning opportunities provide psychological comfort and insight through the camaraderie of others working toward similar goals and facing similar challenges.

The director's job is complex and challenging. Recognizing the importance of self-knowledge and its impact on one's ability to perform well is the beginning of a progression toward greater success in the role. Directors who learn strategies for seeking feedback from a mentor, coach, or colleague expand their developing self-knowledge. It is also crucial for administrators to be open to feedback from the people who work with them—the teachers and other staff. With increasing self-knowledge comes the opportunity to learn to modify your behavior in order to respond more effectively to responsibilities and colleagues. While learning, personal change, and professional growth involve struggle as well as exhilaration, the consequences include success, along with new opportunities for learning and prosperity in the role.

CONCLUSION

The question about what directors of ECE programs need to know in order to succeed has been addressed by discussing four core areas of knowledge: stakeholders, organizations, the external world or community, and self. Discussions in each area reflect on the responsibilities of the director. The four core areas are not hierarchically ordered. The director who moves from novice to expert learns in all areas concurrently, and growth in one area supports growth in the others. For example, when a director grows in understanding of organizations and the interplay between self and organization, he or she finds it easier to communicate and interact professionally with the varied stakeholders she or he meets in daily work. Likewise, when a director grows in knowledge of the external world, understanding the other adults involved in the program is facilitated. Consequently, encouraging professional growth of program personnel may become easier.

Two points serve as an afterword to this discussion. First, it is crucial to understand that no person will come into the position of director with complete competence in all four core knowledge areas. Even when experienced directors enter an existing or a new program, there will be challenges and struggles that are specific to that situation. Novice and experienced directors alike will continue growing in core knowledge. They will have insights to offer one another and should seek camaraderie among themselves.

Second, this is an early analysis of the core knowledge needed. The limited literature and tentativeness of some of the analysis reflects the newness of the conversation. We present this to the ECE field for consideration in the current dialogue about administrators. Conversation about administrators' learning and reflection on practice will lead to more comprehensive and deeper understanding of what the ECE program administrator needs to know.

This discussion has raised issues for consideration about the training of administrators and the director credential. These include the following:

- How can a credential recognize the knowledge that a director has acquired through experience? Specifically, can a credential address both formal and informal avenues of learning?
- What are effective ways to provide leadership and management training that promotes access to self-awareness and unconscious values and assumptions?
- Can the individual be assessed in such a way that the credentialing body both accurately assesses the candidate's knowledge and assists the candidate toward continuing a process of reflective practice?

Successful directors become a part of their program, not just overseers. They are committed to continued reflection and learning for themselves and for all others in the program. In this way they will remain sensitive to their role in determining the quality of caring and learning services provided under their leadership.

REFERENCES

Bloom, P. J. (1988). *A great place to work: Improving conditions for staff in young children's program*. Washington, DC: National Association for the Education of Young Children.

Bloom, P. J. (1996). The quality of work life in early childhood programs: Does accreditation make a difference. In S. Bredekamp & B. A. Willer (Eds.), NAEYC *accreditation: A decade of learning and the years ahead* (pp. 13–24). Washington, DC: National Association for the Education of Young Children.

Bowman, B. T. (1989). Self-reflection as an element of professionalism. *Teachers College Record, 90*(3), 444–451.

Bredekamp, S. (1989). *Regulating child care quality: Evidence from NAEYC's accreditation system*. Washington, DC: National Association for the Education of Young Children.

Bredekamp, S., & Willer, B. (1996). NAEYC *accreditation: A decade of learning and the years ahead*. Washington, DC: National Association for the Education of Young Children.

Buckner, L. M. (1988). *Supervising with communicative competence in early childhood centers: Sociopolitical implications of the legitimation deficit in administrator preparation*. Unpublished doctoral dissertation, University of San Francisco.

Caruso, J. J., & Fawcett, M. T. (1999). *Supervision in early childhood education: A developmental perspective* (2nd ed.). New York: Teachers College Press.

Covey, S. R. (1992). *Principle-centered leadership*. New York: Simon & Schuster.

Culkin, M. (1994). *The administrator/leader in early care and education settings: A qualitative study with implications for theory and practice*. Unpublished Ph.D. dissertation, The Union Institute, Cincinnati, OH. (UMI Abstracts International, No. 9502953)

Decker, C. A., & Decker, J. R. (1988). *Planning and administering early childhood programs*. Columbus, OH: Merrill.

Deming, W. E. (1986). *Out of the crisis*. New York: Cambridge University Press.

Dombro, A. L., O'Donnell, N. S., Galinsky, E., Melcher, S. G., & Farber, A. (1996). *Community mobilization: Strategies to support children and their families*. New York: Families and Work Institute.

Gardner, J. (1990). *On leadership*. New York: Free Press.

Goffin, S., & Lombardi, J. (1988). *Speaking out: Early childhood advocacy*. Washington, DC: National Association for the Education of Young Children.

Gormley, W. T. (1995). *Everybody's children: Child care as a public problem*. Washington, DC: Brookings Institution.

Greenleaf, R. (1977). *Servant leadership: A journey into the nature of legitimate power and greatness*. New York: Paulist Press.

Hewes, D., & Hartman, B. (1972). *Early childhood education: A workbook for administrators*. New York: R&E Publishers, Inc.

Hildebrand, V. (1984). *Management of child development centers.* New York: Macmillan.

Jones, E. P. (1986). *Teaching adults: An active learning approach.* Washington, DC: National Association for the Education of Young Children.

Kagan, S. L. (1991). *United we stand: Collaboration for child care and early childhood education.* New York: Teachers College Press.

Kagan, S. L., & Bowman, B. T. (1997). Leadership in early care and education: Issues and challenges. In S. L. Kagan & B. T. Bowman (Eds.), *Leadership in early care and education* (pp. 3–8). Washington, DC: National Association for the Education of Young Children.

Kagan, S. L., & Cohen, N. E. (1997). *Not by chance: Creating an early care and education system for America's children.* New Haven: The Bush Center in Child Development and Social Policy at Yale University.

Katz, L. G. (1977). *Talks with teachers: Reflections on early childhood education.* Washington, DC: National Association for the Education of Young Children.

Katz, L. G., & Goffin, S. G. (1990). Issues in the preparation of teachers of young children. In B. Spodek & O. N. Saracho (Eds.), *Yearbook in early childhood education: Early childhood teacher preparation* (Vol. 1). New York: Teachers College Press.

Kelley, R. (1992). *The power of followership.* New York: Doubleday.

Larkin, E. (1992). *The preschool administrator.* Unpublished doctoral dissertation, Harvard University, Cambridge, MA.

Manning, J. P. (1998). *The relationship of directors to quality within child care programs in Massachusetts: An exploration into some contributing characteristics.* Unpublished doctoral dissertation, University of Massachusetts, Amherst.

Mitchell, A. (1997). Reflections on early childhood leadership development: Finding your own path. In S. L. Kagan & B. T. Bowman (Eds.), *Leadership in early care and education* (pp. 84–94). Washington, DC: National Association for the Education of Young Children.

Morgan, G. (1982). *Managing the day care dollars: A financial handbook.* Watertown, MA: Steam Press.

Morgan, G. (1997). Historical views of leadership. In S. L. Kagan & B. T. Bowman (Eds.), *Leadership in early care and education* (pp. 9–14). Washington, DC: National Association for the Education of Young Children.

Poster, M. A. (1986). *Identification, classification, and comparison of the work performance requirements and actual work performance of child care center directors in the commonwealth of Pennsylvania.* Unpublished doctoral dissertation, University of Pittsburgh, Pittsburgh. (UMI Abstracts International, No. 8707598)

Reckmeyer, M. C. (1990). *Outstanding child care centers.* Unpublished doctoral dissertation, University of Nebraska, Lincoln.

Schein, E. H. (1991). What is culture? In P. J. Frost, L. F. Moore, M. R. Louis, & J. Martin (Eds.), *Reframing organizational culture* (pp. 243–253). Newbury Park, CA: Sage.

Schön, D. A. (1987). *Educating the reflective practitioner.* San Francisco: Jossey-Bass.

Seplocha, H. (1998). *The good preschool: Profiles of leadership.* Unpublished doctoral dissertation, Rutgers, The State University of New Jersey, New Brunswick. (UMI Abstracts International, No. 9834121)

Springate, K. W., & Steglin, D. S. (1999). *Building school and community partnerships through parent involvement*. Old Tappan, NJ: Prentice Hall.

Tertell, E. A., Klein, S. M., & Jewett, J. L. (1998). *When teachers reflect: Journeys toward effective, inclusive practice*. Washington, DC: National Association for the Education of Young Children.

Tronto, J. C. (1998, Fall). An ethic of care. *Generations* [Special Issue].

VanderVen, K. (1988). Pathways to professional effectiveness for early childhood educators. In B. Spodek, O. N. Saracho, & D. L. Peters (Eds.), *Professionalism and the early childhood practitioner* (pp. 137–160). New York: Teachers College Press.

6

What Is Management Ability?

Roger Neugebauer

As with any small business, the leader of an early care and education (ECE) organization must wear many hats. Because most programs are too small or too poor to afford to hire administrative support staff, a wide range of administrative tasks fall on the shoulders of the center director in addition to the central leadership functions. This chapter expands on the nature of the challenge (starting with a hypothetical telephone message to illustrate the point), provides an overview of the many functions a director must perform, and closes with some suggested resources.

> *Hello, you have reached the Hippety Hop Child Care Center phone system. To speak to the center director, press 1. To speak to the center's accountant, press 1. To speak to the transportation manager, press 1. To speak to the head of marketing, press 1. To speak to the education coordinator, press 1.*

The director of an early care and education program or others children's program must indeed be the master of many tasks. A quick review of the functional responsibilities of directors presented in this chapter demonstrates the breadth of the director's job. A director must be prepared to handle any task from analyzing the center's cash-flow position to placating an angry parent, from resolving a conflict between two teachers to crafting inexpensive yet nutritious lunch menus.

However, a director must be more than a technician. Not only must she be able to master each of her various tasks; she must be able to carry them out at the same time. She must be able to prioritize her time and attention so as to move the organization forward. She must have a firm vision of where the organization is headed and be able to focus organizational resources on achieving this vision.

THE DIRECTOR AS CONDUCTOR

Center directorship is more than the sum of its parts. A director may be able to perform every task in isolation but still fail as a director.

Think of the job of a director in terms of the job of an orchestra conductor. An orchestra could have a world-class violin section, a renowned French horn player, and able performers in every section. But without a skilled conductor, the orchestra could be a dud. The conductor must be able to blend all the talents of the individual performers into a collective sound that is well balanced and moving. An effective conductor knows when to highlight the French horn player, when to let the violin section shine, when to move the tempo forward, and when to slow the pace.

Like an orchestra conductor, an effective director must be able to achieve a productive balance of energies. He must be able to devote enough attention to the curriculum to maintain the quality of services delivered without neglecting attention to building center enrollment. He must be able to attend to the needs of staff without letting accounts receivable get out of control. He must be able to resolve today's crises without neglecting tomorrow's opportunities. In short, he must be able to build the assets of the center and then blend all these assets into a finely tuned, supportive environment for children, parents, and staff.

While a center director functions like a conductor, much of the work he performs requires business, not musical, skills. At the conclusion of this chapter, I provide some suggestions on where to look for help in developing these skills.

THE DIRECTOR'S TASKS

There are myriad ways to categorize the various tasks a director must orchestrate. In general they fall into the eight functional areas I discuss in the following sections.

Setting the Course

In almost every successful performance of a group task, goals and standards must be set clearly in advance, clearly communicated, kept constantly in view, and dramatized along the way.
—Theodore Caplow

To be successful, an early care and education program must be responsive to the needs of its intended customers. It must be proactive to changes in these needs as well as to trends in the social, regulatory, and funding spheres. It must also have a plan of action that guides it into the future. It is the director's responsibility to make sure that these tasks are accomplished.

A program is like a living organism developing in an ever-changing environment, heading off to an uncertain future. It is up to the director to keep the center attuned to the changing environment and to shape a vision that will pull the organization forward.

The director must set the course in order to lay out a vision that all staff can use as a road map to guide their day-to-day efforts. The importance of the director as goal-setter is succinctly put by organizational consultant Warren Bennis (1989): "Leaders' visions are compelling and pull people toward them—intensity coupled with commitment is magnetic" (p. 192).

Not only must the director set the course, but she must also keep her finger on the pulse of the organization. She must continually monitor the performance of the organization to assure that it is not veering off-course and that all parts of the organization are performing as expected.

Leading the Way

See everything, overlook a great deal, correct a little.
—Pope John XXIII

A leader with a vision needs to do more than simply lay the vision out. The captain of a sailing ship not only chooses a destination and sets a course to get there; he also keeps the ship on course by shifting the rudder and continually adjusting the set of the sails. On a day-to-day basis, a center director needs to move the organization forward by making decisions, solving problems, and resolving conflicts.

To keep the center from bogging down or getting sidetracked, the director is constantly negotiating with players inside and outside the organization regarding their performance. In most centers, the director is also accountable to a higher authority, either an owner, a silent partner, a board of directors, or a parent organization. The director must exercise great finesse in controlling the performance of subordinates, maintaining the cooperation of outside stakeholders, and maintaining the support of those in authority.

In carrying out the many tasks of leadership, the director must be cognizant of the tone she is setting with these actions. Every organization has a culture that influences how members behave. A military unit has a culture of rigid authoritarianism where behavior is shaped by fear of punishment. A sports team has a strong sense of team spirit, and behavior is influenced by a strong desire to work together to win games.

The way in which the director makes decisions, solves problems, and resolves conflicts in large part shapes the culture of the organization. If the director solicits staff opinions in making decisions and holds staff responsible for solving problems, this will set a participatory climate in which all staff feel they have a stake in the results. On the other hand, if the director makes all decisions without input and steps in to solve all problems, this will send a very different message and set a more authoritarian tone.

Implementing the Program

The developmental question is not "What can children do?" Rather it is "What should children do that best serves their development and learning in the long term?"

—Lilian Katz

The purpose of ECE programs is to provide nurturing, stimulating, and safe environments for children. This is not likely to be accomplished simply by bringing together a group of well-intentioned, caring individuals and letting them do their thing. In order for children to develop optimally in a center, their daily experiences must be guided by a thoughtful curriculum carried out in an appropriate environment.

While the director may not work regularly with the children, it is her responsibility to oversee what they experience on a daily basis. The director must assure that the center operates under a sound program philosophy with clear curriculum goals. Likewise, she must take responsibility for communicating these goals clearly to all staff and for providing a facility and equipment that make possible the achievement of these goals.

The program responsibility of the director is broad. It not only involves daily classroom experiences; it also involves meeting children's nutritional, health and safety, and, in some cases, transportation needs. Administrators also have the fundamental responsibility for relating to the families who use their program's services. They are generally an initial point of contact for the families and also play ongoing roles with families during the time that a family purchases and uses program services.

In many children's programs, the director's responsibilities are confined to the management arena. In these centers there is usually an assistant director or an educational coordinator who is responsible for the curriculum. While this would appear to be a logical division of labor, it violates a key organizational principle. This principle holds that the person at the helm of an organization must be the keeper of the faith, the person who believes most deeply and cares most passionately for the central mission of the organization.

A director can, of course, delegate major responsibility for the daily implementation of the curriculum to assistant directors, educational coordinators, and teachers. However, when the director totally abdicates final responsibility for the curriculum, this relegates the care of children to a secondary level of concern.

Guiding Staff Performance

The best kept secret today is that people would rather work hard for something they believe in than enjoy a pampered idleness.
—John Gardner

The most demanding, stressful, and yet often most rewarding, responsibility of a director is in working with staff. It is every director's challenge to mold a disparate group of well-intentioned, but often insufficiently trained and nearly always poorly paid, individuals into a well-tuned caregiving team.

The separate tasks of guiding staff performance are not overwhelming. Given some basic training, some helpful counseling from peers or predecessors, and some hands-on experience, most directors can master the tasks of recruiting and selecting staff, training staff, communicating expectations, supervising day-to-day performance, appraising performance, stimulating creativity, and providing motivation.

What is often overwhelming is trying to carry out these supervisory tasks under the pressures of long hours, low pay, staff shortages, high turnover, and scanty resources. A paucity of qualified candidates willing to work for low wages and limited time and resources to support the development of those hired add up to high stress for directors.

The capabilities that often make or break a director's accomplishment in working with staff fall under the category of ingenuity. The successful staff manager is often able to spot talent in a seemingly hopeless candidate; to enable a green staff member to see the value of growth by facilitating a few small successes; to motivate teachers about the importance of their work in spite of the low monetary value placed on it; and to create a sense of team spirit that results in a supportive, enjoyable work environment.

Finally, the director must see to his own needs for growth and satisfaction. For the director to be motivated, he must see the successful results of his efforts. He must see visible evidence that his performance is improving and that this progress has a major impact on the success of the center.

As the organization grows, the director will need to continually upgrade her skills in areas such as staff supervision and financial management. In addition, she will need to master such tricks of the trade as managing time, setting priorities, delegating tasks, and husbanding her personal resources.

Working with Parents

Every company's greatest assets are its customers, because without customers there is no company.

—Michael LeBoeuf

Conventional wisdom holds that child care is a partnership between parents and caregivers—parents and caregivers work hand-in-hand to meet the needs of the child. In reality, centers often do a less than adequate job in making the partnership work.

One of the main concerns raised by the Cost, Quality and Child Outcomes Study was that parents usually have no idea what their children are experiencing when they leave them at child care centers (Helburn, 1995).

It is the director's responsibility, and clearly one that directors have not been executing with great success, to keep real communication flowing between the center and parents and, in the process, build parent trust in the program and teacher respect for parents.

The director has a number of parent relations tasks to accomplish. As with many areas of responsibility, the director may not be the one actually doing the work, but he is ultimately accountable for making it happen.

Parent relations responsibilities start the minute the parent first inquires about enrollment. From the very start, the director is responsible for accurately presenting the center so that the parent can make an informed enrollment decision and so that parent expectations are in line with reality. Once enrolled the director must move quickly to make the parents and child feel welcome and at ease about procedures and expectations.

On an ongoing basis, the director has the daunting task of making sure that caregivers receive all the pertinent information they need from parents to meet their children's needs. At the same time, she must insure that parents are informed about their child's experiences at the center. From the Cost and Quality study results, it is clear that standard forms of communication, monthly newsletters, and annual parent conferences are not enough. One of the best ways to help parents truly understand what goes on is to get parents involved in some aspect of working in the classroom (Helburn, 1995).

An increasingly important aspect of parent relations is assuring that cultural differences are respected. As our nation's population has become diverse, this increasing diversity is reflected in our center enrollments. If cultural differences are understood and taken into account in program activities and interactions, they have an enriching impact for all members of the center community. If these differences are ignored or misunderstood, this can lead to conflict, frustration, and negative experiences for children. Children need to see members of their own communities in positions of influence and power. It is important that the director support education and training efforts to address the local community's diversity issues.

When a director is effective in working with parents, the result is a bond of trust between the center and the parent. Achieving a trusting relationship makes it easier for teachers to provide feedback, both positive and negative, to parents. For parents, being able to trust the center eliminates a major source of anxiety from their lives.

Developing Resources

The lack of money is the root of all evil.

—George Bernard Shaw

Another key finding of the *Cost and Quality* study was that the highest-quality centers had available the most resources per child (Helburn, 1995). High-quality centers may have achieved their above-average resources by securing significant public subsidies, by garnering support from employers, or by charging parents above-average fees.

The director is clearly the key player when it comes to securing resources. Given the vital role of available resources in determining quality, the amount of resources a director is able to secure may be a critical measure of her effectiveness.

The one common challenge for directors of all types of centers is building the center's reputation in the community. Whether the center is seeking to build resources from charging high fees, keeping enrollment high, soliciting donations, or garnering public support, the reputation of the center will have a major impact on the success of this effort.

Likewise, securing and maintaining an adequate location is a key challenge for directors of all centers. In many businesses the three top determinants of success are "location, location, and location." In child care the performance of the staff and the integrity of the curriculum are more important than location. However, securing and maintaining an appropriate, well-maintained facility in a location convenient for parents will go a long way toward ensuring the success of a center.

In addition to engaging in activities designed to build the resources of one's own organization, directors need to play a role in building support for all children, families, and caregivers. The long-term interests of the center are enhanced when the director is involved in profession-building and resource development activities for the entire field.

One focus of advocacy efforts where a director's participation is especially important is in raising staff wages. Clearly the Achilles heel of early care and education is the lack of resources available for teachers' compensation. Directors are remiss if they are not actively engaged in pursuing a solution to this professional challenge. They can pursue it both internally through a fair compensation schedule and externally on the public policy level.

Managing Assets

We are drowning in information but starved for knowledge.
—John Naisbitt

A center director is a caretaker of the resources of his or her children's program. He or she is responsible for protecting the assets of the organization. A director must learn and practice wisdom in managing financial assets and care in protecting human and physical assets.

In managing financial assets, the director has three major responsibilities: developing a plan (budget) for the effective use of limited resources, accounting for the income and expenditures, and monitoring financial performance.

The last responsibility requires the most insight. Anyone can develop a budget and any bean counter can keep track of money, but it takes a perceptive director to analyze the accounting information to determine if the center is living within its budget. A perceptive director can make midcourse adjustments when conditions are changing and can manage cash flow so that the center can always pay its bills and maintain its credit standing.

The director bears final responsibility for safeguarding the assets of the organization. He must guarantee that the center is in compliance with all legal requirements, that physical assets are well maintained, and that the center maintains adequate insurance coverage. On the human assets side, acting as a caring professional person, supporting compensation, and developing career development possibilities for staff are ways a director maintains and strengthens the organization. (See Chapter 8 for a discussion of professionalism.)

Growing the Organization

To stay on the upward growth curve requires a broadening of the management talent base. The manager must begin getting results through others.

—Steven C. Brandt

A key step in a director's maturation occurs when she recognizes that she is responsible for growing an organization, not simply running a center. The director who is running a center focuses energy on the day-to-day tasks of keeping the center afloat. The director who is growing an organization is focused on building the infrastructure of the center so that it can survive into the future.

This is not to demean the challenge of running a center. Keeping a center afloat is a hugely demanding job, requiring all the skills described above combined with huge doses of hard work and perseverance. However, running a center is like renting your living quarters—all the resources you expend add up to little in the long term.

Growing a business requires a director to carry out all the work of running a center, but carrying them out in a planful manner that builds structures and processes that will stand the test of time. A future-oriented director focuses on concretizing administrative systems and policies, and on building a management team.

By systematizing administrative tasks, a director makes an organization more efficient by eliminating the need to continually remake routine decisions. Policies and procedures need to be standardized for personnel, financial, maintenance, crisis management, and customer relations matters. These systems need to be complete without being overly bureaucratic and firm without being static. And these systems must be well communicated so they do have the impact of guiding behavior in desired directions.

The bigger challenge for a director is to build a management team. Center administrators tend to be classic Type A managers who feel impelled to do everything themselves. However, the long-term interests of the organization are best served when its fate is not in the hands of one person.

An administrator concerned with the long-term growth of the organization should be working to make himself dispensable. His goal should be for the organization to move forward without him. This requires not only grooming a successor but also developing team members who are capable of assuming full responsibility for the various tasks of center management.

THE DIMENSIONS OF DIRECTORSHIP

Not all center director jobs are alike. While all administrators bear final responsibility for the eight functions described above, directors in different settings will carry them out in dramatically different ways and attend to them in widely varied levels of emphasis.

There are five dimensions by which child care organizations vary that have a direct impact on the nature of the director's role:

1. *Large versus small centers.* Clearly the work of a director in a center serving 40 children is dramatically different from that of one in a center serving 160 children. The director in a small center must be the jack-of-all-trades, carrying out all the management tasks and even working in the classroom from time to time. The larger the center, the more likely the director accomplishes her work through others—bookkeepers, educational coordinators, assistant directors, and so forth.
2. *Single site versus multisite organizations.* The fastest-growing segment of the child care world is small multisite operations. Increasingly, successful centers are responding to growing demand by adding new sites. Every site an organization adds contributes geometrically to the complexity of the executive director's job. Managing people and programs from afar presents significant challenges to organizational communication, staff motivation, and quality control.
3. *Independent versus dependent programs.* The director's job has an added dimension of complexity when the program is controlled by a parent organization. Commonplace examples of dependent centers are those operated by churches, YMCAs, employers, community action agencies, or local multiservice centers. In any of these situations, not only does the director need to manage the program but he must also seek approval for his plans from, negotiate for resources from, and justify his decisions to the parent organization. When the work of the center is only marginally related to the mission of the parent organization, the director must also invest significant energy in selling the parent organization on the value of the ECE services it provides.

4. *For-profit versus nonprofit programs.* This is the most visible difference among programs, but among these dimensions, it probably has the least impact on the role of the director. In theory, there is a major difference. The director of a center making profits by charging high fees to well-to-do parents has a radically different job from that of an inner-city program serving poor children under public contracts. In reality, such stereotypic models are becoming rare. More and more nonprofit programs are finding it necessary to serve higher-income parents on a fee-paying basis in order to balance their budgets. On the other hand, with the spread of vouchers as a means of distributing public subsidies, more for-profit programs are serving subsidized children. As a result, the differences in the work of administrators in for-profit and nonprofit programs are diminishing. This is true despite the fact that a small single-site center has very different capacity and resources than a large center that is part of either a corporate for–profit or public organization.

5. *Single-service versus full-service centers.* The complexity of the director's work is directly affected by the complexity of the center's program. Centers serving only preschool children present less challenges than those serving children from birth to age 12. Likewise, centers offering only full-day care are much less difficult to administer than organizations offering full-day and part-day care, drop-in care, evening care, and transportation services.

DEVELOPING MANAGEMENT ABILITY

Center directors desiring to improve their management ability can learn much from books on business management. Next to mystery stories and romance novels, these books are the hottest sellers around. Walk into any bookstore and you will be presented with a plethora of choices to begin your business management education. Unfortunately, most of the books will be of little help. Many currently popular business titles are little more than vanity pieces—the leaders of leading corporations telling the often less-than-gripping details of their rise to power. Many other tomes are directed at leaders of large corporations.

Fear not! There are many business books that are insightful and inspiring to leaders of small to midsize social service and education or information organizations. Over the past 20 years, I have been an avid reader in this arena and have identified a number of authors and books that I can wholeheartedly recommend to directors in a range of categories. Most of the books mentioned below are classics in the literature.

Basic Management Principles

If there is a single guru of management theory, it undoubtedly is Peter Drucker. In five decades of publishing management texts, his work has always been ahead of the curve. His writing today on the changing climate of business is as insightful as his basic management tomes of the 1950s. He has even written extensively on nonprofit management. However, I think the book all directors should use for a basic grounding is *Management: Tasks, Responsibilities and Practices* (1974). This immense but highly readable work spells out the key role the manager plays in the success of the organization and describes all the factors the manager needs to take into consideration.

Written at an entirely different level is *Managing Any Organization* by Theodore Caplow (1983). A management consultant, Caplow found that in working with organizations, whether a Boy Scout troop or a *Fortune* 500 company, certain basic principles applied. In this book he attempts to summarize basic rules and roles that govern any organization. Written in everyday English, with a wide range of examples, this book might serve as an excellent jumping-off point in a director's business education.

Leadership—Traditional Theories

There are many classic works focusing on what makes good leaders. Possibly the most respected thinker in this arena is Warren Bennis. His *On Becoming a Leader* (1989) is a classic in the leadership field. Based on research on 90 American leaders ranging from astronauts to football coaches, Bennis outlines and describes the four common abilities of successful leaders: management of attention, meaning, trust, and self.

Another famous book, possibly more famous for its many imitators, is Robert Blake and Jane Mouton's *The Managerial Grid* (1964). In this seminal work the authors describe how to evaluate leaders in terms of the production skills and people skills. Every leader combines these skills at various levels. Some are high in people skills but low in production skills; others have the reverse profile. But clearly the most successful leaders combine abilities in both areas.

Successfully combining theory and practice is Henry Mintzberg. In *The Nature of Managerial Work* (1973), he shares his observations of managers on the job. His identification of the characteristics of managers should sound strikingly familiar to most center directors: They perform great quantities of work at an unrelenting pace; undertake activities marked by variety, brevity, and fragmentation; have a preference for issues that are current, specific, and nonroutine; prefer verbal communication; and are subject to heavy constraints but can exert some control over their work.

Edgar H. Schein was the first organizational consultant to take a close look at the culture of organizations in *Organizational Culture and Organizations* (1985). In this seminal work, Schein describes how the culture of an organization shapes its performance and outlines the stages in the development of an organization's culture.

Finally, the book that had the greatest impact on my management philosophy is *The Human Side of Enterprise* by Douglas McGregor (1960). In this book McGregor posits two approaches to management—Theory X and Theory Y. Theory X is the traditional approach to management, which assumes that workers are inherently lazy and need to be closely supervised and threatened with punishment in order to perform. Theory Y posits that most workers are motivated to perform to the degree that they are committed to the goals of the organization. This theory assumes that people are naturally inclined to work hard if they believe that their efforts contribute to positive results. This book forces leaders to examine their attitudes about work and workers.

Leadership—New Approaches

The current wave of books on leadership tend to focus on examinations of the unique traits of successful leaders in the business world. One of the first to gain wide respect was *Peak Performers: The New Heroes in Business* by Charles Garfield (1986). Garfield identifies the traits of "hardy" leaders. He is persuasive in describing how successful leaders seek opportunities that further their personal growth.

Particularly attuned to the early childhood world is *The Female Advantage: Women's Ways of Leadership* by Sally Helgesen (1990). Based on research comparing male and female executives, this book describes gender differences in management styles. She describes how workplaces managed by women tend to be "webs of inclusion"—communities where sharing information is the key. This book is must reading for all center directors.

Of the many motivational books on the market, one of the most successful and most relevant to the early childhood world is *The 7 Habits of Highly Effective People* by Stephen R. Covey (1989). This book outlines seven guidelines of human contact that have proved to have enduring, permanent value. The seven principles, such as "Begin with an end in mind" and "Seek first to understand, then to be understood," require little translation to apply to the early childhood setting.

Finally, a book that also connects with the soul of most early childhood leaders is *Love & Profit: The Art of Caring Leadership* by James A. Autrey (1991). This book refutes the traditional assumption that successful leaders in business need to be driven solely by the profit motive and not to let personal feelings get in the way. Autrey describes how a successful leader can combine a strong concern for people with the profit motive.

Customer Service

One of the most influential management books of the 1980s was *In Search of Excellence* by Tom Peters and Robert Waterman (1982). The book was based on the now oft-repeated formula of identifying the common traits of successful companies. Peters and Waterman summarized their findings in terms of eight crucial characteristics. Included among these characteristics were "productivity through people," "hands-on value driven," and "stick to the knitting." However, one of the most influential characteristics identified was "close to the customer." This initiated a wave of interest in customer service by American businesses.

This wave of interest was accompanied by a wave of customer service books. One of the most insightful ones was *The Customer Signs Your Paycheck* by Frank Cooper (1984). This book presents the "Ten Commandments of Customer Service," the focal point of the commandments being that a successful business is built on attention first to the needs of customers.

Recently the focus on customer service has broadened into focus on creativity in marketing. One of the most helpful of the books in this genre is *How to Drive Your Competition Crazy: Creating Disruption for Fun and Profit* by Guy Kawasaki (1995). The strategies Kawasaki presents for getting the upper hand against the competition are both clever and doable.

CONCLUSION

A dominant feature of the world of ECE programs is the incredible diversity of organizations that populate it. Centers are small and large, simple and complex, and funded in a myriad of combinations. They offer a wide range of program philosophies and services. They are operated by a plethora of agents from moms and pops to multinational employers, from churches to the U.S. Army, from community boards to national headquarters.

Matching this diversity is the wide variety of demands on directors. However, no matter what the organization looks like, the core of the director's job remains the same. While the manner in which directors carry out their work will, of necessity, vary dramatically, all directors must ultimately carry out, manage, or at least relate to the eight basic functions of center management. If practitioners are working on an administrative path in their career, they will want to master all eight, as well as child development and teaching, in order to have maximum flexibility to move on what the National Association for the Education of Young Children calls the career lattice. These well-prepared administrators link the parts of knowledge necessary for children's services into a whole where professional skills are recognized, portable, and necessary for the provision of child and family services.

REFERENCES

Autrey, J. A. (1991). *Love & profit: The art of caring leadership.* New York: Morrow.

Bennis, W. (1989). *On becoming a leader.* Reading, MA: Addison-Wesley.

Blake, R., & Mouton, J. (1964). *The managerial grid.* New York: Harper.

Caplow, T. (1983). *Managing any organization.* New York: CBS College Publishing.

Cooper, F. (1984). *The customer signs your paycheck.* Everett, WA: Frank Cooper.

Covey, S. R. (1989). *The 7 habits of highly effective people.* New York: Simon & Schuster.

Drucker, P. (1974). *Management: Tasks, responsibilities and practices.* New York: Harper & Row.

Garfield, C. (1986). *Peak performers: The new heroes in business.* New York: Morrow.

Helgesen, S. (1990). *The female advantage: Women's ways of leadership.* New York: Doubleday.

Helburn, S. (Ed.). (1995). *Cost, quality, and child outcomes in child care centers: Technical report.* Denver: University of Colorado, Economics Department.

Kawasaki, G. (1995). *How to drive your competition crazy: Creating disruption for fun and profit.* New York: Hyperion.

McGregor, D. (1960). *The human side of enterprise.* New York: McGraw-Hill.

Mintzberg, H. (1973). *The nature of managerial work.* New York: Harper & Row.

Peters, T., & Waterman, R. (1982). *In search of excellence.* New York: Harper & Row.

Schein, E. H. (1985). *Organizational culture and organizations.* San Francisco: Jossey-Bass.

7

Capturing the Breadth and Depth of the Job: The Administrator as Influential Leader in a Complex World

Karen VanderVen

The future world we must prepare children for is one of increasing complexity and unpredictability. In an earlier era institutions and relationships were stable and predictable (Elkind, 1994; Lifton, 1993). However, in the face of a world in constant flux, children will have to become highly adaptable. They will need to be flexible and resilient in their thinking and action.

The significance of early childhood for laying the groundwork for the ability to grow and adapt is well known to all of us. Thus the early care and education (ECE) field needs to develop organizations and provide settings that will support a child in acquiring these necessary attributes. This will require a cadre of practitioners (some administrators and some teachers) who can understand society's evolving complexities and can reconceptualize the purpose, structure, content, and adaptability of developmental settings such as schools, child care centers, Head Start, and other children's programs. A recognition of ECE settings as organizations operating as complex systems will underlie their work. The ability to understand the conditions that are part of every organization goes beyond an administrator's basic preparation as a manager. A director's capacity to understand and deal with complexity is related to his or her degree of personal and professional maturity. As ECE directors continue to learn and develop professionally over time, they become increasingly skilled and knowledgeable about working as leaders in ECE organizations and systems.

This chapter will:

- Identify the relationship between a director's professional preparation and the interrelated aspects of organizations

- Describe a recent paradigm shift whereby complex systems theory has been recognized as applicable to organizations
- Show the stages of personal and professional development of early childhood practitioners into leadership capacity, relating to the ability to understand the complexities of children's programs
- Suggest how complex systems thinking can enhance the advanced practitioner's influence both within and beyond her or his organization

DIRECTOR PREPARATION AND THE SYSTEMS ASPECTS OF ORGANIZATIONS

To manage and lead effectively, it is crucial that an ECE administrator be competent in such areas as financial administration, plant maintenance, staff development and supervision, establishment of policies, oversight of program and curriculum, parent and community relationships (Vander-Ven, 1994). (See Chapters 3 and 5.) However, preparation in these areas may not include organizational dynamics and systems aspects of organizations.

Administrators of children's programs are always interacting with, and effecting the structure of, the organizations in which they work. The structure of the organization—whether it involves working in a classroom or with a group; balancing a budget; or collaborating with parents, local businessmen, and health consultants—is central to organizational processes. As Senge (1990) puts it in his discussion of structure:

> We tend to think of "structures" as external constraints on the individual. But, "structure" in complex living systems ... *means the basic interrelationships that control behavior.* In human systems, structure includes how people make decisions—the "operating policies" whereby we translate perceptions, goals, rules, and norms into actions. (p. 40)

In an ECE organization the structure exists in the relationships between the people in the program, and it is manifest in the parent handbook, the class schedules, the job descriptions, the budget, and the board protocols. Administrators work with structural issues as a fundamental part of their job.

Structure Is Essential

Sometimes even a well-prepared director may fail to provide sufficient structure within the organization. Certainly an unprepared director with no administrative knowledge is likely to falter in this area. When organizational structures are inadequate, key areas of organizational functioning are at risk. Mission, lines of communication and responsibility, roles and job functions, the working relationships among employees, and the organizational culture that determines the values and norms of the workplace all suffer when the administration does not provide basic structure. Teachers or other staff members may have little understanding of the mission and goals of the organization or of their job responsibilities. Clear ways for staff and clients to share information may be lacking. Procedures for doing business may be neither established nor clear.

In such a program, there is little formal supervision. Nobody knows who is responsible for making final decisions. Directors and teachers may work from different visions of early childhood and appropriate care and education. They may also work with varied levels of knowledge and experience about child development, teaching, family support, program design, and management. Disorganization results from the lack of structure, and this leads to ineffectiveness and constant crisis. Daily, and sometimes moment-to-moment, a director's or teacher's energy is focused on situations that must be attended to immediately. We might call this an unstructured organization where crises occur repeatedly.

Overly Structured Organizations

At other times, although less likely in a humanistic area such as ECE, directors may run things in a way that reflects a traditional or linear organization, making this type of ECE program almost the extreme opposite of an unstructured organization. The organization is hierarchical; that is, there are multiple layers of workers from bottom to top and rigid lines of authority and communication from top to bottom. Job descriptions are highly explicit and inflexible. There are extremely explicit rules and procedures. A director's supervision is constant and highly directive, with little, if any, input from teachers in decision making. In such an organization, morale is often low, with teachers and other staff beginning to avoid the mandates of the administration. Of course, staff performance is usually low, too. But there is a new way of thinking about organizational design that can avoid the pitfalls of either mode.

The hypothesis of this chapter is that a leadership approach to early childhood management will address the challenges of complexity, constant flux, and unpredictability mentioned earlier. Such a leadership approach focuses on the (1) director's understanding of the complex aspects of ECE organizations, (2) the organizational contexts and structures in which practitioners operate, and (3) the phenomenon of complexity.

THE ECE ADMINISTRATOR AND AN ECE ORGANIZATION AS A COMPLEX ADAPTIVE SYSTEM

Increasingly, early care and education has been viewed as a complex system by several researchers in the field. In a national study of ECE training and education, "our findings gave us a heightened understanding of the complexity of early care and education and the systemic nature of the problems in the field" (Morgan et al., 1994, p. 137). The job of the early childhood director must be recognized as "complex" and "multifaceted" (Larkin, 1992) and as one "juxtaposing the most menial of tasks with a range of sophisticated and interpersonal skills" (p. 120). This is in line with a comment by Lynch and Kordis (1988) that in all organizations, "What must change is the quality and quantity of our awareness of complexity and our skills and comfort level in working with it" (p. 13). Understanding the complexity of their ECE organization as a system is precisely the challenge to new administrators.

Complexity Theory

Complexity theory is a branch of the new physical sciences dealing with unpredictability, interconnectedness, and nonequilibrium conditions in systems. It has been applied to a number of phenomena in the social sciences, such as leadership (Eoyang, 1997; Goldstein, 1994; Wheatley, 1992) and early childhood education (Fromberg, 1994; VanderVen, 1998). Early childhood theorists and practitioners can relate this concept to changing ECE leadership development.

According to complexity theory, the world is spontaneous, alive, and disorderly—in other words, complex. This results in organizations where there are no simple answers and where people and programs continually interact with a constantly changing environment.

A key concept in this theory is the *complex adaptive system*, which is an open system interacting with other systems. The complex adaptive system utilizes information received from these other systems on an ongoing basis. Growth and change in the system is continuous, and one result is learning. Complex adaptive systems demonstrate learning. Paradoxically, they may show order, pattern, and coherence, as well as sudden change and rapid transformations.

The concept of a complex adaptive system provides a useful construct to help ECE administrators attain the balance between lack of organizational structure and a control-based management model, which fails to take complexity into consideration. As leaders in their organizations, administrators deal with complexity in all aspects of the program, from the details of developmental and learning issues that emerge in teacher supervision to work with budgets, planning, facilities, and legal or financial issues.

Stages of Personal and Professional Development

New concepts of systems and of human development require that we reconsider the professional development of ECE practitioners, program directors, and other administrators. Human development does not stop with the end of childhood, but rather continues throughout life. This lifelong development does not proceed in linear ages and stages, but rather through phases (Levine, 1989). Phases are an ongoing and repeated process in which individuals constantly revise their thinking in line with new information from their interactions with their world. The administrator, for example, revises as he or she deals with situations in the organization that are complex, because many independent agents are interacting in many different ways.

For example, an early childhood director/trainer might attend a workshop on instructional methods to enhance teachers' ability to transfer their new learning to the workplace (i.e., classroom). The director/trainer would integrate this information into his or her existing knowledge of training methodology. As a result, the director/trainer's concepts of training methodology (and possibly of adult learning) would change in the direction of providing more effective career development experiences to all the teachers on staff.

In a five-phase model of personal and professional development in ECE, a practitioner's increasing understanding of the administrative job is examined in relation to an ecological-systems hierarchy (VanderVen, 1988). While the ecological model could be related to teachers, this chapter examines the administrator's or director's work within the ecological-systems hierarchy. The systems hierarchy is based on Bronfenbrenner's model of child ecology (Bronfenbrenner, 1977).

The model for administrator development—whose five phases are novice, initial, informed, complex, and influential—will be discussed in detail later in the chapter following a discussion of Bronfenbrenner's ecological view of the child's world. The model suggests that administrator development relates to Bronfenbrenner's five ecological levels.

Bronfenbrenner's Model of Development

According to Bronfenbrenner (1977), a child's development is affected by a multiplicity of systems. The systems are hierarchically arranged from those in which the child is actually present to those that affect the child but in which he or she is not directly present.

The first level in the hierarchy is the *microsystem*. The microsystem is the setting that actually contains the child, and it includes the people in it, the physical characteristics, the activities taking place, and the norms or guidelines for conduct that prevail. An early childhood classroom, for example, is a microsystem.

Level 2, the *mesosystem*, relates to the family, the neighborhood, and the organization. The mesosystem is a network of microsystems that interact with each other to create the supportive environment that "situates" children.

The *exosystem*, level 3, is comprised of the institutions of society that strongly affect the quality of child rearing. These include health care, the economy, employment, transportation, religion, the mass media, government, and legislation, among others.

Finally, level 4, the *macrosystem*, is composed of the overarching values of society that shape the exosystem and ultimately filter down and influence the microsystem.

The model for professional leadership in ECE identifies and connects a series of five similar levels for administrator development. As administrators develop in their professional lives, the more they are able to respond effectively to events in the complex world and to act to influence events that have an effect on the staff, children, and families involved in the children's program.

An Ecological Model of Practitioner Development

A model of practitioner development, focused here on administrators, has five phases—novice, initial, informed, complex, and influential. The model of administrative development illustrates how an individual director's ability to address complexity within Bronfenbrenner's model develops with experience and learning. As directors develop more complex mental models about their professional tasks and areas of competence, they are able to relate to the people, activities, and ideas in more spheres of Bronfenbrenner's model. That is, a practitioner in the novice phase will function in the classroom almost all of the time. Later, as a director in the complex phase, she or he will function in all the spheres, from coaching in the classroom to interacting with large systems affecting children, such

as health departments and the public education system. Administrators'
ability to address factors at each ecological level is related to their particular developmental phase.

Novice Phase. Novice practitioners are those at the entry level, such
as teachers' aides. Almost universally, they work directly with children
in the immediate setting (Bronfenbrenner's microsystem) though some
may have very limited administrative responsibilities. They may have little if any formal preparation in child development and teaching, and they
may tend to view the behavior of clients (children and families) without
giving much consideration to context or meaning. Their work is generally
unmodified by such hallmarks of professionalism as formal knowledge,
well-honed practice skills, and personal reflection. Rather, their individual value systems and ideas about childhood determine their practice.
There may be variations in thinking and approaches among individual
practitioners in this phase; however, the perspective of novices tends to
be very grounded in their immediate job assignment. They have little
concern with the organization as a system of services, individuals, values,
or other qualities, or with external systems.

Initial Phase. Initial practitioners are beginning to change. Their
understanding grows as they gain experience and benefit from training,
guidance, and supervision. Through these experiences, initial practitioners address belief systems and acquire new knowledge and skills.
They are developing an understanding of the complexity of the ECE setting. Like those in the novice phase, administrators in the initial phase
generally combine administrative and teaching responsibilities. Initial
phase practitioners are generally teachers and continue to have their focus on the immediate setting (the microsystem) while they work to acquire and apply knowledge of a wider context to their practice. In the
initial phase, a practitioner's worldview, mental models, and understanding of larger external community systems related to ECE, while expanding, are still limited.

Informed Phase. Informed-phase practitioners generally have a degree (associate or bachelor's level), or advanced training and experience.
Their primary work focus is still directly on children, although some may
have some supervisory/administrative responsibilities as well. Informed-
phase practitioners are beginning to move away from linear thinking or
single cause–one effect thinking. They begin to experience what their
preparation has told them: Development is multiply determined by an
interaction of societal, familial, and individual factors. They may have

some beginning understanding of the many variables in the lives of children that affect their development and behavior, or they may consider events in a child's community, neighborhood, family, and culture as important. They are recognizing that interacting multiple factors, both organizational and external, may influence children's development.

An informed-phase practitioner may become an administrator, often as a promotion for good direct teaching skills. However, frequently this new director has little or no formal preparation in administrative core knowledge and competency. The transition may thus be particularly difficult. Such administrators, in the beginning of their development into an administrative role, are likely either to fail to provide sufficient definition and structure to the work of the staff and program, or to overly define and control it. This may be due to the director's incomplete grasp of the organizational or systems dynamics that are operating in the children's program.

Directors in this phase begin to work in their program's service and policy domains. Often they continue to have teaching as well as administrative responsibilities, which adds to the challenge because role boundaries are blurred. Informed-phase practitioners may need a wider array of skills to apply across domains of work than they possess.

Complex Phase. The children's program administrator with formal preparation or experience usually falls in the complex phase. There is likely to be a great deal of variability in terms of the mix of tasks and activities the practitioner performs at this point. Tasks may range from supporting and coaching a new teacher, to negotiating a budget with the school district, to attending an interagency advocacy meeting. Some of the administrator's work in the complex phase begins to involve the institutions of society that so crucially affect children. The administrator may relate to the economy, the transportation system, health care, the mass media, and the like. This work expansion could take any number of forms and foci.

The complex-phase administrator's expanded areas of work may include advanced *direct* practice work or may focus on *indirect* work, that is, administrative and managerial roles. Quite likely, direct and indirect roles will be blended. A newer director in the complex phase practices from the perspective of the basic competency sets and core knowledge that have already been discussed in Chapter 3 and Chapter 5. Such a director keeps a focus on Bronfenbrenner's mesosystem: the internal working of the children's program interfacing with the child's family and neighborhood or community.

There are some complex practitioners with few if any administrative responsibilities who provide a highly skilled level of direct practice to children and families, while others in this phase are solely administrators. But most practitioners in the complex phase assume administrative responsibilities while maintaining some direct contact with young children. More seasoned complex practitioners extend their scope and interact more proactively with the exosystem—the social institutions of the mass media, economy, health care, transportation, employment, education, and recreation—which embraces the child's world of family and neighborhood.

Influential Phase. Practitioners who stay in the field and who are in a constant process of cognitive and personal development may move into the final stage in the model, which is the influential phase. In this phase, administrators may manage some direct services; however, their work also includes dealing with larger system issues such as advocacy and public policy on a local or broader level. Robert Kegan (1994) describes this process of expanded professional capacity as "the personal unfolding of ways of organizing experience that are not simply replaced as we grow but subsumed into more complex systems of mind" (p. 9). Being able to understand complex systems is most likely an attribute of an influential practitioner. Complex systems are the powerful shaping values of the society (Bronfenbrenner's macrosystem) that continually interact with and modify the variables in the other three ecological levels.

Influential practitioners acquire this name because of their ability to think powerfully in the leadership positions they hold in the field. Thus it devolves on the field of early childhood education to ensure that some practitioners actually stay in it until they "make" it to this sophisticated and effective level of practice. In that way the profession's core values—such as the importance of human development in both teaching children and managing staff, and the need for partnerships with parents—can become incorporated into institutional frameworks. When, through the influential practitioner's work and vision, the core values are incorporated into the children's programs, policies, and practitioner training, we can anticipate that the values may influence more children and families.

PROFESSIONAL GROWTH INVOLVES COMPLEX ADAPTATIONS TO THE SYSTEM

The ongoing professional growth of the complex-phase administrator into the influential leader is in itself a cognitive complex adaptive system. In this system, as new connections are developed and new patterns of thinking emerge, practitioners weave their individual values, ideas, and experiences into more complex patterns.

An important observation regarding professional progression from novice to influential is that the mental abilities and worldviews of the practitioner become less and less tied to any particular job or role. An influential practitioner has a multitude of knowledge and skill areas that can selectively, and in an integrated fashion, be applied to a wide range of tasks. This indeed is why the complex or influential practitioner is most likely to have a blended career combining several domains. This career may bridge service, policy, higher education, resource and referral, and research. The more cognitive complexity possessed by a practitioner, the less closely connected his or her abilities are to a particular job or function. Thus, the more practitioners can apply their knowledge and skills to varied situations. As administrators, influential practitioners can deal with complex systems. Their ability to function in this way enables them to integrate social and other factors into more complex programs that support child and family in a more complex world.

Characteristics of Complex Adaptive Systems Thinking and Practice

As administrators develop—becoming advanced complex or influential leaders—they must conceptualize (through practice) and use more complex, multifaceted *mental models* (Senge, 1990) to drive their approach. "Mental model" is a term used to refer to the internal coherent frame of reference we use to represent our worldview, to integrate our experiences, and to draw upon for problem solving and decision making (Senge, 1990). Senge says mental models are "deeply engrained assumptions, generalizations, or even pictures or images that influence how we see the world and how we take action. Very often we are not aware of our mental models or the effects they have on our behavior" (p. 8).

Senge continues with some examples: "None of us can carry an organization in our minds—or a family, or a community. What we carry in our heads are images, assumptions, and stories" (pp. 174–175).

The mental models that administrators use as they make decisions transcend their specific technical skills and competencies. Depending on the efficacy of the mental model, an administrator's decision can result in an organization's effective approach to a problem, or in maintaining the status quo, or even in re-creating current problems. Thus it is important for ECE administrators, in addition to acquiring competence and core knowledge, to transform their mental models to embrace a complex adaptive systems worldview. They can then apply it to their directorship and leadership work. As Senge states, mental models "determine not only how we make sense of the world, but how we take action" (p. 174).

Advanced complex and influential ECE practitioners function from a complex, dynamic worldview. They are able to handle and respond effectively to ongoing change and variety in the systems in their organization. The dynamic systems thinking of the advanced complex and influential ECE practitioner as a worldview or mental mode is expressed in the following list. The characteristics are based on the work of such authors as Gell-Mann (1994), Goldstein (1994), Kaufmann (1995), Morgan (1997), Prigogine and Stengers (1984), and Wheatley (1992).

The advanced complex and influential ECE practitioner:

- Sees things holistically—"the whole picture," rather than just a limited section or component
- Recognizes interconnections among different systems, realizing that a change in one may affect all the others
- Sees situations as multiply caused, rather than in "linear," one cause–one effect terms; meaning that situations may be addressed by multiple actions
- Is not upset by unpredictability; tends to use it to advantage, "going with" the emergent directions
- Recognizes patterns in situations that may seem chaotic, which can lead to productive self-organization
- Sees the value of structure in an organization, as contrasted to lack of definition or formal efforts to overcontrol
- Strikes an appropriate balance between concern with details and letting things evolve
- Does not see things as proportionally additive—recognizes that too much may lead to more of what isn't desired, and that a small action or input into a system may lead to a major outcome
- Sees turbulence as an opportunity for positive change rather than requiring an increased emphasis on control
- Is able to see recursion effects, that is, how a system feeds back on itself and generates new patterns and effects
- Utilizes the concept of "fractal," or scale (Eoyang, 1997), to encourage coherence in an organization; for example, the staff is treated with the same attitudes as the children
- Recognizes "sensitive dependence on initial conditions," or the butterfly effect (Eoyang, 1997)—that a very small input can lead to a very large output—and the implications, both positive and negative, of this phenomenon
- Sets the tone and direction, in order to generate energy around a goal, but does not overdefine or overdirect

Early childhood administrative practitioners must be able to adapt their own thinking so as to understand and approach ECE as a complex adaptive system rather than as a simple personal service system for families and other customers.

Mental models affect the work of the novice as well as the influential practitioner. What changes as a practitioner administrator moves through the leadership phases is awareness of, and capacity to use, personal mental models. Becoming aware of and using their mental models to drive their approach is one of the areas of greater complexity observed in the work of complex and influential practitioners. In the later phases, an administrator's mental model embraces interacting events in different arenas from the microsystem to the macrosystem. This allows the administrator to grasp the complexity in the professional environment, which includes both the ECE program itself as a dynamic adaptive system and a wide variety of external variables and situations that continually affect it.

In line with the concept of a complex adaptive system and changed mental models of practice, I want to emphasize one characteristic of the influential administrator. The gradual growth in thinking capacity that characterizes the influential-stage administrator does not mean that she or he abandons basic knowledge and skills, and then moves onto a separate, higher plane of thought. Rather, the initially acquired knowledge of separate domains of teaching and policy or management increasingly become mentally interconnected. Thus the influential administrator recognizes and acts on these more complex understandings and insights.

Mental Models at the Complex or Influential Phase

In order to embrace new mental models and function at the complex and influential phase, administrators must be sufficiently ready to make the cognitive developmental leap that this requires. Such readiness is related to personal development in thinking ability, in social perception and the like, as well as to professional career growth, resulting in an ability to perform ever broader and more complex tasks. The following examples illustrate how an understanding of complex adaptive systems might actually be applied to an ECE administrator's work. A few examples from ecological levels of early childhood practice analogous to Bronfenbrenner's ecological hierarchy are offered.

Microsystem. Ultimately, all administrative activities directly impact the immediate setting containing children, for example, the classroom setting. An excellent example of influential-level complex adaptive systems thinking applied to a direct practice situation is described in a recent article about time and classroom scheduling, "Untiming the Curriculum: A Case Study of Removing Clocks from the Program" (Wien & Kirby-Smith, (1998). A director in an earlier stage of understanding complex dynamic systems would be more committed to the more controlled schedule of specific inflexible time frames "as scheduled." An advanced thinking director would utilize flexibility, combining fixed events (group times, story, meals) and a sequence of events (the schedule) with varied and changeable time boundaries determined by ongoing circumstances (children's completion of play, weather, an unexpected parent visit). Another example would be handling challenging behavior in children. A non–complex systems thinker would see something like time-out as additive—expecting that the longer a child spent in time-out, the better he might then behave. An influential thinker, aside from sensing that time-out is inappropriate for young children anyway, would recognize that overly long or punitive actions would, rather than securing compliance, encourage anger, resistance, and covert acting out.

Mesosystem. A beginning director, as an approach to staff development, might send staff to formal training so they could meet regulations by getting in the required number of hours—with little concern as to whether that training would actually change direct practice. A complex director, however, showing an attribute of a contemporary leader (Gardner, 1996), might encourage his or her constituencies to see themselves as "co-creating and living a story." To prepare teachers to learn this approach to their work with children, a complex director would not eliminate the training about state regulations. They would coordinate a variety of teacher training experiences, including training about state regulations and child-oriented, even "childlike," approaches, with teaching and classroom organization. These might include storytelling and play and "even what may appear absurd" (Goldstein, 1994, p. 16). The director in the complex phase may also design sessions that include and integrate work and learning about more traditional topics such as cognition, social, emotional, and language development, and activities. Awareness of adult education strategies and adult learning styles is a necessity for the director in a complex mode.

Such an engaging, attention-getting approach can bypass the resistance to change and learning that is so ingrained in human service practitioners—including ECE staff. As another example, staff may consistently be late, using a great deal of energy to "cover." A program of "flextime" might be used by an advanced director as a structured (and more complex) way to approach the situation, generating neither misuse of work schedules nor the resistance that would result from an overly rigid approach.

Or a parent might be continually late to pick up a child. An advanced director might, in a paradoxical sense, offer the parent a selected number of days of lateness, rather than a rigid penalty. An unexpected outcome might be a prompt parent who now does not want to take advantage of staff generosity. Another example would be to utilize contemporary strategic planning models, themselves conceived in complex adaptive systems theory (e.g., Stacey, 1996). These models state that traditional planning in which we "analyze external environments and internal capabilities, and then design organizational structures, processes and behaviors so that they fit the environments" (Stacey, 1996, p. 3) are no longer viable. Such traditional models lead to ever more futile efforts to control, when the pace and dynamics of change are ever on the increase.

Contemporary models of planning for operations in the mesosystem, in contrast, would focus more on establishing short-term goals, being less quantitative, building outward from a current event or activity, and creating new events to meet a prestated intent. Such models and the thinking beyond them allow the organization to be responsive, flexible, and adaptable should trends and other circumstances require this. For example, a primarily preschool program might more readily position itself to include an after-school program should the identified needs and demography of its community change suddenly. Along this line, the advanced complex and influential leader would feel comfortable with the concept of marketing, which involves such activities as trend analysis—that is, determining future trends and needs. The advanced complex and influential thinker would take these into account when positioning the organization's activities, working proactively rather than reactively to promote his or her children's programs.

Exosystem. The influential practitioner will enter the larger exosystem in order to advocate for adequate support for families from the institutions of society. There the practitioner can influence the mass media, transportation, business, shopping facilities, health care, employment, recreation, education, housing, and the like—all entities that provide absolutely essential support to children and families in positive quality of life and development (Bronfenbrenner, 1974). Here, knowledge of complex adaptive systems, with their interdependence, interconnectedness, possibility of rapid change, and the other phenomena already mentioned, would be crucial for working with and within these systems.

An example where knowledge of interconnectedness would be particularly important would be in a systems collaboration such as a "full-service" school. In such a school the components of the wider human service system that have traditionally worked within more narrow and self-defined boundaries (e.g., health and family support services) would be subsumed within another system—the school, which has its own characteristics. Ability to work with all these interrelated dynamics would be an attribute of an advanced complex or influential leader. This leader would actively seek to forge new connections, knowing that to keep a program growing—that is, to continue to evolve as a complex adaptive system—the director must actively seek to develop connections with external units. The collaborations that then result would keep the system dynamic, stronger, and less vulnerable to any one force that could seriously threaten it.

Macrosystem. In the macrosystem—the overarching values of society toward children—the influential leader will be the one who uses transformational approaches to change these values. This requires being "in the public eye," as predecessors such as Erik Erikson, Benjamin Spock, and Fred Rogers have been. The influential director will recognize that disciplines outside of early childhood education, such as health practice, psychology, and social work, will be the source of new ideas and insights. Juxtaposing a new concept against another represents analogical thinking (Gergen, 1994), which is recognized as the mental source of creativity. This requires the mental attribute of constantly being open to new information—indeed, of the mind functioning as a complex adaptive system. It is continuously gathering new knowledge from multiple sources, itself becoming more complex and able to develop more and more powerful and embracing insights and actions.

The mental model driving the practices of a new director—such as "every aspect of the center would comply with regulations," which is certainly a safe and necessary, if unexciting, approach—might be very different in an influential-stage director. This person might carry an embracing vision of transformation in the lives of children and the conception of ways of attaining this (Daniel, 1998, personal communication).

A principle underlying this phase model is the law of requisite variety, which states that, in a system, that element with the greatest amount of variability is the most powerful (King, Novik, & Citrenbaum, 1983). Following this principle, complex and influential leaders are most able to deal with the variety or complexity in their organizations.

More Variability in Complex Systems as Reflected in Practice

In line with their highest level of cognitive complexity, the careers of advanced complex or influential leaders will have the greatest degree of variability and complexity. An individual may or may not hold just one job title. Within their position, advanced complex or influential administrators may have the greatest flexibility. They may also have the greatest number of options for different activities and even hold multiple job titles. There are several common examples. One would be college or university faculty members who teach, administer, perform community service, and are involved in program development, advocacy, research, writing, publication, training, and consultation. Another would be advanced complex state child care directors who, simply with a different core position, perform all of the other functions named above: do some teaching, consultation, advocacy, and the like. A third would be the practitioner in a demonstration program in a community college who teaches children and adults, lectures on child development, and may be called on to testify before the state legislature.

To perform all of these multiple functions, the practitioner must be able to think systemically: to recognize the commonalties and connections among systems, and to be able to apply components of knowledge from one area to another area. What a change of mind-set it is for the early care and education director to embrace the new mental model. This model requires that the practitioner accept unpredictability, turbulence, and the inability to control, while still keeping active and "moving" or creating and responding to events and opportunities in various complex systems. This is how the influential practitioner makes transformational change happen.

As early care and education administrators acquire the understanding of children's programs as complex adaptive systems—constantly learning, constantly creating themselves—they will be in an exciting position. The greatest potential for creativity comes when the organization, far from equilibrium, is operating "at the edge of chaos," or in complexity. Influential administrators will face many challenges as they help create change and also adapt to the increasingly rapid pace of change. The future's children will be the beneficiaries.

REFERENCES

Bronfenbrenner, U. (1974). *A report of longitudinal evaluations of preschool programs: Volume II. Is early intervention effective?* Washington, DC: U.S. Department of Health, Education and Welfare, Office of Human Development, Children's Bureau.

Bronfenbrenner, U. (1977, July). Towards an experimental ecology of human development. *American Psychologist*, pp. 513–530.

Elkind, D. (1994). *Ties that stress: The new family imbalance.* Cambridge, MA: Harvard University Press.

Eoyang, G. (1997). *Coping with chaos: Seven simple tools.* Cheyenne, WY: Lagumo Corporation.

Fromberg, D. (1994). *The full day kindergarten.* New York: Teachers College Press.

Gardner, H. (1996). *Leading minds: An anatomy of leadership.* New York: Basic Books.

Gell-Mann, M. (1994). *The quark and the jaguar.* New York: Freeman.

Gergen, K. (1994). *Realities and relationships: Soundings in social construction.* Cambridge, MA: Harvard University Press.

Goldstein, J. (1994). *The unshackled organization.* Portland: Productivity Press.

Kaufmann, S. (1995). *At home in the universe.* New York: Oxford University Press.

Kegan, R. (1994). *In over our heads: The mental demands of modern life.* Cambridge, MA: Harvard University Press.

King, M., Novik, L., & Citrenbaum, C. (1983). *Irresistible communications: Creative skills for the health profession.* Baltimore: W. B. Saunders.

Larkin, E. (1992). *The preschool administrator: Perspectives in leadership in early childhood education.* Cambridge, MA: Harvard Graduate School of Education.

Levine, S. (1989). *Promoting adult growth in schools.* Boston: Allyn & Bacon.

Lifton, R. (1993). *The Protean self.* New York: Basic Books.

Lynch, D., & Kordis, P. (1988). *Strategy of the dolphin: Scoring a win in a chaotic world.* New York: Fawcett Columbine.

Morgan, G. (1997). *Images of organization* (2nd ed.). Thousand Oaks, CA: Sage.

Morgan, G., Azer, S., Costley, J., Elliott, K., Genser, A., Goodman, I., & McGimsey, B. (1994). Future pursuits: Building early care and education careers. In J. Johnson & J. McCracken (Eds.), *The early childhood career lattice: Perspectives on professional development* (pp. 133–139). Washington, DC: National Association for the Education of Young Children.

Prigogine, I., & Stengers, E. (1984). *Order out of chaos.* New York: Bantam Books.

Senge, P. (1990). *The fifth discipline: The art and practice of the learning organization.* New York: Doubleday.

Stacey, R. (1996). *Complexity and creativity in organizations.* San Francisco: Berrett-Koehler.

VanderVen, K. (1988). Pathways to professional effectiveness for early childhood educators. In B. Spodek, O. N. Saracho & D. Peters, (Eds.), *Professionalism and the early childhood practitioner* (pp. 137–160). New York: Teachers College Press.

VanderVen, K. (1994). Professional development: A contextual model. In J. Johnson & J. McCracken (Eds.), *The early childhood career lattice: Perspectives on professional development* (pp. 79–95). Washington, DC: National Association for the Education of Young Children.

VanderVen, K. (1998). Chaos/complexity theory, constructivism, interdisciplinarity and early childhood teacher education. *Journal of Early Childhood Teacher Education, 18(3),* 43–48.

Wheatley, M. (1992). *Leadership and the new science: Learning about organization from an orderly universe.* San Francisco: Berrett-Koehler.

Wien, C., & Kirby-Smith, S. (1998, September). Untiming the curriculum: A case study of removing clocks from the program. *Young Children, 53(5),* 8–13.

II

A Credential for Program Administrators

The development of a director credential may be a next step for early childhood practitioners. The chapters in Part II are focused on issues for consideration in a dialogue about a director credential.

If we assume that early care and education (ECE) programs are dynamic systems and that an educated director, trained in management and leadership as well as child development, is a key to meeting organizational goals, then it makes sense to investigate the possibility of a credential. Reflection on the content of Part I suggests that we consider the need to develop a credential that allows for expansion of the role. The credential can serve two purposes. It can provide a clear delineation of the specific knowledge and skills involved in a director's daily work in a variety of ECE programs. A credential can also serve as a framework for articulating the knowledge and skills a director will need as she or he moves from work as a novice director to the subsequent role of a complex or an influential director.

Consideration of the promise of the credential leads to an investigation of the challenges of designing, creating, and monitoring an effective credentialing process. Across the country individuals and groups have been working on these issues. Part II makes the point that a credentialing process can be built on a foundation of the work already in place.

The chapters in Part II provide the authors' best description and analysis of issues and considerations as well as what is in place and what may be needed to design effective credentials for directors. The authors review both the promise and the challenges facing the ECE profession in deliberations about the credential.

The authors both acknowledge current director training and education programs and anticipate future demands on ECE organizations and administrators. While the ECE administrator is not considered a sole force for the creation of quality programs, the underlying value reflected in all of these chapters is that a well-prepared director can serve as a major force in the provision of quality services to children and families.

The authors view administrators as facilitators of quality programs and as resource managers who lead their organizations in anticipating, and responding to, the opportunities that are expected to emerge for the ECE field in the near future. The authors expect that changes in the early childhood profession and in the market may offer new administrative opportunities. They consider the future for credentialing administrators as part of professionalization.

In Chapter 8 Gwen G. Morgan examines the assumptions of the traditional sociological definitions of a profession. She concludes that there have been major changes in the ways in which professionals view themselves and are viewed by others; the capacities in which ECE professionals interact with children and families; and the degree of authority granted to professionals by the general public. Professionals interact far more collegially with those they serve than in the past. Also, there have been major changes in approaches to regulation of the workplace, including professional training and credentialing. Morgan cites evidence of the movement toward a new professionalism focused on career development, credentialing, and caring human relationships. She makes recommendations for implementing a director credential based on the new framework.

Anne Mitchell gathers information from other occupations to address several key questions about a credential and the credentialing process in Chapter 9. She examines the professional development systems in eight diverse U.S. occupations and finds similarities that point toward personnel credentialing as a route for improving early childhood education services. Mitchell suggests that administrative credentialing has the potential to make the job of public-sector licensers more efficient, to satisfy consumers regarding the quality of a child's program, to advance the status of the profession, and to upgrade the standards of care for America's children.

In Chapter 10 Sue Bredekamp discusses the strengths and weaknesses of a training approach versus credentialing approach in professional development. She also examines the challenge of implementing a credentialing system without an infrastructure of institutions prepared for students who are obtaining the credential. Bredekamp considers the benefits and challenges of establishing credentialing systems at the national, state, and local levels. Lastly, she addresses the difficulty of promoting higher-quality standards for director performance while maintaining access to the job for diverse groups of people. Bredekamp presents each of these sets of issues as an either/or, but the goal of the chapter is to achieve both/and solutions to these dilemmas.

Marsha Poster and Roger Neugebauer, in Chapter 11, present a selection of the innovative educational and training approaches for directors currently in use (or being developed) in the ECE field. Poster and Neugebauer report on a survey of a cadre of America's most experienced directors who have had long and effective careers. They summarize the insights of this cohort of directors into the training experiences that most dramatically shaped their careers. Poster and Neugebauer then explore some innovative programs across the country that are utilizing education and training formats that have been shown to make a difference.

Karen Hill-Scott examines the confluence of several trends that are reshaping early care and education in the United States in Chapter 12. She also discusses the impacts of these trends on the organization and management of child care services, with a specific emphasis on the child care program director. Hill-Scott suggests that changes in child care and other children's programs will result in entirely new opportunities of advancement for center directors. She makes a case for developing new skills for center directors who work at the program or site level and identifies the implications of these changes for leadership training and director credentialing in developmental programs.

The individual authors' perspectives are thoughtful and may give rise to lively conversation about the merits of a credential. Some of the authors present a broader, market-based view or consider the issue from the vantage point of a new professionalism with expanded leadership opportunities for administrators. Others consider the very precise discussions and dialogues that will be required within ECE organizations and in the larger community to design a credential. Work to inform these discussions is already under way in the practical projects reported throughout the book and particularly in Chapter 11. None of the authors present the director credential as a substitute for other aspects of quality. Rather they give us the opportunity to investigate the role of director as a support for quality to be put in place along with other quality components.

8

A Profession for the 21st Century

Gwen G. Morgan

As the 21st century begins, there are changes in the way the public perceives professions and changes in the way that professions see themselves. It is in this transitional period that we are now discussing a credential for directors. Don Peters (1988) defines profession in two ways: (1) as membership in a group that is recognized as a professional one and (2) in terms of behavior of the individual, where acting professionally means acting "autonomously, rationally, and ethically in exercise of one's knowledge and skills." He points out that "one has to be recognized both by one's self and by others" (p. 93). This chapter explores historical and changing definitions of profession in this century and reflects on their implications for the early care and education profession.

Professionalization is the dynamic process whereby occupations can be observed to change certain crucial characteristics in order to be considered a profession (Vollmer & Mills, 1966). Director credentialing arises in the early care and education field as a subtopic, part of the effort to professionalize the field as a whole. This chapter uses the term *director* interchangeably with *administrator, manager, executive,* or *administrative leader.* Some of the literature on management and leadership separates transactional leadership from transformational leadership, or management from some types of leadership. I believe that the professional preparation of directors should prepare participants for all these management and leadership aspects of their role—and their future roles—which they will need at different times.

The term *early care and education* (ECE) is intended to refer to programs for children younger than school-age as well as programs for school-age children in out-of-school time. Practitioners in this hundred-year-old field incorporate concepts of early education, concepts of caring, and concepts of family support, believing that these elements are intertwined and interdependent.

This chapter begins with an exploration of whether the executive role in administering a program for children is the same profession as or a different profession from that of early childhood teacher, and how the paradigm of profession is changing. It presents a brief history of professionalism, focused on the issues of access and equity of opportunity. The cluster of traditional attributes that are often used to define a profession, as identified by sociologists, is summarized, along with some of the common criticisms and the public's changing view. An analysis is made of which of these traditional attributes of professions have been discarded and which are still strong. A different approach to professionalism, career development, is contrasted with credentialism. Some beliefs important in the ECE field appear more compatible with the emerging professionalism of the future than with the professionalism of the past. Finally, the director credential is placed in the context of credentialing in the ECE field.

WHERE DOES THE DIRECTOR BELONG PROFESSIONALLY?

Preparation for the executive role is similar whether the organization is a child care center, Head Start, school-age program, resource and referral agency, nursery school, school, family child care system, early intervention center, or social service agency. This executive will need knowledge of the same content as does an early childhood teacher; that is, child development theory and best practices, family relationships, inclusion, and diversity. That basic content is necessary but not sufficient for the director. In addition, the director will need preparation in topics such as management and leadership.

In ECE, directors have more college training related to their work than teachers have, but this college preparation is likely to have been for teaching. If we believe that this role requires special competencies over and above those of teachers/caregivers, we need to become clear about which profession "owns" these leaders. Does the ECE field take professional responsibility for the preparation of its administrators, or do we import them from some other field?

There is an extensive academic system that currently prepares managers at the master's level, the bachelor's level, and in the community colleges. In the early childhood field, some of us have generally assumed that a person responsible for the administration of an early childhood program needs to be a member of our profession, rather than a generic administrator belonging to the management profession. State licensing agencies have targeted their required qualifications to assure knowledge of child development theory and practice, often without even requiring knowledge of how to operate a program. A number of states have allowed for the possibility of an outsider, a non–early childhood professional—visualized as not a professional—in the role of administrator, as long as the program also employs an early childhood–qualified program director (under a variety of titles) to make decisions about the program for children and their families. These states, too, fail to require any coursework in managing an organization for either role.

Currently there are a number of unexamined assumptions in our field about the role of the executive. According to one view, early childhood educators are "professionals" who work autonomously and therefore by definition are not managers. The professional preparation has focused primarily on one role—the classroom teacher—without giving much attention to the large number of different roles that are available to the early childhood practitioner and that are generally considered to be professional roles.

Here, the assumption seems to be that early childhood programs should be embedded in larger organizations where there will be other individuals who have management skills, because the early childhood educators will not have the competence to manage their early childhood programs. Management takes place above the program level. Head Start has been largely structured in this way, with some notable spin-offs. Schools, too, have been structured to separate administration from professional early childhood skills.

Contrasting assumptions are held by those who believe that the director of an ECE program should have both early childhood professional competence—in order to work with children and families—and professional administrative competence. From this perspective, to separate policy decision making from the theory and practice of early care and education means to turn quality over to others who do not have the qualifications to make those decisions

Not all directors have the full range of responsibility for financial management that a director of a single center has. In public school systems, program directors are limited in their scope because the structure of the system relies more on rules than on program leadership. However, school-based management, though rarely achieved, does offer some hope for quality. Future directors may need preparation in leadership and administration both in Head Start and even in school-based programs. They will need it in order to have lateral mobility across these different systems. They will need it in order to be leaders in integration of funding to create community-based systems.

Directors' necessary competencies will continue to include substantial knowledge of child growth and development (see Chapter 3 for a list of administrator competencies). They will be more skilled if they have had extensive experience as a qualified classroom teacher, as most of them now have. But there is a long list of additional skills that directors need because their roles are very different. Human development, learning, and relationships are at the heart of the knowledge base for both teachers and directors.

A BRIEF HISTORY OF PROFESSIONS

The growth of professions in the 19th century coincided with a rising middle class with economic and social power, made possible by the development of industry. Professionalism, like business, was a powerful avenue for upward mobility in a previously fixed class system (Larson, 1977). In the United States, opportunity for an individual to advance in life through his or her own efforts was, and still is, a basic value, whether or not it is real.

In the 19th century, American colleges were organized on the assumption that higher learning constituted a single unified culture whose goal was to produce a learned person. The new 20th-century university replaced this model with autonomous departments driven by scientific research within boundaries of the specialized discipline and its subspecializations. There were great gains from this educational system in scientific achievement, preparation for employment, and access for women and minorities. The cost has been a narrowing of focus and a vocabulary shared only by colleagues (Bellah, Madsen, Sullivan, Swidler, & Tipton, 1985).

Equity of Access

Opportunity for social advancement based on individual effort and ability is a key value in the United States. As formal schooling became a part of the paradigm of professionalism, replacing the old apprenticeship system, equity of social opportunity through professionalism became tied to equity of access to college. A profession determines who gets access to the knowledge, through entrance standards for certificate and degree programs, length of study, and requirements for degrees (Hughes, 1965). This country's strong commitment to social mobility has therefore become tied to its commitment to access to higher education.

To the extent that access to college is limited for those who have potential talent and ability, then access to professions is limited, and access to social mobility is limited. Without access, the dream of equal opportunity is flawed, and professionalism becomes a barrier to social mobility and equal opportunity. Lack of access is of particular concern in education. Children in this country are now very diverse, and their own hopes for their own futures will be influenced by whether they see members of their own community in positions of leadership and power. At present the caregivers teaching children in ECE programs almost exactly match the families of the children they serve, in language and culture. Programs for children in out-of-school time, too, have diversity of staffing. Head Start has a good percentage of diversity in its staffing. Child care centers are more likely to be staffed primarily from the dominant culture. Public school teachers are overwhelmingly White. It is easy to see how professional qualifications can serve as a barrier to jobs in this field.

We must reject any professionalization that narrows access to leadership roles only to privileged individuals. Efforts to professionalize must not be based on a 19th-century view of professionalism, but on a 21st-century view. These different views are explored below.

Traditional Attributes of Professions

Experts have viewed professions as characterized by certain traits or functions (Greenwood, 1966; Houle, 1981; Hughes, 1965). This approach has been called the "taxonomic" approach. A profession was defined by having these attributes. In general, the attributes identified as traits or functions can be reduced to three:

1. A specialized knowledge base
2. A service mission
3. Autonomy and control of the work

Specific clusters of characteristics are considered integral to each of the three major attributes. The characteristics associated with the knowledge base include the following:

- An extensive period of required formal education, requiring time and money
- Acceptability of education only if in approved forms and institutions
- Standards of education and training determined by the profession; that is, a monopoly on the knowledge
- A generalized and systematic knowledge base that draws on well-developed theory from which the practitioner can formulate testable propositions

- Esoteric knowledge that the public does not have
- Technical knowledge with a strong scientific basis
- Some form of apprenticeship/supervised practicum
- Use of practical knowledge (effective techniques and specialized skills)
- Capacity to solve problems (application of theoretical knowledge to practical issues)

The characteristics associated with the service mission and orientation include the following:

- Perceived social necessity of the service for client and society
- Unique functions (not performed by other professions)
- Provision of the highest-caliber service, regardless of the identity and finances of the recipient
- Subordination of personal needs and material interests to the client
- Primary orientation to the community interest, not to self-interest
- A system of rewards that symbolize the intrinsic value of work achievement and thus are ends in themselves
- A sense of mission
- Standards of practice
- Distance from the client

The characteristics associated with autonomy and control include the following:

- The formation of professional associations
- Uniform criteria for admitting new members to the field
- Cohesion of the professional community
- Commitment of members to the profession as a lifelong occupation
- Creation of a culture with history, tradition, belonging
- Intensive adult socialization experience for recruits
- Community sanction; laws that protect exclusive monopoly of the work
- Uniform and extensive practitioner licensing
- Shaping of legislation concerned with the profession by the profession
- Professional autonomy and an acceptance of broad personal responsibility for judgments and acts
- Authority granted by the laity based on knowledge
- Public trust

- Codes of ethics
- Self-policing to warrant the public trust

It is important to see these three bundles of characteristics as an interdependent paradigm. The professional has knowledge that is not available to the general public but is necessary to the public's well-being. Only a qualified professional can be trusted to apply this knowledge. The public is therefore dependent on the professional, who knows what is best. To warrant the trust of the public, the profession develops a code of ethics. This rationale is the basis on which professionalism rested at the beginning of and through most of the 20th century. As we enter the next century, there have been changes in attitudes.

Criticisms of the Taxonomic Approaches

Self-Serving. Many of today's policy experts are strongly opposed to legal monopolies and control of markets. In their view, professions emerge only as government offers powerful protection to organized elites. Sociologists were accused of supporting established institutions rather than social activism (Gilbert & Specht, 1978). Newer experts, particularly in the field of social work, pointed out that the knowledge of professions might be only self-protective credentialism; authority might be a means of controlling clients; community sanction may be bestowed in the interests of the established power structure, not the people; ethical codes are developed to protect the profession from interface from outside; and finally the norms, values, and beliefs that constitute the culture of a profession may be no more altruistic than any other group that works for money.

Overemphasis on Rational/Scientific. According to Ritzer and Waltczak (1986), female occupations are prevented from enjoying the benefits of professionalization by powerful male elites who perceive femininity to be antithetical to traditional (i.e., dominant male) definitions. Noddings (1992) points out that the attributes of professions were established by male sociologists studying male occupations. Values and concepts such as caring were relegated to lower status as feminine traits.

The older definitions of the knowledge base for professions emphasized scientific/rational knowledge and de-emphasized caring. Some professions, like social work and nursing, complained of a diminution of caring on their route to professionalism. Barbara Bowman (1989) argued against such a loss:

> One of the most important attributes of a profession is that it have a coherent knowledge base. The discussion about the base for early childhood education has primarily focused on the formal knowledge system—the theories, experiments, and statistical evidence. . . . Less attention has been given to subjective or personal knowledge as a foundation for teaching. Along with many early childhood educators, I contend that the theoretical underpinning for early childhood education must not be restricted to externally validated knowledge.
>
> There is no inherent contradiction in having two knowledge systems for teaching: a formal one that includes information about human beings, and a subjective one that includes experiential knowledge of self and others. Early childhood education has a rich history of valuing the second type of knowledge. (pp. 444–445)

Brain research today is revealing that cognitive learning, inseparably from other forms of development, is dependent on caring relationships. If higher education is not preparing our profession to care, directors must impart this knowledge. Many directors over the years have complained that they sometimes need to retrain the college-trained early childhood educators just as much as they need to train the newcomers to the field.

Authoritarian and Lacking in Family-Friendly Focus. Earlier in the century, when professionalism was at its height, it was assumed that a nonprofessional occupation has customers but a professional occupation has clients (Greenwood, 1966). Customers determine what services and/or commodities they want and have the capacity to appraise their own needs and to judge the potential of the service or of the commodity to satisfy them. In a professional relationship, however, the professional dictates what is good for the clients, who have no choice but to accede to professional judgment. The premise is that, because they lack the requisite theoretical background, clients cannot diagnose their own needs, discriminate among the possibilities for meeting them, or evaluate the caliber of the professional service they receive.

Across all the helping professions, there has now been a major shift in the direction of the client as customer and partner. Interprofessional helping stresses a holistic focus on the family and responsiveness to needs as the family sees them. Today, we have popular psychology, a return to self-responsibility in health, and many influences of consumerism on all the professions and their domains. It is not likely that we will ever return to the older way of thinking about the client relationship. Absolute power of the professional over the user of the service is not a goal that either the society or the professionals any longer embrace.

The Public's View of Professions

Because authority is granted to professionals by those they serve, it is important to try sense how the public views professions as we enter the 21st century. Experts may disagree, but in the end it will be the public's view that determines whether the old taxonomic characteristics continue to define a profession, whether a new paradigm develops, or whether occupations are no longer judged professional or not professional, except by some lay concept of dedication.

Currently, the positive words that appear to be associated with professions in the public eye include: *dedicated, committed, expert, businesslike.* These are words that could be applied to any individual in any occupation, and they often are.

The general public also rejects any status gap between parents and professionals as a concept in public policy. The national number-one goal—that all children should arrive at school ready to learn—stresses parents as first teachers, rather than professionalism, as a guiding principle in policies for young children.

Much of the anti-elitism and anger among citizens stems from the public perception of the illegitimacy of authority and such feelings as the following:

- The professional is imposing solutions on the public.
- The knowledge base may not be relevant or necessary to the solution of the problems.
- The expert has lost touch with the common wisdom.
- The motivation for the elite is self-aggrandizement rather than the common good.
- The access to income, security, and social-class status enjoyed by the professional in a precarious economy is not a fair process open to anyone.

"Professionalism is starting to look like a racket," according to a recent article (Menard, 1995). To the extent that these perceptions have any validity, they will undermine the future of professions.

A CHANGING PARADIGM

As director credentialing is developing in the United States, the policy environment is very different from that of a century ago. We are no longer able to expect the professionalism of the early childhood specialist, including the role of the director, to unfold in the same way that earlier professions emerged. Of all the characteristics traditionally associated with professions, a few appear to have been completely jettisoned. Other characteristics are either on their way to extinction or may be greatly modified. A few may still retain their power and importance. However, if any of the characteristics were no longer accepted, then the entire configuration would lose its viability. We would need a new paradigm.

The old attributes can be sorted into categories: strong, gone, or weakened. Those characteristics that appear to be still strong are the following:

- College credit continues to serve as a kind of currency that gives continuing value to the learning that an individual has experienced.
- The importance of service, and a high degree of dedication in the way the work is performed, continue to be hallmarks of professionalism.

Those characteristics that appear *gone* are the following:

- The professional/client relationship in which the client places trust in the professional because the client does not have the knowledge to evaluate the service is rapidly disappearing, replaced by something closer to a customer relationship. The professional now listens to clients' stories.
- The earlier idea that a professional calling, characterized by service to the community and often by low compensation, was rejected and to some degree replaced by a career approach. The goal was no longer the fulfillment of a commonly valued life of service but the attainment of "success" (Bellah et al., 1985).
- The exclusive control of a profession over entry into roles is unlikely in the future to be fully supported through public regulatory power. Reliance of the public on professionals' codes of ethics is being replaced by consumer-protection measures.

Other characteristics appear to be undergoing rapid change. Some of them, too, may be approaching extinction; others may change or may be greatly *weakened*. They include the following:

- A strong movement toward interprofessional communication and helping is replacing the narrowness of separate specialized professional frameworks. Professionalism is increasingly centered on the

needs expressed by the families and children using the programs, rather than the need as diagnosed from the fragmented perspectives of separate specialists.
- The rigid and permanent social-class distinction between professional education and vocational education has disappeared, and entry-level training for those in assisting roles is seen as an earlier stage of preparation that can later become a part of the extensive formal education required for more responsible roles.
- The knowledge explosion is influencing the previous view of there being a fixed amount of knowledge monopolized by a profession. The skill of seeking and finding information may now be more important than any other competency.
- The idea of distance from the client is being modified by the idea of caring.
- The autonomy of the professional is greatly modified by the fact that many professionals are based in organizational structures.

The last item above requires further examination. According to the 19th-century paradigm, the true professional is never hired (Hughes, 1965): "He is retained, engaged, consulted, etc. by some one who has need of his services. He, the professional, has or should have almost complete control over what he does for the client" (p. 9).

Autonomy has declined, as individual professionals are more and more likely to be associated with agencies and institutions. No longer is professional work done almost entirely by an individual who hangs out his or her own shingle. Further, it may be less clear who the client is or how many clients there are. Professional work is affected by insurance and public payments.

The problem of autonomy becomes complex in an organizational setting. It is an effort to distinguish between the professional's obligations to the child or family or client, and obligations to the employer, as well as obligations to the public good. It is still more difficult to determine the degree of authority that derives from professional knowledge and skills versus the authority of the organizational structure (Barber, 1965). The professional may have been socialized to have a self-concept of autonomous collegiality with a pattern of self-control and colleague control. How to function professionally within an organization or even a government bureaucracy requires new skills in practicing the application of professional knowledge in a setting where there are formal procedures and a need for accountability, both of which create organizational controls, resulting in strain and conflict.

Career Development Approach in Contrast to Credentialism

In the field of ECE, an approach labeled career development, or professional development, takes a modern view of professionalism. Career development rests on an expectation of lifelong learning, with compensation based on the qualifications of the individual. A career lattice or ladder identifies the pathways an individual can follow within ECE to move into more challenging and better-paying roles, either sideways or upward. While promoting milestone credentials and lifelong professional growth, it is not credentialist. There are a number of differences between the career development approach and credentialism.

With the credentialist approach, individuals enter a professional preparation program in a college with the end goal of getting a specific credential, which will define them as "professionals" and separate them from those who are not professionals. The career development approach allows for the gradual unfolding of intentionality, rather than a single declaration upon entry into a 4-year institution or graduate school.

There is some class bias in the credentialist approach. Individuals with advantages of family wealth and educated parents are those who can identify their lifetime goal early. Intentionality unfolds differently in people from low-income families, who cannot see themselves achieving a professional credential until they have passed closer milestones, such as a child development associate credential, an associate's degree. Often they will arrive at an advanced degree and a respected professional status, but they will go about it in a more gradual way, without initially declaring, or having, an intention to earn an advanced degree. We need to design our future credentialing system to encourage this more gradual unfolding of intentionality.

In the career development approach, we stress access to credit-bearing training so that people can apply their training to get milestone credentials. Credit is important in our field, where many receive their college education after employment. We need to care about credit for any high-quality substantial training. We do not want second-class training, or second-class credentials, for anyone. Credits and early credentials become milestones at different stages in a career. They become points of recognition rather than a terminal credential. The career development approach doesn't recognize any credential as terminal, stressing lifelong education and career growth.

A key point that career development planners have stressed, which credentialists sometimes have not, is the central importance of diversity among those who work with diverse children and their families. Quality for children requires that they can see members of their own culture in

Table 8.1. Percentage of Children under 6 Participating in Early Care and
Education Programs by Race/Ethnicity, 1995

Type of Care Arrangement	White	Black	Hispanic	Other	All
Relatives	14%	25%	20%	21%	20%
Family Child Care with Sitters	19%	10%	10%	11%	13%
Centers	28%	29%	15%	24%	24%
Parents	39%	35%	54%	43%	43%
Percent of Total Children	65%	16%	13%	6%	100%

Note: Due to rounding, columns do not necessarily add up to 100%.
Source: Hofferth, Shauman, & Henke (1998).

positions of power and status in the programs they attend. Otherwise, the program itself undermines their own hopes for their own futures.

With the diversity of children served by ECE programs (see Table 8.1), it is essential to assure diversity among the teachers and directors, not just among the teacher assistants. At present, minority population groups are greatly underrepresented in leadership roles in the field (National Black Child Development Institute, 1993). Creating this imbalance is an essential aspect of leadership development in the early childhood and school-age field.

The credentialist approach separates the professionals from the non-professionals by a permanent social-class division. With the professional development approach, all staff members are on a professional track; and the assistants will become teachers, the teachers will become master teachers, and directors are likely to be drawn from this progression. Accessible training programs are essential to this concept.

Reforms in the credentialist system require changes, but not quite as major and not quite as structural as the reforms pursued by the career development groups. For the latter, knowledge is a lifelong process that is increasingly interprofessional, that will increasingly stress caring relationships as at least as important as the rational/scientific approaches to cognitive knowledge that characterized the end of the 19th and most of the 20th century.

The ECE Practitioner's Perspective

The ECE field views itself as professional and yearns for recognition by others. For a number of years, some leaders have tried to adapt the field to the traditional taxonomic definition of professionalism, trying to explain our basic concepts in such a way as to make them compatible with the assumptions in the century-old definition of professions.

Sometimes our knowledge base does not permit us to adapt to the old paradigm. For example, if our knowledge base of child development tells us that a partnership relationship with parents is essential, then the esoteric nature of professional knowledge is an inappropriate concept for our field. Most practitioners are aware of the potential problem and uncomfortable with a relationship that creates a status gap with parents.

One early childhood leader (Porter, 1981) describes her own view and is aware that it deviates from the traditional taxonomy of attributes of professionalism:

> We want to share what we know. We want to make it easy to understand, and we want to demystify it without threatening its complexity or integrity. We have made substantial effort through parent education and family support networks to transmit the knowledge we have about facilitating development because we believe that such information should NOT be confidential. This attitude is clearly outside the realm of professionalism.

Rather than trying to adapt to incompatible ideas from the past, it is entirely likely that we should be asserting our own concepts as strengths and celebrating the ways in which we have always been ahead of the curve. As professionalism redesigns itself for the new century, we may be more compatible with the future redefinition than we have been with the traditional definition. Some strengths that we should celebrate are the following:

- We are a family-friendly profession. We support families and try to share with parents as peers. From our early days in settlement houses, through the strength of the parent cooperative movement, through the strong models of family support developed during World War II that influence us still, we have understood ourselves to be part of the supportive environment of parents' lives. Early childhood practitioners work to improve the quality of parents' time with their children. Most early childhood texts and the research findings on which they are based describe a shared relationship of trust between the teacher and parent as the desirable goal. ECE, in contrast to many other professions, has viewed itself as supplementing, not supplanting, parental responsibility and decision making. Not every practitioner has built on these concepts, but they are a part of our thinking, reflected in many of our leaders, some of our training, much of our history, and all of our best programs.

- We take a holistic view of the child. We know that all aspects of development are inseparable and integrally related. We resist carving knowledge into subject-matter areas, understanding that the tasks of early childhood are to lay down the connections, not separately to master the parts (Damasio, 1994; Frank, 1969; Karmiloff-Smith, 1992).
- We teach in complex ways, responding to each child rather than norming, teaching to a group, or standardizing our expectations.
- We insist that care and education cannot be separated from one another in our work. Caring is a necessary part of teaching. Relationships are central to our work. We use our own selves in teaching, and we encounter the child's self. We have also developed skills in facilitating group development.
- We have not been willing to split the higher-paid "teacher" from the one who cares.

All of these strengths are in some way at odds with the traditional approach of professions, but they may be valued in the new century's approach.

WHY A DIRECTOR CREDENTIAL NOW?

The above discussion of changing professionalism raises questions about whether the time is right for a new effort to credential directors. This chapter has attempted to summarize why it is not likely that we would succeed, even if we wanted to, in implementing new credentials based on restricting access to jobs in the field. However, by designing our credential as part of a career development system, we are consistent with public views of professionalism and closer to our own insights and ideals. Our task is to make the effort right for the time.

The career development approach emphasizes that current training for the already employed can also count as preservice preparation for a more demanding role in a career path. The career development approach creates access for the director credential. Initially, in order to create a supply of credentialed directors and a shared commitment to quality among them, the candidates need to be encouraged with financial aid, reunion meetings, and other supports, such as personal counseling, academic redemption, and mentoring. These supports will sustain the process, identify concerns, and serve as the basis for ongoing research and development during the first years of the credential. Through this process, the quality of administrative processes in children's programs can be expected to change. A credentialed director will have a strong effect on her or his program. The following seven statements (Hill-Scott, 1997) demonstrate a logic for how director credentialing can affect quality and the economics of ECE:

1. A credentialed director is a better director.
2. A credentialed director will create a high-quality program.
3. A high-quality program will be more efficient.
4. High efficiency will permit better compensation.
5. Higher quality will increase willingness to pay.
6. Willingness to pay will permit price increases.
7. Price increases will produce both higher compensation for staff and positive outcomes. (pp. 13–14)

The Elements of a Director Credentialing System

It is a long process to put together the necessary ingredients for credentialing administrators. Each group working on administrative and director credentialing initiatives across the country will have to answer for itself. Each initiative will institutionalize its answer to each of the elements of a director credentialing system. Fortunately, those groups creating such a credential can benefit from one another's learnings through a national network, Taking the Lead. The availability of materials from one another will cut down on the time it will take to make all these decisions, and it will also enable them to build on one another's discussions and work. In no particular order, each of these groups will have to decide about the following:

- A granting organization
- A system for recruitment that can reach many groups
- Accessibility for the credential: financially within reach, geographically within reach; hours the coursework is offered; appropriate design for adult learners
- Development of criteria applied to applicants for credential and method of assessment
- Decision on any prerequisite training

- Decision on how much coursework, content, and theory are applicable to professional responsibilities, as well as levels offered
- Decisions on the training delivery (courses at college, college courses in the community, distance learning, etc.)
- Faculty development
- Decisions on credit for prior learning experiences and method of assessment for credentialed directors; decisions on equivalencies with other credentials
- Decision on what changes to make in licensing and subsidy policy to encourage more credentialed directors
- Evaluation of the training and of the system

The Director Credential in a Professional Context

The discussion of history, along with changes in the concept of a professional, leads to proposing a cautious definition for the 21st century. An ECE professional is: *anyone who is working with young children and/or their parents, and who is on a professional path toward commitment and further learning.*

There are many interdependent roles in ECE. We need competent ECE specialists to move into them, through them, and back and forth across them. We need to see the big picture of our field. As we try to visualize our future, we need to advocate for high-quality ECE training and required qualifications appropriate for each role, ·with training while employed to qualify for the next role and clear pathways for career mobility.

As in the past, traditional college students can prepare in advance for these roles. The career development approach does not replace traditional education, but it expands participants to include the already employed as well and makes it possible to recruit more diverse staff into leadership roles.

A director credential is an important missing piece in the ECE career development system. The administrator role is an especially important one, too important to be neglected by higher education. Quality for children will depend on the competence of this person. It is the administrator who creates the working conditions, salary policy, vision, family support, supervision, orientation to continued professional growth, and developmental philosophy for the program as a whole.

REFERENCES

Barber, B. (1965). Some problems in the sociology of the professions. In K. Lynn (Ed.), *The professions in America* (pp. 15–34). Boston: Houghton Mifflin.

Bellah, R. N., Madsen, R., Sullivan, W. M., Swidler, A., & Tipton, S. M. (1985). *Habits of the heart: Individualism and commitment in American life*. Berkeley: University of California Press.

Bowman, B. (1989, Spring). Self reflection as an element of professionalism. *Teachers College Record, 90*(2), 444–451.

Damasio, A. (1994). *Descartes' error: Emotion, reason, and the human brain*. New York: Grosset/Putnam.

Frank, L. K. (1969). Evaluation of educational programs for young children. *Young Children, 24*(3), 167–174.

Gilbert, N., & Specht, H. (Eds.). (1978). *The emergence of social welfare and social work* (3rd ed.). Itasca, IL: Peacock.

Greenwood, E. (1966). The elements of professionalization. In H. M. Vollmer & D. L. Mills (Eds.), *Professionalization* (pp. 45–55). Englewood Cliffs, NJ: Prentice-Hall.

Hill-Scott, K. (1997, April 24–25). *Executive summary of the Illinois Director Credential Symposium* (pp. 13–14). Chicago: National-Louis University, Early Childhood Professional Development Project.

Hofferth, S. L., Shauman, K. A., & Henke, R. R. (1998). *National Center for Education Statistics, statistical analysis report: Characteristics of children's early care and education programs: Data from the 1995 national household education survey*. Washington, DC: U.S. Department of Education, Office of Educational Research and Improvement.

Houle, C. O. (1981). *Continuing learning in the professions*. San Francisco: Jossey-Bass.

Hughes, E. (1965). Professions. In K. Lynn (Ed.), *Professions in America* (pp. 1–14). Boston: Houghton Mifflin.

Karmiloff-Smith, A. (1992). *Beyond modularity: A developmental perspective on cognitive science*. Cambridge, MA: MIT Press.

Larson, M. S. (1977). *The rise of professionalism*. Berkeley: University of California Press.

Menard, L. (1995, March 5). The trashing of professionalism. *New York Times Magazine*, pp. 41–43.

National Black Child Development Institute. (1993). *Paths to African American leadership positions in early childhood education: Constraints and opportunities*. Washington, DC: Author.

National Center for Education Statistics. (1995). *Child care and early education program participation of infants, toddlers, and preschoolers*. Washington, D.C.: U.S. Department of Education, Office of Educational Research and Improvement. (NCES No. 95–824)

Noddings, N. (1992). In defense of caring. *Journal of Clinical Ethics,3*, 15–18.

Peters, D. L. (1988). The child development associate credential and the educationally disenfranchised. In B. Spodek, O. Saracho, & D. L. Peters (Eds.), *Pro-*

fessionalism and the early childhood practitioner (pp. 93–104). New York: Teachers College Press.

Porter, C. (1981, November). *Professionalization and day care: Friend or foe.* Paper presented at conference on Child Care Education, University of Miami, Coral Gables, FL.

Ritzer, G., & Waltczak, D. (1986). *Working: Conflict and change* (3rd ed.). Englewood Cliffs, NJ: Prentice-Hall.

Vollmer, H. M., & Mills, D. L. (Eds.). (1966). *Professionalization.* Englewood Cliffs, NJ: Prentice-Hall.

9

The Case for Credentialing Directors Now and Considerations for the Future

Anne Mitchell

The quality of children's experiences in early care and education (ECE) programs has been on the decline. The majority of ECE today is judged to be poor or mediocre. Given the importance of ECE to school entry and later success, policy makers are now concerned about whether current programs are capable of achieving a level of service quality that supports school success. Concerns about the outcomes of early education, especially those related to school entry and success in learning, are increasing. Simultaneously, we understand better than ever the clear and direct link between the quality of children's ECE experiences and the outcomes that result from the children's participation. There is overwhelming evidence that practitioners who have attained higher levels of education and have been educated specifically about children in the age range they work with can produce better child outcomes. Additionally, there is evidence that the director's experience contributes to a higher level of service quality. Furthermore, it is the administrator who makes the decisions that create the conditions for good child outcomes. Administrators create program conditions when they set the adult–child ratios, limit group sizes, and, most important, hire well-trained teachers.

The United States is unique among developed nations in not having national funding for a universal early care and education program and, as a result, not having any national standards for the preparation of early care and education personnel. Many other countries have national standards and accessible training systems to prepare personnel to meet their standards as part of a national ECE system. In the United States, the profession of early care and education is unlike many older professions in that there are no national requirements set by the profession itself for individuals to enter the profession. Instead, the issue of personnel standards for early care and education is the responsibility of each state. State government carries out this responsibility through facility licensing regulations rather than through the state's system for granting individual licenses[1] to other professionals, such as plumbers, architects, social workers, or dental hygienists.

THE CASE FOR LICENSING INDIVIDUALS IN ECE

Developing a credential for directors may be one strategy for working toward higher-quality services. It is part of a larger move toward licensing individuals—teachers as well as directors in children's programs. Other countries use individual licensure, and it has been discussed at the national level in several recent reports (Kagan & Cohen, 1997). Because teachers have been the central practitioner recognized and valued in ECE programs, there has been more activity focused toward teacher credentialing and licensing than toward administrative credentialing.

Taken together, lessons from other countries and other occupations combine to make a strong case for licensing individuals in early care and education in the United States. In fact, one of the eight recommendations—to be achieved by 2010—advanced in a recent national report (Kagan & Cohen, 1997) is to license all practitioners responsible for children using a three-tiered approach: early childhood administrator, early childhood educator, and early childhood associate educator. While current conditions place us far from that goal, several factors and forces within the field and in society push in that direction. The movement to create voluntary credentials for directors is one bold step forward.

Preparing Early Care and Education
Personnel in Other Countries

Drawing on information from Brazil, Canada, China, Finland, France, Japan, Kenya, New Zealand, Norway, Sweden, and the United Kingdom, it is clear that preparing ECE personnel is a common challenge (Pritchard, 1996). Although personnel preparation and continuing training are addressed in ways unique to each nation, there are many similarities among the training systems of different countries. Many countries (e.g., France, England, Finland, Japan, Norway, Sweden) have established specified training requirements that individuals must meet before they begin the practice of early care and education. In many Western European countries, these requirements are at the college level (e.g., Finland, France, Sweden,

Norway). Training of ECE personnel is mainly preservice and offered in institutions of higher education, clearly for academic credit. Further, in at least two countries (Finland and the United Kingdom), family child care providers are required to complete preservice vocational training.

In most countries, the locus of control for personnel requirements and preparation content is differentiated by the age of the child. For children from birth to about age 3, the personnel preparation content is more health-related and governance is under the ministry for health or social welfare. For children from about age 3 to school-entry age (which varies from 5 to 8 years), personnel preparation is education-related and programs are governed by the ministry of education.

In some countries, preschool teachers typically undergo more extensive training at the university level, while child care personnel working with younger children may be prepared in postsecondary vocational schools. The distinction is not so stark in practice. For example, in Sweden, ECE programs are required to have a combination of personnel from both sources so as to meet children's needs holistically. Both Sweden and Japan have developed coordinated routes into the early education profession such that different types of preparation build upon each other. New Zealand has developed a coherent training system that incorporates vocational and academic training as well as an apprenticeship-type preparatory system historically centered in cooperative nursery schools.

The general status of ECE personnel, and their compensation relative to teachers in the public education system in their nation, appears to mirror closely the situation in the United States, with the notable exception of France. Preschool teachers in France receive salaries and recognition on a par with elementary school teachers (and operate with typical elementary school ratios); moreover, both sets of teachers are required to complete preparation programs equivalent in duration and academic level. Issues affecting teachers' professional training and credentialing situations serve as a stage (and/or backdrop) for the queries raised later in this chapter regarding possible values and strategies in administrative credentialing.

Compared to their counterparts in the United States, ECE personnel in other countries are required to meet higher standards of preparation, typically preservice (and inservice continuing education), and the training offered to meet standards is provided in academic and/or vocational postsecondary institutions.

Preparation and Entry into Other Occupations in the United States

To gather lessons for early care and education, occupations across a spectrum of professional, service, sales, technical, and construction trades were selected for study. They were chosen to cover a wide range of occupational categories that have some relationship to ECE because ECE has often been regarded as partly a profession and partly a service occupation. Diverse occupations have been examined, ranging from technical professions (e.g., architecture and engineering), to helping professions (e.g., social work and nursing), service occupations (e.g., travel agents and cosmetologists), and trades (e.g., electricians) (Mitchell, 1996).

With the exception of travel agents, these occupations are characterized by a common set of conditions. To practice the occupation, an individual must do the following:

- Meet certain requirements that are established by those already practicing the occupation
- Acquire a license to practice that is granted by a public authority, usually a state, through a board of professionals

The exams are designed by national organizations for the occupation or profession, and are used in all states with necessary modifications to match state regulations. Preparation for an occupation usually involves a formal education program and may also require an apprenticeship. A national body associated with each occupation accredits the preparation programs. Each occupation has a professional organization(s) whose role is to promote the occupation, to set standards for entry, and often also to offer advanced credentials beyond licensure.

These occupational conditions are interrelated and serve to reinforce one another. For example, in the processes reviewed, licensing standards affect the content and nature of preparation programs, which in turn are affected by professional organizations. The cornerstone of these approaches is the individual license. ECE credentialing—for teachers or administrators—can be established from this model. Alternatively, credentialing could follow a different sequence of steps leading either directly to a credential or to set of sequential steps that lead to a credential.

The justification for public (government) involvement in licensing individuals rests on one or more of several underlying rationales. One rationale is to protect clients from personal harm—which applies to occupations dealing directly with people, such as registered nurses and beauticians. Another is to ensure the competence of independent practitioners—which applies to occupations in which individuals may practice unsupervised, such as social workers or engineers. A third is to protect public safety and welfare—which applies to occupations such as electricians and architects.

Travel agents, having no license and no standard preparation programs, are an exception to the pattern outlined above. Their conditions most closely resemble the preschool/child care occupations of the early care and education field, with one exception. All of the studied occupations (including travel agents) have median salary levels that are nearly double those of ECE personnel in the United States.

Compared to early care and education, other occupations have a more organized preparation system and established entry standards. They require more training to enter (training is provided in higher education institutions for those that are more professional). A license is required to practice—medicine or law for instance—and one recognized national organization represents the profession and grants the credential.

Salient Characteristics of ECE in the United States

Several assumptions about the current status and desired future characteristics of the ECE field are useful to keep in mind while considering the insights from other countries and other occupations.

In the United States, the field of early care and education encompasses children from birth through age 8 and their families, many settings, and a wide variety of roles. The settings may be centers, schools, and homes. As outlined in Chapter 1, roles include (but are not limited to) lead teacher, teacher, assistant teacher, small-group family child care provider, large-group family child care provider, family child care assistant, school-age child care worker (for young school-age children under age 9), family support worker, home visitor, child life specialist, early intervention specialist, resource and referral counselor, Head Start component coordinator, program director, executive director, mentor, teacher educator (or trainer), or youth worker.

There is a core body of knowledge that underlies practice in the whole field. Specialized knowledge relates to children in specific age ranges, generally birth through 2, 3–5, 5–8 (and for school-age programs, ages 8–12 or 12–18). Most states have developed core competency or core knowledge documents through their efforts to build professional development systems. The child development associate (CDA)[2] competencies articulate basic areas of knowledge and skills required for ECE professionals in teaching roles with children under age 5 in home and center settings.

The ECE field is currently characterized by multiple entry points to its occupations. Ensuring that entrants are qualified for their roles will require easy access to preparation and continuing education. Given multiple entry points, a common knowledge base, and accessible preparation/development, the process could result in multiple connected pathways for individual movement within the different roles, ages, and settings. Thus, pathways are created that produce a career "lattice" of lateral and upward mobility—rather than the traditional career "ladder" of hierarchical progression within a single setting or program type (Bredekamp & Willer, 1992).

Internationally, there seems to be a distinction made between personnel working with children under age 3 and those working with children over age 3 that is roughly a health/education split. In the United States, the split is somewhat different. It is related not so much to the ages of children as to a combination of the sponsorship and historical mission of programs. Generally, personnel working under public education sponsorship (e.g., teachers in public schools, early interventionists, special educators) have higher education preparation requirements and must have individual licenses. In nonpublic school-sponsored ECE programs, teachers have to meet personnel requirements contained in the state's child care facility regulations; these may be minimal and typically do not require higher education. For example, public prekindergarten teachers working with 3- and 4-year-olds or early intervention teachers working with infants and toddlers have to meet state education standards and possess an appropriate teaching license, while teachers of children these ages in child care centers typically do not.

One clear characteristic that emerges from both international and other occupational perspectives is standards for individuals. This characteristic is absent in much of the U.S. early care and education field. Individual licensing of practitioners—required in public law and/or regulation, and specifying high levels of competence—could move the field toward higher-quality practice. Individual licensing by itself is probably not sufficient to achieve higher quality. To ensure the advancement of quality, the compensation of those who work in early childhood occupations must be improved so that it promotes equity among early childhood staff within the field who fill comparable roles and have comparable qualifications. Given that academic achievement is widely regarded as valuable (and usually influences compensation), and that there is a direct relationship between the level of a practitioner's educational attainment and the quality of ECE teaching, preparation for all credentials should carry (or be transformable to) academic credit. In this career lattice, a teacher's ongoing training while employed can be preservice training for another more demanding role, such as an administrative role.

The conditions that characterize many other occupations in the United States could be a powerful force for improving quality in early care and education. These conditions are the individual license granted by a state board of licensing, with board standards set by the profession; accreditation of preparatory schools by a national organization; and advanced credentials offered by professional organizations. In early care and education, as in other fields such as health care, individual licensing can be reinforced through the staffing requirements prescribed in facility licensing regulations.

Developments and Trends Affecting Individual Licensure

Positive developments for establishing individual licensure are occurring in the ECE field, while significant barriers to the establishment of licensure exist simultaneously.

Supportive Forces and Factors. The concept of licensing individuals in early care and education is not entirely new. Facility licensing regulations in many states require personnel to possess specified qualifications.

New York City and California have required individual credentials for many years. Recently, there has been movement in a few other states toward requiring individual credentials of personnel in child care settings (within facility licensing). In 1991, Florida passed legislation requiring that by July 1995 every child care center have at least one teaching staff person possessing the CDA or its equivalent for every 20 children enrolled. To date, dozens of "CDA equivalents" have been identified and presented to the state's Department of Health and Rehabilitative Services.

Since 1989, Massachusetts has required that group child care center personnel possess a certificate of qualification. The certificates of qualification require both work experience and college-level coursework in early childhood education. Certificates reflect the positions for which the individual is qualified: teacher (infant/toddler or preschool), lead teacher (infant/toddler or preschool), director I, and director II.

Head Start performance standards include requirements for individual credentials for Head Start staff. Currently, at least one teacher per classroom must have a CDA. By 2003, Head Start must meet a congressionally mandated goal that 50% of all Head Start teachers have an associate degree. Head Start social service staff will soon be required to have the newly developed social service competency-based credential, which is a form of the CDA.

Potential Barriers, Considerations, and Constraints. Taking note of the situation in France, if teachers (meaning those persons in charge of a group of children), regardless of setting, are to enjoy equal compensation and status, they must meet the same qualifications and have the same credential. Institutionalizing inequality by setting will likely guarantee inequity of compensation. If personnel qualifications are established that encourage lower levels of education in non–public school settings, the field of early care and education could split permanently into two fields. One way to avoid this split is to link the efforts to advance individual credentialing for the whole field to the movement toward establishment of (public school) teaching standards boards, which are being established in states. There is an opportunity to acquire national advanced certifications through the National Board for Professional Teaching Standards. Another avenue for addressing standards for staffing will be the evolving accreditation standards for centers, school-age programs, and family child care centers. The accreditation standards are, in effect, national standards, and they can be expected to affect individual training, licensure, and overall program funding. As states begin to require individual licensure and as accreditation processes designate higher levels of education for teaching staff, many changes can be expected to occur in higher education scope and sequence and in other types of training.

In many occupations, there is one major professional organization whose members are the practitioners (ECE professional teachers and administrators) of that occupation. Typically, this organization works to advance the occupation, set standards for its practice, and offer a variety of advanced professional credentials. In contrast to other occupations, the field of early care and education has many organizations. There is one organization—the National Association for the Education of Young Children (NAEYC)—that spans multiple issues, roles, and sectors of the field but does not focus solely on the ECE profession. There are also many distinct professional organizations, each related to different roles and sectors of the field. Many of these organizations are composed of role-alike professionals (e.g., the National Association for Family Child Care [NAFCC], the National Association of Child Care Resource and Referral Agencies [NACCRRA], or the National School Age Care Alliance [NSACA]) and/or setting-alike professionals (e.g., the National Head Start Association or the National Child Care Association) and are committed to advancing the professionals in their sector of the field. As professional organizations in other occupations do, at least four of these organizations (NAEYC, NCCA, NSACA, and NAFCC) have established or are developing accreditation procedures. NSACA will soon offer an individual credential as well as program accreditation.

While there is some movement in the direction of individual licensing, there are also some significant barriers. There are only a handful of states and one city in which individual licensing now exists for center-based personnel. The CDA is firmly embedded in Head Start, with adaptations made for renewal and ongoing training, and it is noted in many states' facility licensing regulations. However, there are issues regarding its use, since it is not widely understood (or valued) outside Head Start and it is sometimes used inappropriately for directors, even though its administrative criterion addresses only a portion of director competencies. The CDA credential is now somewhat linked to the higher education system in associate-degree-granting colleges, but the links are weak or nonexistent to bachelor-degree-granting college programs. There is a system for accrediting teacher education programs in bachelor- and master-degree-granting colleges, but none for programs at other levels of higher education. To achieve large-scale change, greater public understanding of the value of well-educated teachers for our youngest children will be necessary to generate public will and public funds.

Individual licensure has great potential to improve outcomes for children who participate in ECE programs. Licensure will ensure that persons working with children have the kinds of preparation and continuing development that are closely linked with the quality practices that lead to better child outcomes. The public and families who entrust their children to these persons will be assured that children are not only protected from harm, but are more likely to thrive and prosper.

THE CASE FOR FOCUSING ON DIRECTORS

While a case can be made for licensing individual practitioners of early care and education, questions remain about which level of license to attempt first. A strong case can be made for starting with directors. Anyone who has ever worked in, or enrolled a child in, a good early childhood program knows that leadership is critical. Administrative actions create a healthy organization that functions as a supportive community for children and staff. The director, often working within the framework set by a sponsoring organization, makes the decisions that create the conditions for good child outcomes. Competent administrators create these conditions by structuring and maintaining the adult–child ratios, setting group sizes, hiring well-trained teachers, and deploying resources efficiently to get the best staff compensation possible while maintaining affordability for parents. These are the aspects of early childhood programs that are known to have powerful influence on program quality and child outcomes.

Research evidence supports the sensible belief that directors strongly influence program quality. The status of leadership training in the ECE field and policy developments in the public and private sectors also argue for focusing some of our efforts on directors.

Research Evidence in Support of Directors

Recent research confirms the influence of leadership on program quality. Specific characteristics of directors are associated with higher program quality and better child outcomes.

While the Cost, Quality and Child Outcomes study (Cost, Quality and Child Outcomes Study Team, 1995) clearly confirmed earlier research demonstrating the strong relationship between program quality and both adult–child ratios and teaching staff wages, the study's findings also revealed important new information about the relationship of administrator characteristics to program quality and child outcomes. According to the study team, their "analyses provide some limited, but intriguing evidence that characteristics of the administrator influence child care quality" (Mocan, Burchinal, Morris, & Helburn, 1995, p. 287). Data on the directors was provided by the directors themselves and each center's teaching staff. Three characteristics of directors were found to be associated with higher-quality child environments and better child outcomes: (1) more years of education, (2) more administrative experience, and (3) greater involvement in curriculum planning.

An earlier national study of exemplary public school early childhood programs predated these findings and suggested the importance of an administrator's contribution to program success. Case studies of a dozen programs across the country revealed that the best programs shared a common denominator: a director with particular characteristics. While all the directors had extensive years of education, better-quality programs were found to have directors who were specifically well prepared in early education/child development. Better programs had ECE administrators who practiced hands-on responsive management, that is, were in close daily contact with their teaching staffs regardless of the size of the district's programs. This aspect is similar to the involvement in curriculum planning found in the study above. Finally, the better programs had administrators who demonstrated the political skills necessary for success at operating within bureaucracies (Mitchell, Seligson, & Marx, 1989).

Studies of early childhood program accreditation offer more evidence for the influence of directors on quality. The characteristics that distinguish nationally accredited programs from nonaccredited ones are mainly those program aspects that are strongly influenced by the director. A national study found that four areas best differentiate between accredited and nonaccredited programs: (1) innovation and acceptance of change, (2) goal consensus (or common vision), (3) opportunities for staff professional growth, and (4) clarity about policies, procedures, and communication. While the staff of a program clearly make major contributions to creating these characteristics, the director sets the tone and constructs the framework that makes them possible through budgetary, scheduling, and other resource decisions to support teachers (Bloom, 1995).

The evaluation of educational programs designed to improve a director's leadership and management skills offers further evidence of the director's effects on quality. Early results from evaluation of a major effort to improve the management skills of Head Start directors show that graduates of the management program improve significantly in their knowledge and their ability to put into practice planning skills, financial administration, management of change, and marketing, among other areas. As an administrator masters and implements new knowledge, there are measurable improvements in the programs they direct (A. Osborne, personal communication, February 1, 1996).[3]

Good programs have good leaders. The extent of the director's education and experience plays a part in producing program quality, along with characteristics that are developed through specialized training. Leadership training increases director competence, which improves the organizational climate for staff and the quality of the program for children, which in turn leads to better child outcomes. Practical and theoretical learning leads to director competence.

Factors and Forces in the Field Favoring Directors

Certain conditions of the ECE field lend support to the case for credentialing directors. Director training has been around for a long time and is often associated with higher education. Trends in regulatory policy increasingly recognize the necessity of administrative qualifications for directors. Credentials for directors are being created in several states and by national organizations. Directors themselves are strongly in favor of credentials.

Director training has long been an integral part of the Head Start training and technical assistance system. Since the early 1980s, each federal region has annually offered a week-long training for new Head Start directors that covers planning, financial and facility management, supervision, and communication. In 1997, national new director training resumed and is offered annually. The national, state, and regional Head

Start Directors' Associations offer regular training as well as networking and support opportunities for directors. The Head Start Bureau has contracted for the development of a curriculum series on management to be used in Head Start training throughout the nation; the full set of modules will be available in 2000.

The Military Child Care Act of 1989 laid the groundwork for the Army Child Development Services to upgrade the qualifications of center and program directors. All directors receive initial training through a 2-week (80-hour) early childhood administration course; access to the Army's basic management courses covering personnel, finance, and facility management supervision; and access to ongoing training in early childhood/child development administration.

Trends in Regulation. The number of states requiring, in their child care facility regulations, that all directors have administrative qualifications has increased over the last decade. Six states now require managerial training of all directors and other states require a combination of managerial, supervisory, and/or administrative experience or training.[4] While the amounts vary widely from 20 clock hours to nine course credits, the trend is toward recognizing that skills and knowledge in both child development/early education and administration/management are necessary for directors of early care and education programs.

Experience with Credentialing. Director credentialing is in practice or development in a number of states. In Texas, the professional administrator credential, which requires 40 hours of classroom time (or home study), has been available since 1984. The state's facility licensing regulations include it as one way of qualifying to be a child care center director. In 1996, the National Child Care Association launched their director credential; the association has developed a curriculum guide and begun offering preparatory training. The Professional Administrator's Credential is also offered nationally. On a smaller scale, the Christian Director's Child Development Education Credential is awarded nationally. (See Chapter 1 for a review of the director credentialing projects.)

Support from the Profession. Directors themselves express strong support for credentialing. A survey of directors reviewed in Chapter 11 (Poster & Neugebauer, 1998) reveals intense interest in a voluntary and nationally recognized credential. The vast majority of directors say that a credential would be an extremely valuable mechanism for improving the quality of child care and a valuable tool for marketing a center to parents. Overwhelmingly, directors believe a credential should be voluntary and nationally recognized.

Private-Sector Business and Philanthropic Support. The business community is also interested in credentialing and in directors. Employers have a strong business interest in strategies to improve the quality of child care centers used by their employees. Working through the American Business Collaboration for Quality Dependent Care (ABC), employers have supported numerous improvement initiatives across the country. To the business community, it is self-evident that directors have a strong influence on producing and improving child care quality. Foundations have also shown strong support for director training leading to a recognized credential, and the support comes from many sources.

The handful of vital training programs in the higher education system and the commitment of national organizations are a solid foundation for an effective preparation and continuing development program for ECE administrative leaders. State-by-state efforts to create credentials for directors are amassing valuable information, which is being shared and adapted from state to state. Private funders and the business community support director credentialing and leadership development.

CONSIDERATIONS AS WE MOVE AHEAD

While a mandatory license for directors (and other ECE practitioners) may be a logical long-term goal for the ECE field, I believe that a voluntary credential is the better approach now for several reasons. Developing a credential is more appropriate now than instituting an individual license, given the early developmental stage of director training and performance measurement. In other fields, licenses have evolved from credentials. Instituting individual licensure requires widespread agreement within the field and among the public that such a consumer-protection mechanism is necessary and feasible. Widespread discussions and dialogue can lead to creative solutions that are appropriate and desirable in today's political environment and that also reflect ECE practitioners' values and realities, such as limited resources, valuing diversity, and giving human relations values a key piece in training.

A credential can be structured to reflect these issues and concerns. Some parts of a credential (say the first 40 hours) could be required for facility licenses as a criteria for higher funding. These types of standards (along with the movement to make accreditation a standard) could be incorporated into both public funding policy and into a center's setting of client fees for parent consumers.

The Social and Political Climate

The current social and political climate offers mixed messages. Consumers of child care (mistakenly) believe that directors are required to have education and some kind of credential to be the director of a program. Many parents assume the required education level is a master's degree, and most think there are already some state requirements specifically for directors.[5] At the same time, there is widespread public concern about the efficiency and size of government, which plays out as deregulation of various industries and privatization of formerly public responsibilities. These trends point toward voluntary efforts overseen by the profession itself rather than mandatory government-based approaches. To satisfy parent-consumers, a voluntary credential should have high academic standards.

The combination of new research on the brain and continuing national emphasis on school readiness is making prekindergarten programs a hot topic for governors and state legislatures. The recent trend seems to be toward programs that are universal and that use all sectors of the ECE community as the delivery system, such as exist in Georgia and New York and have been proposed in California. These programs will require increases in the qualified ECE labor force. While the prekindergarten delivery system is diverse, the personnel qualifications for prekindergarten staff usually reflect those of the public school. This is not only an opportunity to argue for better early childhood teacher certification and recognition of the CDA; it is also an opportunity to introduce the director credential as the appropriate qualification for administrators of these programs.

Parents as Advocates for Director Credentials

Parents could be an important constituency in advocating for professional preparation, especially of directors. Strategies to engage parents usually include emphasizing the results and outcomes of professional preparation for teachers and directors in terms of the benefits for children in ECE programs. Programs also educate parents and the public on what early childhood development is all about. Practitioners thereby demonstrate the important knowledge teachers and directors gain in preparation programs and involve parents in parenting education so they can experience firsthand the benefits of training. The issues that have prevented parents from being powerful advocates for improving the quality of care need to be kept in mind. Because the need for ECE services is fleeting, rather than chronic, parents do not stay as interested in early childhood issues when their children enter school.

Parents believe (correctly) that higher professional preparation will increase the cost of programs. They have a fixed amount of resources and are often reluctant (or unable) to pay for higher quality. Parents often don't see any need for training early childhood teachers, believing that early care and education resembles parenting and that more training will transform teachers into dehumanized technicians or ivory tower intellectuals. Parents do not have the same concerns about directors. Managing a program is not viewed as equivalent to parenting, and parents believe both education and special skills are required.

A State-by-State Movement

With the exception of the three credentials mentioned earlier, overall director credentialing programs are developing state by state. As the movement advances, it is crucial that lessons be shared among states and that community-based credentialing efforts (such as the pilot projects associated with Taking the Lead) be linked to state credentialing efforts. At present, state-by-state development seems to be proceeding with adequate communication among the designers. When there are enough fully functioning statewide credentialing systems—perhaps six or seven would be enough—questions of equivalence among them and reciprocity between states will be raised.

Judging from the experience of licensing professionals in other occupations, there is an interaction between state-level and national professional concerns. Each state government typically sets the requirements that allow an individual to practice a profession, while the national organizations in the field and national leaders in the field set the standards and create the examination process (which is used by each state).

The route from voluntary credential to required license is not a monolithic path. For example, consider the social work field. In 1980, when about half the states (23) had social work licensure laws, the national professional organization (the National Association of Social Workers) promoted a model licensure law and advocated through its state chapters for enactment in all states. This goal was achieved in 1992.

If licensing is the long-term goal for early care and education, should each state group developing a credential seek to get the credential into the state's facility licensing (as in Texas)? Or can the credential move smoothly into being the state-granted license (when the state's political climate changes to favor state regulation of a profession)? Or is a campaign led by one or more of our national professional organizations a better route? When the ECE field progresses to the point where a director credential becomes a required license in several states, discussion of these matters and the kind of national–state interaction evident in other professions will be needed. Through these discussions, a standard of intrastate equivalency will be reached, allowing administrators to apply their credential in different states.

Reflecting the Diversity of the Field

Early childhood administrative leadership involves the management, supervision, and direction of the full range of early childhood programs. (See Chapter 1 for a list of ECE programs and Chapter 7 for a discussion of ECE leadership.) The ECE industry is large, diverse, and growing; however, it is not large enough (or well-financed enough) to be able to support several different director credentials. To promote unity and for efficiency's sake, the field needs one comprehensive credential that is adaptable across settings. One step in this direction is that New York state expanded the scope of its proposed credential to include school-age program directors and is exploring how to link it to public school administrator certification.

Preparation—Essential for Any Credential

Administrative competence can best be developed through training that combines theoretical and practical learning experiences and that addresses the multiplicity of knowledge, skills, and attitudes necessary to perform well as an early childhood director. (To ensure access, training can be designed to follow both the standard professional and the career development models presented in Chapter 8.) Awarding a credential for directors who successfully complete a program and/or demonstrate their acquired competence recognizes a director for his or her achievements. The credential can both commend directors for their accomplishments and act as an incentive for pursuit of training. Developing effective and efficient training methods and the delivery systems to make them widely accessible are equal in importance to developing a director's credential. The viability of any credentialing system rests on the field's acceptance and ownership of the credential and on easy access to preparation for the credential.

The current social and political climate bodes well for developing a voluntary credential for administrators state by state. The high interest in states in early care and education evidenced by expanding prekindergarten programs and increasing funding for child care offers opportunities. Critical considerations in creating credentials are to promote unity of the early care and education field, ensure that preparation for a credential is easily accessible, and think now about how the various state credentials will fit together and ultimately reflect a national standard for early child-hood administrative leaders.

NOTES

1. The terms *license, certificate,* and *credential* each have distinct meanings. *License* is the official permission granted by a competent authority (usually government) to engage in a business or activity that would otherwise be illegal, for example, a public school teacher license or child care center facility licenses. *Certificate* is a document certifying that one has fulfilled the requirements of a field and may practice particular roles in the field, for example, the child development associate (CDA). (Currently there is a national board certification process for licensed teachers [K–12] being developed. It will apply to teachers in each specialty area. Some districts pay either a one-time bonus or increase salaries for teachers who hold the certificate.) The word *credential* means that which gives title to credit or to confidence; it is a general term encompassing all types of certificates and licenses.

2. The CDA program is a national effort to credential qualified caregivers who work with children from birth to age 5. The program is operated by the Council for Early Childhood Professional Recognition. To receive this credential, an individual must be at least 18 years old, have recent work experience with young children, have at least 120 clock hours of formal education in child development/child care, and be able to document and demonstrate competence in working with children of specific ages in a particular setting. The credentials available are: CDA-center-based infant/toddler, CDA-center-based preschool, CDA-family day care, and CDA-home visitor.

3. Al Osborne, Jr., is director of the Entrepreneurial Study Center of the Anderson Graduate School of Management at the University of California at Los Angeles, which includes the Head Start Management Fellows program.

4. According to information from the Center for Career Development in Early Care and Education at Wheelock College.

5. These findings are from a small survey conducted at Starting Point, the child care resource and referral agency in Cuyahoga County (Cleveland, OH).

REFERENCES

Bloom, P. J. (1995). The quality of work life in early childhood programs: Does accreditation make a difference? In S. Bredekamp & B. Willer (Eds.), *NAEYC accreditation: A decade of learning and the years ahead* (pp. 13–24). Washington, DC: National Association for the Education of Young Children.

Bredekamp, S., & Willer, B. (1992). Of ladders and lattices, cores and cones: Conceptualizing an early childhood professional development system. *Young Children, 47*(3), 47–50.

Cost, Quality and Child Outcomes Study Team. (1995). *Cost, quality and child outcomes in child care centers.* Denver, CO: University of Colorado, Department of Economics.

Kagan, S. L., & Cohen, N. E. (1997). *Not by chance: Creating an early care and education system for America's children.* New Haven, CT: Yale University Press, Bush Center in Child Development and Social Policy.

Mitchell, A. (1996). Licensing: Lessons from other occupations. In S. L. Kagan & N. E. Cohen (Eds.), *Reinventing early care and education: A vision for a quality system* (pp. 101–123). San Francisco: Jossey-Bass.

Mitchell, A. W., Seligson, M., & Marx, F. (1989). *Between promise and practice: Early childhood programs and the public schools.* Westport, CT: Greenwood.

Mocan, H. N., Burchinal, M., Morris, J. R., & Helburn, S. W. (1995). Models of quality in early childhood care and education. In S. W. Helburn (Ed.), *Cost, quality and child outcomes in child care centers: Technical report* (pp. 287–295). Denver: University of Colorado, Department of Economics.

Poster, M., & Neugebauer, R. (1998). How experienced directors have developed their skills. *Child Care Information Exchange, 1*(21), 90–93.

Pritchard, E. (1996). Training and professional development: International approaches. In S. L. Kagan & N. E. Cohen (Eds.), *Reinventing early care and education: A vision for a quality system* (pp. 124–141). San Francisco: Jossey-Bass.

10

Issues and Barriers in the Credentialing Process

Sue Bredekamp

The role of the director in an early childhood education program is pivotal. As pointed out in earlier chapters, research now substantiates what practitioners have known for some time. The skills and leadership ability of the program administrator directly affect the quality of programs provided for children and families and, concomitantly, the nature of the work environment experienced by staff (Bloom, 1989, 1996; Bloom & Sheerer, 1992). Given the importance of the administrative role, the need increases for systems that ensure that qualified directors are available to fill the demand. The purpose of this chapter is to identify and discuss the various issues and barriers that exist to establishing such systems for ensuring qualified directors in the United States.

Four major sets of issues as well as the advantages and disadvantages of alternative strategies are addressed in this chapter. These issues are (1) credentialing versus training (professional development), (2) national versus state versus local (the level of the credential), (3) access and equity versus quality, and (4) assessment systems versus training systems. Each of these sets of issues is listed here as an *either/or* dilemma. However, the goal of this chapter is to address these issues in tandem in the hopes of achieving *both/and* solutions that are assumed to be more likely to overcome the inherent (or perceived) obstacles in any forced choice.

Thorough exploration of the pros and cons of the various options in director credentialing is needed so that the field does not later regret decisions or investments that are made now. The dictum "Be careful what you wish for, because you might get it" is an appropriate caution when planning and implementing costly systems such as director credentialing that, if mandated, would have a major impact on professionals and program budgets.

CREDENTIALING VERSUS TRAINING

The word *credentialing* has multiple meanings that contribute to some of the misunderstandings in discussions about director credentialing and to disagreements within the field regarding the benefits of requiring credentials for directors. In a generic sense, credentials are simply qualifications. *Credential* has its origin in the word *creed*, which means "belief" or "trust." In short, one who possesses credentials is one who can be trusted to exercise official power. The general category of credentials is often applied to diplomas or certificates of completion of some form of professional preparation. Not surprisingly, *credential* and *credit* have similar origins in the word *creed*. Granting credit for training implies that the public can trust that the student has learned something from the educational experience.

Credential also has a more narrow interpretation. In the field of early childhood education, the word is most often associated with the child development associate (CDA) credential. Developed in the 1970s by the federal government's Administration for Children, Youth and Families, CDA is a national assessment system for entry-level personnel (see also Chapter 9, note 2). The CDA credential is used most often for Head Start and is also broadly available to early childhood personnel working with children from birth through age 5 (Council for Early Childhood Professional Recognition, 1996). Perhaps because of the early childhood profession's experience with the CDA credential, some early childhood professionals assume that director credentialing implies a uniform, consistent, singular entity or outcome (the director credential or perhaps the CDD— the child development director credential).

Lessons from the CDA Credential

Given that the CDA is the best-known national early childhood personnel credentialing system, its history is worth exploring for possible lessons relevant to director credentialing (Trickett, 1979). That history is especially relevant because it illustrates clearly the challenges that the first major issue—credentialing versus training—presents. The child development associate credential was launched in the early 1970s as a strategy to provide recognition to competent early childhood practitioners. The credentialing system is a competency-based assessment system that assesses a candidate's ability to perform the job of an early childhood professional working directly with children. In some ways the initial premise of the credential was that there are large numbers of individuals who are competent practitioners who do not possess formal academic credentials. This competence was presumably acquired on the job and through informal training mechanisms. The CDA provided a strategy for identifying and granting professional recognition to these individuals. Because the CDA was competency-based, for many years it did not require any specific prior academic or professional preparation. Perhaps the greatest contribution of the CDA to the field was the development of the CDA competencies, which provided a clear set of guidelines for professional practice and also goals for professional development programs (Granger & Gleason, 1981).

From the outset, however, it was clear that competent early childhood professionals are not just born, they are trained. A wide variety of training programs and materials were developed, some with federal funding through Head Start, to address the training needs of CDA candidates. As a result, some candidates took short-term, specially designed training courses of varying durations, while others achieved an associate degree or more (Powell & Dunn, 1990). The lack of specificity about the amount of training a CDA credential reflects led to great variety in applying the qualification in state child care licensing requirements. For instance, some states list the CDA as a qualification to be a classroom teacher, others as an aide, and some even as a director (despite the fact that the CDA includes no administrative competencies).

Not until the Council for Early Childhood Professional Recognition assumed administration of the CDA in the mid-1980s did the national system have a specified mandated academic and training requirement. The current requirements are a high school diploma or GED and 120 clock hours of formal professional preparation distributed across the 6 goals and 13 functional areas of the competencies (Phillips, 1991). The requirement that training be "formal" was a major leap for the field because it provided the much-needed link between CDA training and higher education systems.

Relationship Between Training and Credentialing

Essentially, the CDA history contains two key lessons relevant to a director credentialing effort. The first is that a credentialing system cannot exist apart from a training system. There is an inherent "chicken-and-egg" phenomenon of whether a credentialing system can be implemented without an infrastructure of preparation for acquiring the knowledge and skills necessary to obtain the credential (Powell & Dunn, 1990). Of course, people cannot become competent without training; but, at the same time, training programs tend to be responsive to the demands of credentialing systems. The latter phenomenon has been clearly illustrated in the case of state certification of public school teachers. In structuring their programs, colleges of teacher education follow almost religiously the dictates of the state certification standards. As a result, early childhood teacher preparation programs at the baccalaureate level vary enormously both in content and in availability because the field of early childhood education has not enjoyed specialized certification status in many states (Bredekamp, 1990; Morgan et al., 1993). For example, in a state that does not have any early childhood certification, it can be almost impossible to major in early childhood education in a 4-year institution, whereas an associate's degree in early childhood may be available.

Institutions of higher education of every type are naturally market-driven. If an institution or professional preparation program does not perceive that there are sufficient numbers of students to justify a program, they are unlikely to offer one. Certification requirements of various types propel students to obtain specific preparation; hence, the inextricable link between credentialing and training, and the hard question of which must comes first—the training programs or the credentialing regulation? Here a both/and approach is possible. As opportunities for careers in early care and education (ECE) programs expand, and as professional requirements change, candidates will seek credentials. We can expect institutions of higher education to respond to this demand with new programs appropriate for the student's demand.

A second issue that is raised by exploring the CDA's history is the outcome that results when the training requirements for the credential are too loosely defined. For many years, it was virtually impossible to answer the simple question: How much training does an individual need to become a CDA? Because the system is competency-based, the answer will always vary with the individuals' capacities, experience, and other factors. Nevertheless, it was almost unethical to leave the question so open that an individual had no idea what the credential required in terms of up-front investment of time and energy. CDA candidates also were unclear about what the potential benefit of obtaining the credential would be (i.e., for what employment does the credential qualify an individual?). Programs or agencies offering some form of administrative credential do have an ethical obligation to acknowledge the magnitude of the candidate's investment of time and energy by clarifying the opportunities available to those seeking the credential as a means to enhance their professional skill.

Implications for Director Credentialing

The foregoing discussion of the CDA's history has implications for the future of director credentialing. Much like early childhood education in the late 1960s and early 1970s, early childhood program administration (as a field of study) lacks an infrastructure of existing preparation and professional development programs. A survey conducted by the Center for Career Development in Early Care and Education (Morgan et al., 1993) found a handful of baccalaureate- or master-level programs designed to prepare early childhood directors. Most administrators obtain early childhood preparation, just as teachers do. They study within some existing system designed specifically to prepare for a role working directly with children (most often as a classroom teacher). At the present time, there are no widely available systematic means for individuals to obtain expertise in fulfilling the responsibilities of an administrator in addition to understanding the core content of good early childhood practice (Morgan et al., 1993).

One could argue that based on the CDA experience, launching a national director credential would provide incentive to institutions to offer such preparation. However, such incentives operate very slowly, and unless considerable pressure were brought to bear to require such a credential of every possible candidate, it is unlikely that institutions would be sufficiently motivated to create a new major and change course offerings. One deterrent is the size of the potential market. There are approximately 120,000 ECE programs, including preschool programs, Head Start, school-age child care programs, and licensed child care centers in the country. Even requiring every one of them to hire a credentialed director would not create sufficient demand to drive higher education programs. Obviously there are exponentially more classroom teachers than directors required to staff early childhood programs, and yet despite this large potential market, early childhood teacher preparation programs have been slow to materialize.

Perhaps a more viable strategy relevant to the size of the market is to create programs and a credential that more broadly address the work of early childhood administration. There are many other kinds of organizations and institutions that require administrators in addition to child care or preschool programs. These include but are not limited to child care resource and referral agencies, state and local government agencies, child welfare entities, and nonprofit agencies and organizations. One legitimate question is whether a generic human services administrator program and/or credential could be designed that would be sufficiently specific for early childhood education but sufficiently general to be a viable option for institutions of higher education and potential candidates.

An alternative to a more generic administrative program might be broader early childhood education programs and degrees. Unlike elementary or secondary education, early childhood "teachers" in child care and preschool do not need a baccalaureate degree to obtain a teaching position. The lack of uniform standards for early childhood teaching is often lamented and has the undesired consequence of making baccalaureate-level preparation relatively scarce. But if the early childhood education programs in colleges and universities were more broadly conceived to prepare graduates for multiple roles, including administrative roles, the marketability of the degrees would be increased. Many institutions will not offer baccalaureate-level programs if the job market does not require the degree or does not adequately compensate the graduates. But the flexibility of a degree can greatly enhance its marketability. The early childhood profession already recognizes the range of positions the field requires by including administrative competencies in its standards for professional preparation at the baccalaureate and advanced levels (National Association for the Education of Young Children [NAEYC], Division for Early Childhood [DEC], & National Board for Professional Teaching Standards [NBPTS], 1996). The challenge is for institutions to design and market programs that go beyond teacher education.

The mutually dependent relationship that exists between credentialing and training requires that decisions regarding director credentialing must address both credentialing and training simultaneously. Given the current state of early childhood administrator training programs in the country, it follows that whatever director credentialing efforts emerge, they should be training/credentialing or certificate-type programs in which an individual completes a training and obtains a credential or certificate as an outcome. Of course, the training should include a mechanism for assessing what the candidate knows and is able to do (knowledge and performance). But to establish director credentialing divorced from training or to establish training apart from incentives or mandates in the form of marketable credentials required for jobs is unlikely to be effective and may actually create more problems for the work force (some of which will be discussed later in this chapter).

NATIONAL VERSUS STATE VERSUS LOCAL

Whatever decision results from the above dilemma (credentialing versus training or credentialing and training), the next major issue confronting planners is the level of delivery for the credential. In the United States, basically three options are available for credentialing systems—national, state, or local. Each choice carries with it inherent problems.

National credentials for early childhood personnel (such as the CDA credential and the newly established early childhood certificate of the National Board for Professional Teaching Standards) have several advantages. First, they are based on the reasonable assumption that the educational and developmental needs of young children are relatively stable throughout the country and that the knowledge base that drives practice does not vary geographically. Second, national systems permit transferability and recognizability of the credential in different contexts. For instance, most Americans, regardless of where they live, know what a certified public accountant is; the same holds true for certified physicians and attorneys.

Analogies with other professionals, unfortunately, break down quickly when applied to early childhood education. Historically, early childhood education programs have been regulated at the state level through licensing of programs. States set very different requirements, which, along with other factors, create differing markets within which child care programs operate. Given the history of diversity of state standards regarding all areas of early childhood programming, state-level credentialing systems for directors would ultimately be responsive to state demands but would vary enormously from state to state. This phenomenon is already apparent in the various director credentialing efforts throughout the country. For instance, one voluntary credentialing effort in Wisconsin consists of 18 semester hours of credit for a director credential. Massachusetts licensing calls for five courses for the director of a small program and six for the director of a larger program. Georgia and Texas require a 40-clock-hour training for a credential. There is something inherently illogical in establishing such different standards for essentially the same job. Other professions would never allow it on either economic, political, or pedagogical grounds. Nevertheless, individuals in states that find the standards either unrealistically high or absurdly low would reject a national standard set at either end of this continuum of training. The credential processes in place at this time are voluntary, and as a director credential is voluntary, at this point it is difficult to compare a voluntary credential to a licensing requirement.

To complicate matters even more, some efforts in director credentialing are occurring at the local level, often propelled by third-party funders (foundations or corporations) that wish to improve program quality by raising director qualifications. Such funding sources do not need to be convinced of the value of well-qualified administrators to the quality of service delivery in any industry. To the degree that these efforts seed the development of potential models of training and credentialing, they can be important contributions. However, adding the variable of local community contexts and markets to the already widely varying state situation will only add to the confusion on the part of consumers (both potential directors and parents or funders seeking programs that employ qualified administrators). An ongoing national dialogue is underway through the Taking the Lead initiative, and this dialogue may serve as a necessary network linking efforts at the local level with individuals and groups working at the state and national levels.

Here again, the best-case scenario is probably not to choose one of these options—national, state, or local—but rather to develop systems that draw on the strengths of each. There is certainly a place for a well-conceptualized project to define and describe the necessary competencies for early childhood directors, and to delineate those competencies into a national credential. This task is best done through a consensus-building process at the national level, as characterized by such prior efforts as developing the CDA competencies and NAEYC's accreditation criteria (NAEYC, 1984, 1991). There is increasing clarity about the range and types of competencies needed for the role (Culkin, 1997; Morgan, 1997; see Chapter 3 for a review of director competencies). What is needed is a sense of ownership of the standards by the individuals to whom they will be applied. Such a perspective comes from a broad-based process of public review and comment that culminates in an official imprimatur by the appropriate professional organization(s). Because there is no national director's association per se, the group to spearhead this work is not readily apparent, but there are many possible candidates, including NAEYC, the Council for Early Childhood Professional Recognition, and Taking the Lead. The product of such an effort could then be used in several ways, either to form the basis for a nationally or locally administered credentialing system or, at the very least, to provide the framework for training/certificate programs at local and state levels.

ACCESS AND EQUITY VERSUS QUALITY

Most credentialing systems by definition are designed to improve the quality and, therefore, the credibility of the professionals that strive for and/or achieve the credential. Implicit in this assumption is that the holders of the credential will somehow be more qualified and better able to provide high-quality service than those who do not hold the credential. Therefore, credentialing systems are also by definition discriminatory; they control access to employment in certain positions that the public and/ or the profession has deemed necessary. For instance, more than a century ago physicians deemed it necessary to control access to the medical profession on the basis of educational qualifications and demonstrated competence. Over time, this control by the profession gained sufficient acceptance among the general public and third party payers (insurance companies) to make it mandatory.

Other professional groups have similarly designed standards and assessments for qualifying members. In fact, in recent years there has been a proliferation of certification programs among professional and trade associations. For instance, there is even an association of associations (American Society of Association Executives) through which an individual can become a CAE (certified association executive). This credential probably does enhance the skills of the individual, but no association has made it a requirement for hiring an association executive. Such programs become benefits for association members and revenue-producing projects for the groups, but they fail to have any real impact on the marketplace.

On the other hand, credentialing mechanisms that are mandated raise the stakes considerably. In public education, for example, an individual must possess at least a baccalaureate degree that covers the required content necessary to become a licensed teacher in the state. Without this credential, one cannot be hired. Controlling access to the profession in this way presumably improves the quality of service provided but also helps increase compensation; as long as there is an unlimited supply of unqualified people to perform any job, wages for performing such a job will naturally be suppressed.

Consequences of Limiting Access

But achieving the goal of limiting access to jobs to credentialed persons can have unintended consequences as well. Because of our nation's history of oppression of people of color and individuals with limited income, such systems can work to exclude individuals from diverse cultural and linguistic backgrounds from upward advancement (Moore, 1997). When credentials are tied to academic qualifications that require substantial financial investment prior to achieving one's earning potential, the record is clear that fewer people of color or low-income individuals are able to advance (National Black Child Development Institute, 1993).

The profession should be unwilling to launch into systems that may trade off access and equity for presumed quality through credentialing. The public school system is a counterexample; teachers' unions and state certification/licensure boards have been very effective in limiting job access to credentialed personnel, but, at the same time, the public's confidence in the quality of public education has declined rather than increased. In the early childhood field, in which the service is closer to the family and community context, consumers have been especially reluctant to embrace formal qualifications and other mechanisms that limit their access to choosing the program or individual they feel most comfortable with. Families from diverse linguistic and cultural backgrounds have been found to have diverse perspectives on what constitutes high-quality early childhood services (Mallory & New, 1994). If the standards for credentialing reflect a dominant cultural perspective, as they often do, then many families might not be happy with the quality of services they receive from credentialed personnel. A credentialing initiative and model of training need to include supports that allow individuals from diverse backgrounds and in varied life circumstances (e.g., part-time teacher, full-time student, and former second-grade teacher or social worker) to successfully utilize the career development system. Access to the career development process will require the availability of financial resources to assist interested individuals. (See Chapter 8 for a discussion of career development training models.)

Diversity and Quality

An examination of the knowledge base of early childhood education as summarized in CDA competencies (Phillips, 1991) and NAEYC's guidelines for preparation of early childhood professionals (NAEYC, DEC, & NBPTS, 1996) reveals that knowledge of cultural and linguistic diversity is an integral part of qualifying as a professional in this field. Therefore, one would not want to take actions that might lessen opportunities for people of diverse linguistic and cultural backgrounds.

More pragmatically, young children from diverse cultural backgrounds need role models of people who are like them in positions of power and responsibility. The director role in the early childhood program as well as the elementary school principal are roles that have a major impact on children both directly and indirectly.

Many people justifiably would argue that setting access and equity versus quality is a false choice. Quality for children and families cannot be achieved if diversity in leadership is sacrificed. Early childhood educators must take a strong stand on this point—a major determinant of program quality is responsiveness to diversity; in short, there is no quality without diversity. The only real solution is to require both access and equity for diverse individuals *and* quality. Training systems that enhance individuals' knowledge and skills but are also affordable and accessible in all geographic areas (such as through technology or distance learning) may be the best strategy. Individuals benefit by improving their skills;

opportunities for professional development remain open to diverse individuals; and programs improve as a result.

ASSESSMENT SYSTEMS VERSUS TRAINING SYSTEMS

National and state certification systems of all types are moving toward becoming performance-based. By that we mean that the marketplace is no longer interested in how someone acquires competence but is interested in the fact that the credentialed individual must perform competently. As a result, we see a trend toward performance-based licensure of teachers (Wise & Leibbrand, 1993), whereby to achieve a license to practice, teachers must successfully demonstrate teaching competence rather than just graduate from an accredited college. The National Board for Professional Teaching Standards operates an assessment system for granting board certification to highly accomplished teachers in various certification areas. Most of the various certifying programs that are administered by professional associations are similar to the CDA credentialing system in that they are assessment systems. Moreover, many of them are closer to testing services than performance-based assessments (National Certification Commission, 1995). Such credentialing mechanisms are strictly assessment systems with no directly related training component.

As described in more detail above, assessment systems depend on the existence of training systems, but it is quite possible to separate the systems in practice and, in fact, there is a trend to do so. Partly because educational institutions have not always been successful at gaining public trust, people seem to believe that individuals need to have their competence assessed independently from the institution that trains them.

Setting assessment systems versus training systems is not as farfetched as it seems. In reality, assessment systems are gatekeeping mechanisms that limit access to advancement while training systems (like all educational endeavors) are more properly viewed as gate-opening strategies. Assessment systems are threatening because the stakes related to them are very high. In designing and administering an assessment system, an organization must demonstrate that its tools and procedures are reliable and valid, and that the decisions that result are legally defensible. This is a high standard, especially in a litigious society such as the United States. In the case of credentialing directors, a gatekeeping assessment system could only be justified if research demonstrates that the performance of the director (as measured by the assessment) affects outcomes for children in the program.

In addition to the legal barriers regarding assessment systems, the resources necessary to adequately implement an assessment system are great. The best such systems are very expensive for the participants as well as the administering organization. The incentives to become credentialed must be in place if individuals are going to commit resources and subject themselves to the assessment. The inevitable question will be whether those resources could be better spent elsewhere.

Likewise, training is costly. Gaining access to professional development through any means inevitably demands a commitment of time and money. In the case of director credentialing, at this point in the profession's development the more urgent need appears to be developing a systematic knowledge base and an infrastructure of preparation and professional development opportunities. Given limited resources and competing demands throughout early childhood education, it seems hard to justify the administrative expense of an assessment system, whereas investments in training systems are absolutely essential—both to improve the skills of the current and future work force and as a prerequisite to moving forward with any assessment system.

CONCLUSION

This chapter begins with the premise that the skill and expertise of the program director are direct determinants of quality in programs for children. Although empirical evidence in support of this point is somewhat limited, anecdotal evidence as well as practical experience are overwhelming. The foregoing discussion of issues and barriers in director credentialing should not lead to the conclusion that the issues are too complex or the barriers too great to take action. If anything, examining these issues in more detail leads me (and perhaps some of the readers) to the conclusion that work must proceed on setting standards for directors. Such standards can stimulate and guide preparation and professional development programs that become more widely accessible and through which an individual's skills and knowledge can be assessed.

Until this work is more advanced (and I believe it should be prioritized in the order in which it is listed), it seems premature to talk about a national director credential. Moving to such a step too quickly could create more problems for the field than it solves. A more achievable scenario might be to conceptualize early childhood administration as one layer of the career lattice as proposed by NAEYC (1994) and others (Bredekamp & Willer, 1992; Johnson & McCracken, 1994). The lattice is a framework that acknowledges that early childhood educators work in various settings and roles, but what connects them as a profession is knowledge of core content plus specialized expertise. In this conceptualization, individuals are presumed to function in various roles with differing levels of expertise, and professional development is assumed to be a lifelong endeavor. The knowledge and skills needed by the early childhood administrator cut across various strands of the lattice (infant/toddler, preschool, school-age) and go beyond to include management and leadership skills. The requirements of the administrator also imply a level of preparation that is at least baccalaureate- and perhaps master-degree level.

If a career lattice is a framework that is acceptable to the field, the biggest challenge will be both to define the minimal qualification for a director and to outline and then delineate the optimal qualification. Currently the requirement is usually the state child care licensing standard (which is too minimal in most cases) and the fact that one is hired to do the job. The current situation is unacceptable, and the future solution must be carefully crafted to ensure that it succeeds in improving the quality of programs and supporting the professional development of early care and education administrators.

REFERENCES

Bloom, P. (1989). *The Illinois directors' study.* Springfield, IL: Illinois Department of Children and Family Services.

Bloom, P. J. (1996). The quality of work life in early childhood programs: Does accreditation make a difference? In S. Bredekamp & B. Willer (Eds.), NAEYC *accreditation: A decade of learning and the years ahead* (pp. 13–24). Washington, DC: National Association for the Education of Young Children.

Bloom, P. J., & Sheerer, M. (1992). The effect of leadership training on child care program quality. *Early Childhood Research Quarterly, 7*(4), 579–594.

Bredekamp, S. (1990). Setting and maintaining professional standards. In B. Spodek & O. N. Saracho (Eds.), *Yearbook in Early Childhood Education: Vol. 1. Early childhood teacher preparation* (pp. 138–152). New York: Teachers College Press.

Bredekamp, S., & Willer, B. (1992). Of ladders and lattices, cores and cones: Conceptualizing an early childhood professional development system. *Young Children, 47*(3), 47–50.

Council for Early Childhood Professional Recognition. (1996). *The Child Development Association assessment system and competency standards.* Washington, DC: Author.

Culkin, M. (1997). Administrative leadership. In S. L. Kagan & B. Bowman (Eds.), *Leadership in early care and education* (pp. 23–38). Washington, DC: National Association for the Education of Young Children.

Granger, R. C., & Gleason, D. J. (1981). A review of the Child Development Associate credential: Corrections and comments. *Child Care Quarterly, 10,* 63–73.

Johnson, J., & McCracken, J. (Eds.). (1994). *The early childhood career lattice: Perspectives on professional development.* Washington, DC: National Association for the Education of Young Children.

Mallory, B., & New, R. (Eds.). (1994). *Diversity and developmentally appropriate practices: Challenges for early childhood education.* New York: Teachers College Press.

McCarthy, J. (1988). *State certification of early childhood teachers: An analysis of the 50 states and the District of Columbia.* Washington, DC: National Association for the Education of Young Children.

Moore, E. (1997). Race, class, and education. In S. L. Kagan & B. Bowman (Eds.), *Leadership in early care and education* (pp. 69–74). Washington, DC: National Association for the Education of Young Children.

Morgan, G. (1997). *Competencies of early care and education administrators.* Boston: Taking the Lead Initiative, Wheelock College.

Morgan, G., Azer, S. L., Costley, J. B., Genser, A., Goodman, I. F., Lombardi, J., & McGimsey, B. (1993). *Making a career of it.* Boston: Center for Career Development in Early Care and Education, Wheelock College.

National Association for the Education of Young Children (NAEYC). (1984). *Accreditation criteria and procedures of the National Academy of Early Childhood programs.* Washington, DC: Author.

National Association for the Education of Young Children (NAEYC). (1991). *Accreditation criteria and procedures of the National Academy of Early Childhood programs* (rev. ed.). Washington, DC: Author.

National Association for the Education of Young Children (NAEYC). (1994). A conceptual framework for early childhood professional development. In J. Johnson & J. B. McCracken (Eds.), *The early childhood career lattice: Perspectives on professional development* (pp. 4–23). Washington, DC: Author.

National Association for the Education of Young Children (NAEYC), Division for Early Childhood (DEC) of the Council for Exceptional Children, and National Board for Professional Teaching Standards (NBPTS). (1996). *Guidelines for preparation of early childhood professionals.* Washington, DC: National Association for the Education of Young Children.

National Black Child Development Institute. (1993). *Paths to African American leadership positions in early childhood education: Constraints and opportunities.* Washington, DC: Author.

National Certification Commission. (1995). *Certification program development guide.* Chevy Chase, MD: Author.

Phillips, C. B. (Ed.). (1991). *Essentials for child development associates working with young children.* Washington, DC: Council for Early Childhood Professional Recognition.

Powell, D., & Dunn, L. (1990). Non-baccalaureate teacher education in early childhood education. In B. Spodek & O. N. Saracho (Eds.), *Yearbook in Early Childhood Education: Vol. 1. Early childhood teacher preparation* (pp. 45–66). New York: Teachers College Press.

Trickett, P. (1979). Career development in Head Start. In E. Zigler & J. Valentine (Eds.), *Project Head Start: A legacy of the War on Poverty* (pp. 315–336). New York: Free Press.

Wise, A. E., & Leibbrand, J. (1993). Accreditation and the creation of a profession of teaching. *Phi Delta Kappan, 75*(2), 133–136, 154–157.

11

Innovative Ideas from the Field

Marsha Poster and Roger Neugebauer

It is quite clear that an individual in an early care and education (ECE) administrative position needs special training and a career development system that acknowledges the many responsibilities of the job. During the mid-1970s, throughout the 1980s and the 1990s, the ECE administrative position was relatively new in education. In recent years leaders in the profession have come to acknowledge not only the complexity of the administrator's job but also the crucial role the director plays in shaping program quality.

In the past ECE administrators had few opportunities to refine their skills through intense, systematic training. There were a number of top-notch director training programs—at Wheelock College, Bank Street College, and Nova University, for example—but these programs were not available or accessible to the vast majority of directors. As a result, without the support of professional development opportunities or informal networks acknowledging the combination of skills necessary to perform this role, the issue of director burnout and turnover held back the professionalism of the field.

However, as appreciation for the role of administrators has grown, so have efforts to address their training needs on a systematic basis, as evidenced by the work presented in this volume. Such training will better qualify future generations of ECE professionals, offer solutions to problems like burnout, and reduce turnover by providing ongoing professional support to those in the field.

This chapter discusses the preparation and training of directors and other children's program administrators (1) by looking at the impact of training on current directors and (2) by reviewing research on the causes, consequences, and cures for administrators' burnout. Finally, we forecast some future solutions by examining innovative career development programs for training and supporting directors.

HOW EXPERIENCED DIRECTORS—AND OTHER
ADMINISTRATORS—HAVE DEVELOPED THEIR SKILLS

When we started to work on this chapter, we decided it would be useful to learn how long-term directors developed the skills that enabled them to have such long and successful careers. We surveyed 41 administrators who have been directing centers for more than 20 years (some as many as 50 years!). We assumed that if we asked these directors what training experiences had had the most impact on shaping their skills, we would be able to isolate a few key training approaches that really make a difference (Poster & Neugebauer, 1998).

We were wrong. What we discovered was that the responding directors survived and thrived by taking their training wherever and whenever they could find it.

In the survey we presented the directors with a list of 15 training opportunities ranging from a Ph.D. in early childhood education or a related field to administrative workshops at early childhood education conferences to support from other experienced directors. The majority of the directors had participated in 11 of these training opportunities, with the most commonplace forms of training being administrative workshops provided at early childhood conferences and local director support groups. Overall this was a well-educated group, with more than 60% having earned at least a master's degree in early childhood or a related field. Surprisingly, more than 80% of the directors had participated in administrative training by organizations outside of the early childhood field (such as Chamber of Commerce training, leadership training by a women's group, or courses in higher education settings such as policy institutes or business schools).

We also asked the experienced directors to rate the value of their various training experiences on a scale of 1 to 10 (with 10 representing "extremely helpful"). Again, we were surprised to discover that all forms of training were rated relatively high. Every form of training listed received an average rating above 6. Overall formal training programs were ranked somewhat higher than informal opportunities. Highest ranked in terms of value overall were a Ph.D. (9.5), a master's degree (7.9), and a bachelor's degree (7.9). However, informal opportunities were not far behind. For example, support from another experienced director had an average rating of 7.4, working with an experienced director 7.3, administrative workshops at national early childhood education conferences 7.3, and participation in a center accreditation effort 7.0.

Finally, we invited participants to describe the training experiences that most positively impacted their performance. This yielded some interesting insights:

- Until recently, most directors had to learn on the job.

    I opened my first school in 1949, when there were no training oppor-
    tunities. I pioneered and learned by trial-and-error. I believe an indi-
    vidual must have the motivation and inborn talent to be successful
    as a director.

    Just being on the job—trying, failing, and trying again—has been
    my primary learning experience.

- Previous life experiences strongly shape performance as director.

    My years of working as a preschool teacher were so valuable. I think
    a director *must* have had direct classroom experience to be an effec-
    tive director.

    I grew up with a salesman father and absorbed without knowing it
    lessons on meeting and greeting, compromising, dealing with angry
    customers, and so forth.

    Being a parent probably had the biggest influence. I started parenting
    during the age of transactional analysis and bought strongly into the
    importance of good self-image. This continues to shape my thinking
    about developing children.

    My religion is a major influence on my work. I have always used
    truth and honesty as basic foundations for dealing with customers
    and employees. This is highly important in a time when parents are
    looking for safety and security for their children.

- Until recently, directors had to look outside the field for interdisciplinary training opportunities.

    The most valuable training experiences I have had have been inter-
    disciplinary in nature: human relations training, training in social
    work, and courses in human behavior and development.

    I learned how to educate children in ECE courses, but when it came
    to directing I had to look far afield for helpful courses—to business
    schools, to Chamber of Commerce programs, and to seminars on
    leadership for women.

Many years ago a local bank sponsored a 6-week training program for new managers. The instructor had a banking background, but years of experience in the nonprofit setting gave him a tremendous understanding of both sides.

I remember an incredibly helpful summer course for principalship certification that offered hands-on training for everyday situations. It was a revelation for me as a new director to see how much the organization of a full-day ECE program mirrored the administrative components of an elementary school. The course was invaluable so early in my career for my understanding and growth within the administrative arena. Being promoted from teacher to administrator meant I often doubted my administrative decisions. Confirmation for decisions and theory, grounding practice, changed everything for me.

- Management training is most helpful when it is experienced after already working as a director.

Attending graduate school certainly reinforced my years of experience.

When I was in college I took two courses in early childhood administration. However, my first day as a director I realized that these courses were pitifully simplistic. I really benefited from some graduate courses I took years later when I had a clear idea what I needed to learn.

- Conferences are most beneficial when they focus solely on management issues.

All in all what has been most helpful is being able to access the administrative courses in business schools and attending early childhood conferences that focus on management issues.

Most early childhood conferences are too basic for me at this stage of my career. The conferences that are aimed just for directors and owners are the only ones that inspire me with new ideas.

- Continuous training not only develops skills, but more importantly serves to keep one challenged and excited.

I think the needs of new and experienced directors are different. In the early years I needed to learn everything. The schooling I look for now isn't needed to run a good center, now it's for my head. It keeps me from burning out as it keeps me thinking and growing.

I think I would wither away if I stopped attending seminars and conferences. Every time I attend, I come away charged up about some new idea to try or some new theory to consider.

- Peer support, and support from colleagues outside ECE, is vital to promoting growth and maintaining motivation.

Our local NAEYC [National Association for the Education of Young Children] chapter has a very informal directors' roundtable which is invaluable for small independent centers like ours.

Meeting with other directors, especially with a mentor team of three other directors, has been most influential.

Working with an experienced center director on a day-to-day basis was the best experience for me. She let me understudy her role. She patiently explained the rationale behind every decision. She let me make decisions gradually.

I have always been fortunate to have licensing evaluators who provided personal support and technical assistance. In addition, I have learned a great deal from members of my board with business experience.

I found that my friendships with directors in other states have been more helpful than working locally. It seems people from afar feel more open to discuss issues without fearing the competition is looking over your shoulder.

For many years I have been a member of an organization dedicated to women in development. As part of the membership services we initiated a mentor program. Sitting on both sides of the mentor/ mentee situation has been a wonderful learning experience.

THE CAUSES AND CONSEQUENCES OF DIRECTOR BURNOUT

During the late 1980s and early 1990s, "director burnout" was such a popular workshop topic at early childhood gatherings that there was a tendency to dismiss it as just a trendy notion. However, research in the broad human services arena, as well as in the ECE field, has demonstrated that burnout is a legitimate concern. Fortunately, this research has also identified approaches for avoiding burnout.

Cary Cherniss (1995) has been in the forefront of those studying the concept of burnout. He consistently emphasizes that there are sources of burnout at the individual, organizational, and societal levels; he reports that human service professionals need the experience of success to sustain their commitments. In interviewing teachers, social workers, psychologists, nurses, and poverty lawyers, he found that the majority of the subjects were considerably more satisfied with their work situations in mid-career than they had been earlier. Because they were more senior, their working conditions had improved. In addition, because they had lowered their expectations, they were less vulnerable to frustration, and—as a consequence of their growing self-awareness—these professionals were better able to identify and engage in those aspects of their work that felt most personally satisfying.

All professionals, Cherniss (1995) notes, need to adopt a realistic time perspective in order to vitiate the impact of the inevitable frustrations of human service work. Those individuals who cultivated special interests (like special projects) in their setting felt more committed to their work and were, as a consequence, less vulnerable to boredom and job dissatisfaction. It is important to note that the child care center director's position seems to support many avenues for "special projects"; however, for many directors, time and a myriad of duties (those tasks that should be delegated to others, e.g., secretarial work, subbing in classrooms) often create barriers. This is especially true when lack of finances prevents the hiring of additional staff to effectively perform all necessary tasks.

Several other factors were found to diminish the vulnerability of professionals to stress and burnout. These include an active rather than a passive response to work frustrations, a drive to continue to learn new skills, an ability to balance the needs of family and career, and a work setting that offers both support and the opportunity for autonomy. All of these factors influence planning, designing, and implementing effective training and educational opportunities for directors.

The Journal of Child Care Administration conducted an interview about dealing with stress with Sue Baldwin (1997), owner of INSIGHTS Training & Consulting, an organization serving early childhood professionals in Minnesota. Baldwin believes there are two major areas of stress for directors: an inability to separate their personal and professional lives, and the personnel-oriented tasks of finding qualified staff, dealing with high turnover, and doing whatever is possible to keep good staff. Poster (1986) identified personnel administration, including staffing, training, turnover, and retention issues, as the tasks that consumed the largest portion of the director's time. These issues continue to be pivotal concerns challenging program quality and creating stress for directors.

In another study Maslach and Pines (1977) studied the burnout process among staff members of several early childhood programs. The causes of burnout, they found, lie less in individual personality traits and more in the situational pressures arising from the job definition. Their solutions, therefore, concern situational remedies, and these are applicable to the director's position. For instance, they suggest a social–professional support system that can provide advice, comfort, and a sense of context. Such a support system provides opportunities both for analysis of the problems to be faced and for addressing personal feelings about them—opportunities for humor, for comfort, and for social comparison. Since burnout rates are lower among those who are willing to share their feelings and receive feedback from others, Maslach and Pines suggest working closely with others in such a way that the professional can identify and analyze stress and solutions to stress. Their study certainly supports the findings of our survey of long-term directors and accentuates the need for building support groups and relationships (Poster & Neugebauer, 1998).

Our discussions with directors confirmed Maslach and Pines's (1997) finding that the following variables are "life-lines" of support for combatting, rather than avoiding, burnout:

- *Having support for the transition.* When professionals who become directors have transitional support upon entering the position and ongoing support for establishing networks with other directors thereafter, turnover and burnout can be positively addressed in order to ensure a longer commitment to the position. Many agencies stress that they hire directors who have already had experience in direct teaching and caregiving, a practice that most in the field would highly support. However, little recognition has been given to the fact that directors are often removed from the support and connectedness with their peer group as they move into an administrative position. This is a problem because the new position not only puts them in isolation; often it also places them in a position of authority vis-à-vis their friends. Human connec-

tions with other administrators are vital at the point of entry into a
new role. Connections and collegiality with other administrators can be
initiated, maintained, and enhanced through director support groups
and networks.

- *Cultivating a suitable temperament.* Most early childhood practitioners
  come into the field due to their fondness for children and their wish to
  be nurturing. Their daily opportunity to provide care for children utilizes such personal qualities as warmth, flexibility, and openness. In
  displaying these attributes, they continue to develop a cluster of attributes that are very valuable in direct work. However, these same attributes may pose difficulties once the professionals assume a managerial
  role. This is particularly true if a practitioner moves to a director position without the benefit of administrative training. The role of the director requires a variety of personal styles. To name just a few key areas,
  a director position includes responsibilities that require individuals
  who are comfortable with authority, directing others, marketing and
  promotion, political issues, and strategic planning. The fact that early
  childhood administrators are overwhelmingly female, of course, brings
  into play the phenomenon that women's socialization is often congruent
  with the demands of direct practice but not with the demands of management. In today's business thinking, organizational leaders understand that they need managers. Specifically, today's managers must be
  nurturant, participatory, mission-driven, and team oriented. The goal is
  for a manager (administrator) to combine these abilities with traits such
  as the skills to act in more proactive, assertive ways. The latter are traditionally those of the more instrumental, proactive, assertive professional, and it is these attributes that need to be cultivated via training
  and support mechanisms.
- *Training and education.* A study conducted by Paula Bloom (1989) found
  that 78% of directors hold baccalaureate degrees and 38% have a master's or doctoral degree. The survey conducted for this chapter supports
  this finding, in that 41% of the directors hold master's or doctoral degrees. Directors reported that they had held their positions for more
  than 20 years because of the training and support systems that were
  available to them. Bloom found that there is one overarching contribu-
  tor to director turnover—lack of "position-specific" training for the job.
  It appears that sufficient formal preparation in the knowledge, skills,
  and attributes relevant to the job of director can contribute to an administrator's sense of confidence and promote the actual ability to transcend those daily challenges that otherwise increase the probability of
  burnout and turnover.

PROMISING PRACTICES AND FUTURE POSSIBILITIES

Keeping in mind the importance of ongoing training and support as antidotes to high turnover and an inoculation for burnout, we now turn to an examination of some actual training approaches and support mechanisms that offer promising directions. Although much work still needs to be accomplished to bring coherence into available training and education for directors, innovative projects of great promise are already underway across the nation. Some of the most significant of these are the director credential projects underway in a number of states. In what follows, we discuss those and a number of other innovative programs. They have been selected for their contributions to the diversity of a future blueprint for director training.

Director Support Groups and Mentoring Programs

A major way in which directors have been gaining support from one another and exchanging information has been through director support groups. Because directors are most often the only person in their organization in an administrative role, they need to reach out to their professional peers, to meet with colleagues. In director support groups, administrators gain ideas and solve problems together.

Although mentors have traditionally been older, more experienced persons who advise the young and inexperienced, individual mentoring relationships differ widely. Particularly for new directors, mentoring is proving to be a highly successful means for a novice or beginner to enter an administrative role. Generally, mentoring programs involve coaching, teaching, guiding, or acting as a role model. Within a one-to-one relationship, a mentor promotes the growth of skills and knowledge within her or his protégé/mentee. Mentoring enables both parties to step back from the intensity of direct practice and take time to think about their actions and observations. Mentoring thus addresses the gaps found in more traditional inservice or supervision training models. Although mentoring is not intended to replace existing methods, its hallmark principles—reflection, collaboration, and regularity—can be used as guiding principles for practice (Abrams, 1995). Examples of such programs are described below.

The California Early Childhood Mentor Program. This program for direct caregiving staff, in operation since 1988, has as its primary project objectives improving child care quality, staff training, and compensation. In late 1996, a director mentor component was added to the program. The project operates as a three-way collaborative initiative between the California Department of Education, Chabot–Las Positas Community College District, and individual community colleges (a total of 50 colleges).

The director mentor component has the following goals: to assist trained and experienced directors to become mentors; to allow less experienced center directors access to the knowledge and insight of "veteran" directors; to increase awareness in the community on issues related to quality; and to involve the community college with others in the community to improve standards of quality. The unique aspects of this project include a reciprocity in training by means of which director mentors and novice directors benefit from a "learning through relationships" model.

Director mentors are early childhood administrators with at least 3 years of administrative experience, currently or formerly employed as directors or site supervisors in center-based child development programs. They provide a one-on-one learning relationship with novice directors by offering technical support in the practical and theoretical aspects of center administration and leadership. In return, they receive a stipend for a minimum of 20 hours. Director mentors are also offered support for their own professional development through a monthly director mentor seminar (on a credit-optional basis), which focuses on supervision, leadership, and advocacy strategies. Once director mentors are selected, their availability is advertised within the professional community.

There are three steps to becoming a mentor director: First, candidates interested in becoming director mentors register for a 2-day regional "directors' institute" provided by the Child Development Training Consortium in collaboration with the mentor program. Second, following completion of the directors' institute, qualified candidates may apply to their community's mentor coordinator, who operates a local mentor selection committee. Third, after the visit to the applicant's worksite, the selection committee reviews all the material and makes the final determination about selection.

In summary, this model does the following:

- Offers an avenue for networking to enhance the ongoing professional development of the mentor directors
- Supports accreditation and other quality initiatives
- Affirms the complexity of the job
- Offers optional credit to foster articulation and documentation for training
- Provides a stipend for sharing knowledge about the profession with new directors

• Fosters mentoring through an established system supporting a coach/consultant relationship

The ART of Teaching. The ART of Teaching™ (administrators form relationships with teachers) is a director and teaching staff project based in Colorado. The project focuses on training and career development services for directors working in "reciprocal learning teams"™ with teachers and others in their organization. While the primary recipient of services is the director, the program provides a measure of education and training services to faculty at all levels in the enrolled early care and education programs. A program evaluation using the Harms, Clifford, and Cryer (1998) instrument initiates the quality improvement process. Training is provided in twice-monthly training seminars for directors, in regular classroom team planning meetings at centers, and through a series of seminars and workshops designed to address directors' and teachers' interests.

Over a 2-year time span, directors work with teachers to raise the quality of services in classrooms through improved communication, management, coaching for practitioners, work with families, and the development of leadership skills. A director and teachers at a program form classroom or centerwide curriculum planning teams in order to work more consistently with teachers. The "reciprocal learning teams," which are central to the process, evaluate classroom quality, set goals, and focus on improved classroom services and activities.

Typically, in the first year of The ART of Teaching, the program teams focus on improved child and family experiences in classrooms and throughout the organization. In the second-year program, entitled the Organizational ARC™ (Administrators form Relationships with Community), directors continue their service improvement work in their program and also focus externally on their community and colleagues.

The program bases learning in the relationships developed between the participants and the faculty to develop a supportive professional arena where directors can address difficult issues, such working with minimally trained staff, teacher turnover, personnel issues, community and marketing, and licensing issues. The ART of Teaching has several particular features. It uses a coach-consultant rather than a traditional mentor model, engages classroom teams in learning strategies for observation and program evaluation, and features a series of seminars for the director and the teaching teams. Specific workshop and seminar topics include child observation, communication, evaluation, diversity issues, literacy, and curriculum planning. Higher education credit is available for interested participants committed to remaining with their program.

Director Growth Opportunities

The following two projects have larger goals than director training but provide great opportunities for directors to expand their skills.

The Managing Turnover in Child Care Centers Program. This program, coordinated by the National Center for the Early Childhood Workforce, involves directors and staff from 20 centers in the San Francisco Bay Area. The project attempts to calculate the direct and indirect expenses incurred when a staff member leaves; to identify ways to reduce these expenses and invest in staff stability; and to explore promising practices for minimizing the stress that children, staff, and parents experience when turnover occurs. The lessons learned have been combined in a training resource book entitled *Taking on Turnover: A Handbook for Teachers and Directors* (Whitebook & Bellon, 1999).

The Managing Turnover project is an outgrowth of an examination of how other industries assess turnover costs and their impact on service quality, and how they intervene to reduce employee departures. By applying lessons from other industries, the goal is to break through the silence and inertia that surround the problem of child care staff turnover. The program fosters training through collaborations with directors and teachers through regular, structured sessions and informal brown-bag seminars.

Director Training and the Bottom Line

Children's World Management Development Program. This program is an example of a director training initiative launched by a national for-profit child care system. Children's World Learning Centers is a nationwide child care provider headquartered in Golden, Colorado, with more than 500 programs spread across 21 states. In 1989, when Duane Larson (a former human resource development professional) was hired as CEO, he identified training as a key part of his strategy for developing the organization. He felt that until the company could guarantee consistent service delivery, they weren't going to be able to progress. Larson said, "I believe that high productivity boils down to a company's commitment to the training process" (Galagan, 1992, p. 47).

The story of how Children's World started a centralized management development program from scratch and had its first graduation 16 months later makes the case for these often-touted but more often ignored principles of success: link your program to corporate goals, design it to meet real needs, and be able to demonstrate its link to performance and the bottom line.

As is characteristic in the profession, Children's World recruited center directors with strong teaching backgrounds. The directors were responsible for the educational component of the program as well as food service, transportation, accounting, marketing, managing a staff of 30 to 40 people, and running a $1-million operation. Noting these strenuous demands, the corporate director of organizational development stated, "We had been putting these young people in a situation where they were almost set up for failure" (Galagan, 1992, p. 47). Turnover among center directors was at about 32%, which in 1989 was lower than the child care industry average for managers, but it was still unacceptable to Larson. In 1992, 1 year after the new training began, turnover among center directors dropped by 5%. According to Larson, the quantitative data showed that "it cost less to train a center director than to replace one, so training that would help to reduce turnover made economic sense" (Galagan, 1992, p. 50). And decreased director turnover also resulted in less customer turnover.

Director Training and Technology

As the field of early care and education enters the new millennium, a variety of enabling technologies and promising applications for distance learning and videoconferencing are unfolding. They provide new opportunities for dissemination of information, interaction among early childhood practitioners, and the delivery of "just-in–time" training and professional development offered directly to early childhood programs.

In using technological approaches, the goal is to use enabling technology, proven distance education methods, and "best practices" in early childhood education and care in order to deliver training that is available, convenient, cost-effective, and high-quality. To make a difference in job performance and program quality, these technologies must be effective at teaching what "quality" early childhood education and care is, how to provide it, and why it is important. Multiple teaching strategies using multiple technologies are needed to create the optimum adult learning environment.

Learning Options. With more than 94 million people in the United States on the Internet, Web-delivered education is now mainstream. Learning Options, owned by NACCRRA, publishes affordable, on-line , on-demand, interactive, quality curricula for ECE professionals. Most of its content can be aggregated to qualify for continuing education units (CEUs) and/or college credit. In addition to covering parenting, preservice licensing, continuing education, elementary and high school equivalency, and an on-line AA child care degree, Learning Options has a number of credentialing courses (over 60 hours and growing). These include: A National Administrator's Certificate, by the National Child Care Association; Leadership: Is It For Me, by Dr. Tim Nolan; and A Hitchhiker's Guide to the Child Care Universe, by Gwen Morgan. A long-term goal is the development of a B.A. degree program. Administrators can use these educational resources to complete their own education and to support the career development efforts of the teachers on their staff.

Access to the training on the Internet offers early childhood administrators the ability to expand professional connections to include association Web sites, ongoing communications and networking with other directors or early childhood educators, and infinite possibilities for personal, professional, and staff training.

In light of these programs, early childhood professionals and adult educators must continue to ask hard questions about the effectiveness and appropriateness of technology and distance education as a delivery system for teaching the "art and science" of caregiving and relational care. Learning at a distance has become more content-rich with the advent of multimedia presentation tools, and it can now become more interactive, even with the instructor and students at different sites. Real-time audio, two-way video, and the Internet links to the instructor allow for interactive questions and answers, and the Internet discussion groups can continue after the class has ended.

Graduate Programs

Not all innovative learning takes places via technological relay. There are several important graduate programs that offer career development for the ECE administrator.

H. John Heinz III School of Public Policy and Management at Carnegie Mellon University. This program will prepare ECE professionals for positions as elementary school principals and/or child care administrators. The program, still under development, is open to educators with a degree in the field of education or child development, and it will offer graduate training in organizational theory, leadership styles, staff development, administration, community relations, and group dynamics. A unique aspect of this program is the building of relationships within the ECE profession as well as with administrators of other organizations outside the profession. All participants study a core of organizational management courses together and thereby learn the similarities administrators face in managing varied types of organizations. Insights gained from this experience are a major influence in the student's development of respect for the complexities of the role of the ECE administrator.

One major tenet of the program is that "principals are really managers of organizations" who are not simply "superteachers," but professionals who need management abilities and training. This program responds to Gould's (1982) study of early childhood administrators, which found that many directors have teaching backgrounds but little or no administrative preparation for the job.

The Center for Early Childhood Leadership at National Louis University. The National Louis University in Evanston, Illinois, is another notable graduate program for directors. Here, Paula Jorde Bloom and others have developed a master's of education program in early childhood leadership and advocacy. This program responds to the fact that "current licensing standards do not reflect the educational expertise needed to effectively administrate an early childhood program" by providing quality training and career development (Bloom & Rafanello, 1995). In addition to the Center's educational programs, faculty have developed a newsletter for administrators and a series of research briefs focused on administrator demographics and professional preparation issues.

Nova University. Nova University in Fort Lauderdale, Florida, has developed a model for director master's and doctoral programs, taking advantage of technology through computer networking and regional cluster group meetings to offer a training option for full-time working directors. This is a format that other universities committed to director training have found to be a workable format and offered over the years.

The Forum for Early Childhood Organization and Leadership Development. The Forum for Early Childhood Organization and Leadership Development in Kansas City, Missouri, builds the capacity of early childhood care and education leaders by providing training in leadership, supervision, strategic planning, budgeting, governance, board development, and fund-raiding. Programs and courses of the Forum serve a six-state region in the midwest and focus on three areas: education and professional development, community-oriented applied research, and community collaboration and problem solving. Two overriding purposes of the program are to bring new knowledge of management and leadership to the ECE field, and to enable early childhood practitioners to link with others providing services to children and families. The Center Director's Institute (CDI), a program of the Forum, is an experientially based hands-on curricula designed by Forum faculty. This curriculum is specifically oriented to developing management, leadership, and advocacy skills for ECE administrators. Programs at the Forum are a part of the Midwest Center for Nonprofit Leadership, an outreach and education unit of the Henry W. Bloch School of Business and Public Administration at the University of Missouri-Kansas City, and offer students the opportunity to earn higher education degrees at the master's level and above.

Summer Institutes

Aside from graduate programs, there are also several innovative summer programs worth mentioning.

Wheelock College and Bank Street College. Wheelock College located in Boston has provided summer seminars for child care professionals since 1975. The seminars began as director training programs but have expanded to include policy makers, consultants, and others in the field. Although the work is offered at the graduate level, participants can receive credit regardless of their prior education. These summer sessions include courses in Child Care Administration, Mentoring, Leadership, and Financial and Legal Aspects of Child Care. Bank Street College in New York City is also sensitive to the issue of accessible training and offers summer institutes and seminars on leadership on weekends.

The Head Start—Johnson & Johnson Management Fellows Program at UCLA. This Head Start program, which operates under the Anderson Graduate School of Management, is another example of a summer institute. The 2-week summer sessions in Los Angeles are designed to provide Head Start directors with "modern management theories and principles," entrepreneurial competence, and the ability to assist other Head Start directors nationwide. Course units include computer labs, finance, marketing, and networking. This hallmark program has gained national prominence and detailed coverage in the *New York Times* (Chira, 1992) and *Education Week* (Cohen, 1992). With the conclusion of the 1998 program, more than 517 professionals have completed training. The program provides admirable networking and support mechanisms through its newsletter (titled *Fellowship*) and publications such as its *Profile Book*, which provides accessible and user-friendly profiles of all the fellows who have participated over the years.

CONCLUSION

In a number of powerful ways, directors influence the climate of their centers both as a workplace for the teaching staff and as an educational and nurturing environment for young children and their families. Directors play a critical leadership role in ECE programs, and they influence the growth of children, the well-being of families, and the professional growth of their staff members. To be effective in carrying out these major responsibilities, center directors need to be well trained for the wide variety of tasks they confront. They also need to have ongoing support to carry them through times of high stress.

Since directors who are willing to grow are a master key to quality, they need the education and training in management and administration that will complement their knowledge of child development, teaching, and family systems. As is apparent in the above description of some innovative programs, this training is already under way in some places. In addition, on the national level there are many promising recent developments. For example, the Taking the Lead project, funded by a consortium of foundations and housed at Wheelock College's Center for Career Development, has launched a number of pilot credentialling and leadership projects. (See Chapter 1 for an overview of the projects.) The projects promise to offer insights into improving the nature of director development as well as to highlight the importance of this training and the need for greater diversity in the leadership pool. The National Black Child Development Institute has also launched a leadership development initiative designed to strengthen the leadership opportunities for diverse populations. On an even broader scale, *Child Care Information Exchange* has initiated an annual World Forum on Early Care and Education with the purpose of bringing together early childhood leaders from around the world to share ideas on improving the delivery of ECE services in diverse settings.

Given the urgency of quality concerns in early childhood programs and the significance of the administrator's role in ensuring that quality, we look forward to the growth of innovative training mechanisms for supporting future generations of ECE directors in their career development at the local, regional, national, and international levels. Ongoing professional association networks, mentors, coaching, professional journals, electronic journals, books, magazines, computer support technologies, and relevant and specific training are all necessary to sustain and refuel an early childhood program director.

REFERENCES

Abrams, J. A. (1995). *Mentoring: Just a buzzword or a boon to training and progessional development?* Unpublished manuscript, University of Pittsburgh, Pittsburgh, PA.

Baldwin, S. (1997). Dealing with stress: Interview with Sue Baldwin. *Journal of Child Care Administration* Issue 213, p. 11.

Bloom, P. (1989). *Child care directors' training and qualifications.* Washington, DC: Office of Educational Research and Improvement.

Bloom, P., & Rafanello, D. (1995). The professional development of early childhood center directors: Key elements of effective training models. *Journal of Early Childhood Teacher Education, 16*(1), 3–8.

Cherniss, C. C. (1995). *Beyond burn-out: How teachers, nurses, therapists, and lawyers recover from stress and burnout.* New York: Routledge.

Chira, S. (1992, August 19). Learning the business side of a social service venture. *The New York Times,* p. B-7.

Cohen, D. L. (1992, August 5). At management school, Head Start directors acquire business acumen for new challenges. *Education Week,* pp. 6–7.

Galagan, P. A. (1992). When the CEO is on your side. *Training and Development,* 46(46–51).

Gould, N. P. (1982). *Women caregivers in licensed day care centers: Who are they? A study.* (ERIC Document Reproduction Service No. ED 224 594)

Harms, T., Clifford, R. M., & Cryer, D. (1998). *Early childhood environment rating scale* (rev. ed.). New York: Teachers College Press.

Maslach, C., & Pines, A. (1997). The burn-out syndrome in the day care setting. *Child Care Quarterly* 6(2).

Poster, M. A. (1986). *Identification classification and comparison of the work performance requirements and actual work performance of child care center directors in the commonwealth of Pennsylvania.* Unpublished doctoral dissertation, University of Pittsburgh. (UMI Abstracts International, No. 870 75 98)

Poster, M., & Neugebauer, R. (1998). How experienced directors have developed their skills. *Child Care Information Exchange,* Issue 121, 90–93. Redmond, WA: Child Care Information Exchange.

Whitebook, M., & Bellon, D. (1999). *Taking on turnover: A handbook for teachers and directors.* Washington, DC: National Center for the Child Care Workforce.

12

Leadership in Child Development Programs: Prospects for the Future

Karen Hill-Scott

The field of child development is at a crossroads. In the past two decades, wide-ranging opportunities for careers in the management and leadership of early care and education (ECE) programs have emerged. Some professional positions that didn't exist 20 years ago—such as municipal child care coordinators, or information and referral directors—are now commonplace. Other jobs, especially those related to developing and managing large systems of ECE providers, are still evolving, parallel to public policy changes that have created the opportunity for these systems to develop.

The center director position, which was once the career terminus for an early childhood professional, is becoming one of a fluid array of management roles in the ECE leadership. There are positive new developments ahead for center directors, but there is also a formidable challenge to respond and adapt to a changing professional environment. Credentialing or management certification is but one of the changes that will flow from current trends in the organization and delivery of ECE services.

This chapter makes some projections about the overall future of early care and education, drawing specific attention to the content of management in ECE programs. The projections flow from an analysis of the political and environmental context of ECE, as well as an analysis of four trends that are shaping a future of better-quality, multimodal, and professionally managed delivery systems across the nation.

Taken together, the projections for the future in early care and education are threefold. ECE will have more complex models of organization, with an emphasis on systems. Quality production will be much more important than it is today, as the base of support for quality broadens beyond the profession. The role and content of management in ECE will undergo an expansion and transformation as new systems emerge and new career ladders develop.

The analysis begins with the 20-year shift in demand for ECE, particularly center-based programs. During the same period, public policy also shifted, and an exponential increase in the flow of child care subsidy funds followed. Today, the increased funding is creating pressure for an expansion of ECE supply and the development of capacities to manage that supply. Given this context, these are the four trends we can expect

1. Employer-supported child care
2. Consumer awareness
3. Public policy trends, such as welfare reform and universal preschool programs
4. Pressure for professional management

CONTEXT

Contrast and Change

For context, let's look at how the societal need for and priority for ECE have done an about-face in just two decades. From 1977 to 1993, the number of preschool children with employed mothers who were enrolled in centers increased from 568,000 to more than 3 million (Casper, 1997; Casper & O'Connell, 1998). In 1976, it was the exception, rather than the rule, for mothers of preschool children to be in the labor force. In 1996, not only were 65% of these mothers in the labor force full and part time, but the Personal Responsibility and Work Opportunity Reconciliation Act (Public Law 104-193) required all mothers on public assistance to find a job, no matter what age their child.

In 1976, national child development legislation could not get through a congressional committee. By 1992, bipartisan sponsors in both Houses of Congress had passed the Federal Child Care and Development Block Grant, tripling federal spending from $3 billion to $9.5 billion. Moreover, by 1997, federal spending had gone up to almost $14 billion (U.S. General Accounting Office [USGAO], 1998) and the president proudly hosted the history-making White House Conference on Child Care.

In the 1970s, the trend was for the government to contract with an ECE center directly. The idea was to directly control operations through the funding process. Advocates were fighting to establish national standards. By 1980, though, the concept of national standards had been politically defeated, paving the way for greater decentralization in the management of public child development funds. By 1990, most federal funds were being funneled into certificate or voucher programs instead of center contracts, so parents could purchase ECE services directly.

In 1976, if a mother worked, she was almost as likely to care for the child herself while working (11.4%) as to use an ECE center (13%) (Casper, 1995). In 1995, whether or not a mother worked, the center was the single most desired option for early education. About 28% of all preschoolers were enrolled in ECE centers *full time*, numbering close to 6 million children (National Center for Education Statistics [NCES], 1998).

ECE has definitely entered a new era. The annual and consistent increases in maternal labor force participation have driven overall utilization of programs. Shifts in public policy have also changed the market dynamics and created the potential for ECE expansion. Consumers definitely have a preference for center-based models of ECE. This will have several impacts on the development of management talent and on the job content of program management.

The New Importance of Child Development Programs

While most ECE professionals wouldn't label child development as an *industry*, these programs do represent a panoply of services that, combined, have a multibillion-dollar cash flow and employ close to 1 million workers. By any standard, ECE is not an insignificant service sector. However, the following description demonstrates its financial significance in the American economy.

If the federal contribution to ECE represented a company, this $14-billion investment would position ECE at number 100 on the *Fortune* 500 list, right behind Archer Daniels Midland, the fourth-largest food producer in America ("The 1997 *Fortune* 500 List," 1998). Federal spending, however, is less than 40% of the total spent on care (Mitchell, Stoney, & Dichter, 1997). Based on the Census Bureau's 1995 estimate of average weekly fees ($79), basic revenues are estimated to be more than $33 billion (Casper, 1995), and a variety of state and local financing mechanisms contribute another $8 billion. The total revenue base for ECE is probably at least $55 billion, similar to the gross revenues of *Fortune* magazine's entire entertainment industry sector. This sector, which included Disney, Viacom, CBS and Time Warner, posted combined earnings of $59 billion in 1997 ("The 1997 *Fortune* 500 List," 1998).

The sheer size of the gross revenues and the potential for their growth signal that ECE is a major component of the social infrastructure. No wonder there are new investors and entrepreneurs interested in early education and that there have been several mergers and acquisitions among national chains. Of course, rapid growth of any industry can result in thin coverage of essential services. Family and child development advocates are rightfully concerned about service quality for the children in this large but highly fragmented industry. After all, ECE is not an industry selling units of hamburgers, autos, or movies. This industry is supporting child development, the legacy of a civilized society. Thus the current context of ECE has an extraordinary polarity of great opportunity accompanied by very difficult challenges.

Opportunity

The overall ECE sector—private for-profit, private nonprofit, and public—is slated for additional growth, fed by at least three phenomena. First, there is the continued labor force participation of mothers, including the new labor force participation of former welfare recipients. Over the past two decades, children of working mothers have entered centers at the average rate of about 143,000 per year. This will increase dramatically with the influx of new employed welfare recipients. Second, consumer preference for center care will continue to drive a recomposition of service delivery within the industry away from home-based nonrelative care. Third, there is a nascent drive to leverage and increase public resources for ECE services into an integrated system that provides full coverage to the preschool population.

   In the private for-profit sector, expansion is most likely to be targeted toward well-educated, moderate- to high-earning families that already have the highest child care center utilization rates, from 40% to 50% (NCES, 1996). This group seems to have a reciprocal relationship to the industry; as center care becomes available, they fill the spaces. Both employer-supported and community-based facilities are likely to be developed. Using child care participation rates from the NCES study, this target population numbers from a conservative 500,000 preschoolers to a high of 1.5 million children under the age of 6. Many are currently in home-based nonrelative care and would be likely to make the shift to center care if it were available.

   According to the U.S. Department of Health and Human Services, close to half of low-income families transitioning off welfare to work will also choose center care. In an analysis of consumers purchasing care with certificates under the Child Care and Development Block Grant, and Title IV-A Care for welfare recipients, the agency found that center utilization ranged from 42% to 68% (National Child Care Information Center, 1997). There were 9 million children on welfare in 1992. At the rates of parental job participation required by law (25% in year 1 and 5% increase annually until 2002), we could have an influx of 1 million increasing to 2 million preschool children in this target population

The generalized consumer preference for centers means that with adequate financing from federal/state/local subsidies or through private/public partnerships, there will be immediate development opportunities for new programs. Capacity cannot expand without management to plan, implement, and maintain services, so the prospect for becoming a center director in this growth phase is exceptional. However, the simplicity of the numbers belies the complexity of actually managing in the new ECE environment.

Challenge

The gross revenues for ECE suggest a financially robust industry. However, the numbers don't reveal what most professionals in the field already know: Per capita spending per child is too low to produce a high-quality program or good outcomes for children. Even high-earning parents who pay top market rates may not be purchasing high-quality care for their children (Cost, Quality and Child Outcomes Study Team, 1995).

Efforts at self-regulation—through advocacy, training, professional development, and accreditation—are making a positive impact on the industry. About 5% of all centers are accredited, and another 5% have applications pending (Bredekamp & Willer, 1996).

We know that quality production doesn't happen by osmosis. The National Association for the Education of Young Children (NAEYC) study on accreditation (Bredekamp & Willer, 1996) showed that quality enhancement requires a significant and sustained investment in the organizations and people that provide child care services. Intensive support—including an infusion of management-level resources, custom-designed training for staff and directors, facilitated support groups, and professional technical assistance—is necessary to upgrade quality.

These data suggest that to reduce the polarity between the opportunity and the challenge we must secure adequate per capita funding to support high-quality care. This is a very long term and politically complicated proposition. In the meantime, we should continue to exploit multiple approaches to create a better patchwork of financing than we have today. Thus we might be able to support high-quality services for different consumer sectors and different age groups of children in the coming years.

Whether or not the investment comes from the public sector, higher parent fees, or other private-sector contributions, we must manage growth effectively so that resources are deployed strategically. This is the main reason that management development from within the industry is so critical. If a priority is going to be put on quality production in child care centers, it takes knowledge of child development to get the job done. Conversely, the child development professional needs to understand how to achieve efficiencies in order to produce and sustain requisite quality levels.

TRENDS

As we enter the next decade, several trends indicate that management talent is critical, if not pivotal, to development of the industry. These trends emerge from the growth in employer-supported child care, new public policies, consumer behavior, and pressure from within the child development profession.

Employer-Supported Child Care Trends

In 1998, Roger Neugebauer, publisher of the *Child Care Information Exchange,* called employer-supported child care "Overblown Trend #1." He correctly pointed out that from early announcements in the 1970s, employer-supported care was slated to be the child care solution of the decade. After 20 years of publicity, this subsector is still only 3% of all centers. However, as a very high profile group, employer-supported child care centers (and other employer collaboration to support ECE services for their employees through such services as resource and referral or support for family child care services) have impacts far beyond their number. Administrators of business-supported programs are appropriate candidates for the administrative credential. Business investments in ECE—and particularly in child care—are important not just because of the amount of the investment but because of the magnitude of the effect created due to the role of business in the world. Businesses have a high profile in their communities—and often in the larger state community and beyond. The impact of business involvement in ECE has a ripple effect outside a specific project. It extends out into the larger community, affecting both the larger business and the ECE education communities.

Employer-supported centers typically have financial support packages that make it possible to run a high-quality program. Parents pay market or higher rates for their services. In addition, the employer also pays for infrastructure, supplies and equipment, wage subsidies, other support, *and* a management fee. As a result of the additional funding and in-kind contributions, per capita funding is much higher than in the marketplace, in some cases as much as 100% over par value. Many of these centers attract the better staff within local markets, operate at ideal ratios and group sizes, provide staff training and development, and show a profit or at least break even. In this sense, good employer-supported ECE definitely represents "the art of the possible."

Employer-supported ECE, whether sponsored by one company or a collaborative, is uniquely different from other community programs such as sole-site centers, Head Start, or publicly sponsored programs. Employer-supported ECE stands out in the market while the other programs may seem more alike to the consumer. The business context and client relationship create an expectation that the child care vendor will mirror the behavior and operating culture of the corporate world. The center administrator, by extension, must become proficient at managing a business operation and function as a corporate liaison.

The management skills of planning, anticipation, and constructive conflict resolution are of extraordinary importance in these settings. The employer who has paid a premium to the child care vendor expects the on-site director to have rehearsed and responsive solutions to every problem that can occur.

High expectations and a sense of authority as consumers are universal characteristics of ECE consumers in employer-supported centers. This operating environment forces the center administrator and his or her parents to implement and regularly fine-tune strong organizational systems. The systems improve program quality and consistency, help the provider realize operating efficiencies, and improve the program's competitive position and marketing.

The broader applicability of practices being developed in the employer-supported sector is threefold. First, rather than instilling rigidity, the development of integrated operating systems opens up the process of management and builds trust with the consumer. It also reduces crises, increases consistency, and makes the center an easier place to work for staff. Second, the director functions as both a business manager and as an educator. In addition to managing the week-to-week survival of the center, the employer-supported ECE director is often part of a team focused on long-term planning, staff development, and overall program improvement for enrolled children and families as well as staff. Third, the director develops technical and personnel management skills comparable to management in other industries. This increases competence and the ability to attract and develop the best staff. To reiterate, one factor of importance in the employer-supported-program work environment is access to substantially more dollars to apply to the per child cost of quality.

Public Policy Trends

Often public policies seem very removed from day-to-day management of a center. Administrators don't see much relationship between what happens at the legislative level and their jobs unless the policy relates to licensing or their center's funding. Since more than 80% of the revenues in centers come from parent fees, only a small minority of directors may perceive that they are affected by broad public policies. That is changing as public policy in the ECE arena continues to evolve at the federal, state, and local levels.

Welfare reform at the federal level could flood the market with new consumers who have certificates to purchase ECE services under the Temporary Assistance to Needy Families (TANF) program. The value of the certificate will vary from state to state, since the federal contribution is not sufficient to cover the cost of market-rate care. Some state policies are combining the federal allocation for TANF child care with new state funds. This is the case in California, Connecticut, and Wisconsin, for example (USGAO, 1998). However, data from the 1997 staffing study (Whitebook, Howes, & Phillips, 1998) suggest that the subsidies are not being used for quality production or higher wages.

It would be feasible to creatively finance center care expansion for the TANF population and provide care at a high-quality level if subsidies were high enough. ECE advocates, and center administrators especially, must continue their dogged pursuit of higher basic rates and/or set-asides for quality production. An example is the success in 10 states for a policy that pays a higher subsidy rate for an accredited program (Warman, 1998). Several other states pay higher reimbursement rates to programs meeting other specified standards, in addition to accreditation, that go beyond regulation.

Another parallel development is an education reform that will have huge impacts on ECE centers. This is the prekindergarten movement, which has been approved or has generated serious interest in Connecticut, New Jersey, New York, Ohio, Georgia (Children's Defense Fund, 1998), and, most recently, California (California Department of Education, 1998). In three of these states, high-quality child care providers will be certified to provide prekindergarten services with state funding at fully funded rates. Some states will offer universal preschool with state funding, while others are targeting services to low-income children first.

Prekindergarten programs are definitely an opportunity for enterprising center administrators to improve quality and expand capacity. Bond financing and public loan programs for child care facility construction are related developments also under consideration or in implementation in several states and municipalities (Mitchell et al., 1997).

There are at least four impacts of these policies on administrators. (1) Program directors will need to learn how to price ECE services closer to the real cost of quality production. (2) Administrators must learn to make linkages to the new resource streams. (3) Directors will need to learn how to market quality to consumers who have access to child care certificates. (4) Directors will need to develop financial management and fiscal accountability skills to produce quality efficiently and meet reporting requirements of public agencies.

Consumer Trends

Parents and ECE providers are entwined in an ironic relationship. Parents purchase services to facilitate their labor force participation and benefit their children. They love their children and appreciate their early care and education programs. But for most, the price for care seems expensive.

Providers offer the care at the lowest price possible, because they don't want to burden the parents with cost issues and are dedicated to working with children. In fact, the provider community, not parents, spearheads the advocacy for affordable early care and education. The result of this structural relationship is that parents (and the public) think market rates cover the full cost of quality, while providers feel denigrated because they live with unworthy wages and poor benefits.

On the average, market-rate services demand just under 10% of the typical user's income (Casper, 1995). This may not be a burden to high-income parents. However, about half of all child care consumers have annual incomes below $40,000 a year. For them, the cost of care is definitely a financial burden, claiming up to 25% of income.

The problem is that as long as the fee-for-service model dominates the industry, there will be an inherent drive on the part of consumers to suppress price. One insidious result is that the economists who help set policy will continue to confuse consumer ability to pay with willingness to pay (and thereby not support quality production). Market prices will continue to be confused with true costs.

Administrators, who are often in the position of setting price, must be the first to consider and promote a fairer valuation of the work product. Administrators must also be the first to put any fee or subsidy increases into staff salaries and quality enhancements.

This is a difficult and uncomfortable role, but directors may find less consumer opposition than they think. Coincidentally, census data on costs for care show that parents are willing to pay more for care in adjusted dollars than they did 20 years ago (Casper, 1955). In 1977, parents paid an average of $55 a week (in 1993 dollars); in 1993, they paid an average of $79 a week. More recently, the Cost, Quality and Child Outcomes Study Team (1995) found that average weekly rates ranged from $85 to $99 in fee-for-service centers.

Unfortunately, operational costs more than doubled during a comparable period (Benson, 1996), so the increase in parent fees did not go to potential salary increases for staff. This is substantiated by the National Child Care Staffing Study, which showed stunning wage stagnation over the past decade (Whitebook et al., 1998).

However, there has to be a way to bring about a closer match between the price of care and the cost of quality production—*and it must involve consumers*. The data clearly show that parents express a strong interest in quality, place a high value on educational programs, and have a widespread preference for center care. In both the Cost and Quality Study (Cost, Quality and Child Outcomes Study Team, 1995) and the NCES survey (1998), parents expressed similar values to child care professionals in rating attributes of care.

It seems only logical that parents could be engaged in the advocacy effort for expanding public finance models that support quality care. It's up to management to devise ways of engaging parents in advocacy for higher quality.

One caveat affecting the ability to engage a parent in advocacy, however, is that consumers consistently overrate the quality of care they purchase. Parents seem to prefer to believe that an ECE program is good until proven to be bad. In the NCES survey (1998), parents tended to believe a center performed well on the dimensions they valued, even if, in reality, the center did not.

The management and leadership of the profession needs to let consumers know the truth from the report by the Cost, Quality and Child Outcomes Study Team (1995). What people think is quality often is not. Maybe the problem for parents is that comparative choices really aren't available. Both mediocre and good-quality care are expensive from parents' point of view. But parents also appear to be deeply uninformed when it comes to recognizing what quality care looks like and what it would really cost if they were to purchase it at full cost in the marketplace

Directions for the Profession in Response to Current Trends

Within the child development profession, the role of monitor, protector, and advocate for the child's developmental interest has reigned supreme. And well it should.

Parents' overarching need for "peace of mind" combined with their inadequate knowledge about quality has created a silent assent to the prevalence of mediocre and low-quality programs. Policy makers are mainly concerned with resource allocation and price suppression. Thus the profession's commitment to self-examination and good child development is more than a blessing. It is an achievement.

There are countless ways in which the profession has evolved that have upgraded the frequency and consistency of quality in ECE programs. However, there remain three related concerns for the future that are worth an exploration.

First, there seems to be a major contradiction between the qualifications the profession defines as necessary for the work force and the qualifications that are held by the work force in the real world. Second, it seems to be a difficult challenge to concurrently achieve both high standards and diversity among the work force and the leadership. Third, there is comparatively less emphasis on the development of management and leadership as a goal for the profession. This is the case even though it takes insightful and capable management to plan for the future and train successive generations of workers.

Not By Chance, a report of the Quality 2000 Initiative (Kagan & Cohen, 1997), is a defining work for the future of the profession. As noted in Chapter 9, it contains an extensive and thoughtful recommendation to license personnel who work with children at three levels—associate educator, educator, and administrator. Postsecondary education is essential for both the educator and the administrator levels. The theory of the system is excellent. It is based, in part, on research findings that show college-educated personnel produce better child outcomes. However, reality will severely jar implementation of a system based on this model.

Thousands of workers are currently classified as higher-level personnel than their training and experience would warrant. In many states, personnel who are currently "teachers" would not qualify for the lowest-level license, associate educator. Many current directors would not qualify for the center administrator license. For example, a recent study on work and wages (Whitebook et al., 1998) indicated that 35% of the centers in their sample employed TANF clients who had no formal work preparation. Also, overall teacher requirements had declined over the decade. Among the director credential programs reviewed by Wheelock College, some did not require a college degree for the center administrator.

Staff development may be a financing issue rather than a selectivity issue, but the profession still seems quite conflicted about basic qualifications for classroom and management personnel. The profession is caught in the gap between high aspirations for the work force, a desire to promote inclusion, and a price structure that won't sustain skilled labor.

A related problem is that efforts to increase diversity, particularly cultural and ethnic diversity, are misconstrued as a rationale for emphasizing practical skills over postsecondary education. Some have even questioned the necessity of basic literacy as a prerequisite for working with young children, especially infants and toddlers.

Let's not confuse the issues. We don't have to compromise basic standards in order to achieve diversity and inclusion. The qualifications floor can't get any lower than it is now, yet diversity in the work force has not been achieved. What is essential is creating access to education and training and welcoming a wide range of perspectives to the profession. When it comes to promoting high standards, we are not precluding diversity as one of the necessary ingredients of quality.

Greater emphasis will need to be put on strategies that fund multiple models of staff and career development. For example, we should consider 10-year timelines to upgrade existing staff and develop management skills from entry level to certified positions. On-site and on-line training by accredited postsecondary institutions may need to become standard operating procedure for this process.

The analysis presented in this chapter definitely suggests that the director of an ECE program needs a level of skill far beyond the teaching fundamentals that are currently the core qualifications for the job. An even greater level of sophistication will be necessary for managing ECE systems. The top job in program center operations is long overdue for greater discussion within the profession.

FUTURE PROJECTIONS FOR ECE
AND DIRECTOR PREPARATION

Political advocacy and the struggle for adequate financing for ECE services are assumed to be contextual constants that will not diminish. The recurring maneuverings at the policy table will always dictate whether or not services are funded, at what level and department of government, and with what regulatory structure. However, assuming a continuation of the trends that have been discussed in this chapter, the profession will be involved in three important domains of substantive activity. Each domain has implications for the role, function, and certification of competency in ECE management.

One domain is the development of multimodal service models and systems of early care and education. Another is the production of higher-quality processes and child outcomes in programs. Third, and perhaps most important, is the development of a pipeline of fairly compensated skilled labor and creative management to staff and guide a wide array of expanded services.

Service Models

The fee-for-service model is the bedrock of ECE funding. However, who pays how much, what the funding maximum is, and who gets to partici- pate are still open questions. Many states will consider market-rate–based formulas for funding as an improvement over their current funding mod- els. Conversely, ECE advocates will push for a higher base rate and for broader benefit coverage so all income groups can have access to service.

In a protracted and gradual process, the full cost of quality care will be purchased with a combination of parent fees and publicly funded child care certificates that are completely portable. This will, in turn, cre- ate a natural opportunity for the widespread emergence of ECE vendor networks on one side of the equation and payment systems on the other. Several states already have well-organized precursors for these systems. In California, for example, the Alternative Payment Programs now man- age 50% of child development revenues, contrasted with just 4% in 1990 (California Department of Education, 1998). These kinds of payment sys- tems may be the embryos of a universal system of administering ECE funds and increasing program coverage all over the country.

Instead of the diffuse fragmentation that exists today, delivery sys- tems may be multimodal, permitting the participation of home-based providers, centers, and public schools in ECE programs. The rates paid (which will consist of a parent fee and subsidy formula) will be deter- mined based on the qualifications of the personnel. In Georgia, for ex- ample, an eligible prekindergarten program must have certified person- nel and a certified curriculum (Raden, 1999). The recommendations for a proposed California system are similar. And the Quality 2000 report (Ka- gan & Cohen, 1997), mentioned earlier, calls for individual licensing.

The implications for center directors and other administrators are complex. First, there is participation in advocacy to assure that the value of certificates, fees, and supplements can purchase quality care. Then, there is learning how to network and function in an interorganizational and interagency context, not in the insulated world of parents, owner/ boards, and children. The director may need to begin marketing to a di- verse consumer base and to produce an externally defined level of quality in a rate-driven system. Fiscal accountability and adhering to additional regulations that come with organized payment systems will be a standard part of the job description. Finally, some directors will want to develop and manage the delivery systems or provide resource and referral or tech- nical services to these systems. However, as will be discussed, formal training that anticipates these future projections is in short supply.

Quality Production

Several forces will support quality production. First, any public policy that ties funding to a quality standard, as is the case with the Georgia prekindergarten program, will reinforce the trend for quality care. Next, as market saturation is reached for center-based ECE, the competition for customers will position the more efficient and high-quality programs at the top of the heap. Also, states will be developing voluntary rating systems to guide the providers and consumers of care toward quality. With increased information and higher quality available, consumers will become better at recognizing quality indicators in the real-world setting and will push for high child outcomes. Finally, professional self-evaluation and accreditation will provide independent verification and certification that both programs and individuals meet a quality standard.

This future will be the protracted reward of the profession's investment in quality production. However, getting there will require new levels of preparation for many directors. Meeting higher standards will also provide new management opportunities for those who want to develop capacity within the ECE profession.

There are several well-documented models for producing higher-quality programs. While most of these quality production models focus on teacher training, not management development, they all depend on professional management to implement. The Smart Start Program in North Carolina, for example, has formally considered quality production as an essential component of a new system. Salary increments and provider payment rates are tied to increases in quality. Technical assistance and training for the teaching work force have to be provided by experienced professionals. Competent administrators looking for a growth opportunity may find new positions as consultants, training coordinators, and evaluators in a quality-based system.

The Labor Pipeline and Management Certification

The time has come to consider a flexible career ladder (or lattice) with horizontal mobility across segments of the ECE industry. Professional managers may work as program directors in centers, as systems developers, as consultants, as resource and referral coordinators, as training consultants, or as evaluators in an enlarged array of related child development services.

A good teacher will always have the foundation to become a good administrator. But supporting teaching, working with families, and teaching one's staff probably comprise between 15 and 30% of a center director's job description. If none of the projected changes in the organization of early care and education services ever happened, the core of directing a center would still be management, not curriculum.

The following list identifies the managerial content areas that are essential for directors. Of nineteen content areas listed, the typical ECE administration classes address only the first five.

1. Child development and curriculum planning
2. Staff training
3. Regulatory compliance
4. Developmentally appropriate practice
5. Quality control
6. Systems integration
7. Operations and efficiencies
8. Corporate liaison
9. Interorganization linkage
10. Customer service
11. Planning and forecasting
12. Advocacy
13. Human resource management
14. Compensation practices
15. External communications
16. Internal communications
17. Financial planning and budgeting
18. Evaluation and accountability
19. Technology applications

We can consider several possibilities for improving management training among early childhood educators. The easiest approach is to encourage child development professionals to obtain graduate training in fields other than child development so they can balance their knowledge of program content with schooling on management or administration.

A second approach would be to create a management and leadership specialization in existing graduate programs in early childhood education. This is much more difficult, requiring the identification and expansion of faculty in these programs nationwide. The approach would support the development of an ECE administrator's capacity to integrate management disciplines into a base of knowledge about child development and teaching. (See Chapter 11 for a discussion of programs.)

A third approach is to create certificate or credential programs that offer concentrated training for management skills specifically applicable to child development programs. This is the fundamental basis for the director credential. In this model, building on child development knowledge a current director or candidate for an administrative position would be exposed to a series of classes or learning experiences that result in the credential. There are several credential initiatives nationwide, but they vary widely in content and time commitment.

Based on a review of training content in credential programs compiled by the Wheelock College Center for Career Development, only three of the fifteen certification efforts appear to cover all the domains identified in the previous list and require a project that integrates the learning (Taking the Lead Initiative, 1998). These were the Wisconsin administrative credential, the Minnesota child care administration certificate, and the proposed New York children's program administrator credential. Another program, offered at the UCLA School of Management but not leading to a credential, also offers this kind of content. All four of the programs required more than 120 clock hours of instruction.

Most of the other programs definitely appeared to provide varying levels of preparation for a management career. No suggestion that the other credential or certificate programs are inadequate is intended. When we consider that very few directors enter their jobs with any real preparation for managerial reality, all fifteen starting points represented in the Wheelock analysis have merit.

If the ECE profession is to be prepared for the future, we must project to the world at large that there exist a professional capacity for first-rate organization as well as first-rate quality in services to children. A director's credential, which addresses management content and which measures performance outcomes, could be a significant step in that direction.

At this juncture, the major danger faced by the field is to reject what has to be done and not develop the capacity to grow. The projections are going to happen, and we must put a priority on developing management while simultaneously building new systems. The proven accomplishments of the profession over the past 20 years show we have the capacity to continue moving forward. We can embrace what works for managing organizations as well as do what is right for the children in our care.

REFERENCES

Benson, B. (1996). A capsule history of for profit child care. *Inside child care 1997–1998 trend report* (pp. 45–46). Redmond, WA: Child Care Information Exchange.

Bredekamp, S., & Willer, B. A. (1996). NAEYC *accreditation: A decade of learning and the years ahead*. Washington, DC: National Association for the Education of Young Children.

California Department of Education. (1998). *Ready to learn. Quality preschools for California in the 21st century* (The report of the Superintendent's Universal Preschool Task Force). Sacramento, CA: Author.

Casper, L. M. (1995). *What does it cost to mind our preschoolers?* (U.S. Census Current Population Reports, pp. 70–52). Washington, DC: Household Economic Studies.

Casper, L. M. (1997). *Who's minding our preschoolers?* Fall 1994 (update) (U.S. Census Current Population Reports, pp. 70–64). Washington, DC: Household Economic Studies.

Casper, L. M., & O'Connell, M. (1998). *State estimates of organized child care facilities*. Washington, DC: U.S. Bureau of the Census, Population Division.

Children's Defense Fund. (1998). *The state of America's children: Yearbook 1998*. Washington, DC: Author.

Cost, Quality and Child Outcomes Study Team. (1995). *Cost, quality, and child outcomes in child care centers: Public report* (2nd ed.). Denver: University of Colorado at Denver, Economics Department.

The 1997 *Fortune* 500 list. (1998, August). *Fortune* magazine (www.fortune/fortune500.com)

The *Fortune* industry list. (1998, August). *Fortune* magazine (www.fortune/fortune500/ind3.com)

Kagan, S. L., & Cohen, N. E. (1997). *Not by chance. Creating an early care and education system for America's children*. New Haven, CT: Bush Center in Child Development and Social Policy, Yale University.

Mitchell, A., Stoney, L., & Dichter, H. (1997). *Financing child care in the United States: An illustrative catalog of current strategies*. Philadelphia: Ewing Marion Kauffman Foundation and The Pew Charitable Trusts.

National Center for Education Statistics (NCES). (1996). *Statistics in brief: Child care and early education program participation of infants, toddlers, and preschoolers*. Washington, DC: Author.

National Center for Education Statistics (NCES). (1998). *Statistical analysis report: Characteristics of children's early care and educational programs: Data from the 1995 National Household Education Survey*. Washington, DC: Author.

National Child Care Information Center. (1997, February). *Child care program figures for 1995. Federal child care programs in FY1*. Vienna, VA: Administration for Children and Families, U.S. Department of Health and Human Services.

Neugebauer, R. (Ed.). (1998). Hits and myths of early childhood education. *Inside child care 1997–1998 trend report* (p. 7). Redmond, WA: Child Care Information Exchange.

Raden, A. (1999). *Universal preschool in Georgia. A case study on the development and implementation of Georgia's lottery-funded prekindergarten program*. New York: Foundation for Child Development.

Taking the Lead Initiative. (1998). *An overview of director credentialing initiatives*.

Boston: Taking the Lead Initiative, The Center for Career Development in Early Care and Education, Wheelock College.

U.S. General Accounting Office (USGAO). (1998). *Child care: States' effort to expand programs under welfare reform* (Testimony before the Subcommittee on Social Security and Family Policy, Committee on Finance, U.S. Senate). Washington, DC: United States General Accounting Office, Health, Education, and Human Services Division.

Warman, B. (1998). Trends in state accreditation policies. *Young Children, 53*(5), 52–55.

Whitebook, M., Howes, C., & Phillips, D. (1998). *Worthy work, unlivable wages: The National Child Care Staffing Study, 1988–1997.* Washington, DC: Center for the Child Care Workforce.

Resources for Directors

Center for Career Development in Early Care and Education
Taking the Lead Initiative
Wheelock College
200 The Riverway
Boston, MA 02215
617-734-5200
Fax: 617-738-0643
http://ericps.crc.uiuc.edu/ccdece/ccdece.html

Early Childhood Mentoring Alliance
Center for the Child Care Workforce
733 15th St., NW, Suite 800
Washington, DC 2005
202-737-7799
Fax: 202-737-0370
http://www.ccw.org

Management Development Series
Children's World Learning Centers
ARAMARK Educational Resources
573 Park Point Drive
Golden, CO 80401
303-526-3400
Fax: 303-526-3393
http://www.childrensworld.com

Learning Options™
1319 F Street NW, Suite 810
Washington, DC 20004-1106
202-393-5501
Fax: 202-393-1109
http://www.naccrra.net

National Association of Child Care Resource and Referral Agencies
(NACCRRA)
1319 F Street, NW, Suite 810
Washington, DC 20004-1106
202-393-5501
Fax: 202-393-1109
http://www.naccrra.net

Child, Youth, and Family Studies
Fischler Graduate School of Education and Human Services
Nova Southeastern University
1750 Northeast 167th Street
North Miami Beach, FL 33162-3017
1-800-986-3223 Ext. 8550
Fax: 954-262-3879
http://www.nova.edu

The Forum for Early Childhood Organization and Leadership
Development
The Midwest Center for Nonprofit Leadership
Henry W. Bloch School of Business and Public Administration
University of Missouri—Kansas City
5100 Rockhill Road
Kansas City, MO 64110-2499
816-235-2305
Fax: 816-235-1169
http://cctr.umkc.edu/user/mcnl/

Leadership Development Program
Bank St. College of Education
Graduate School
210 West 112th Street
New York, NY 10025
212-875-4467
Fax: 212-875-4753
www.bnkst.edu

The Center for Early Childhood Leadership
National Louis University
1000 Capitol Drive
Wheeling, IL 60090-7201
847-475-1100 Ext. 5252
Fax: 847-465-5617
www.nl.edu/cecl

Head Start—Johnson and Johnson Management Fellows Program
University of California Los Angeles
110 Westwood Plaza
Box 951481
Los Angeles, CA 90095-1481
310-825-6306
Fax: 310-206-3924
http://www.anderson.ucla.edu/

National Black Child Development Institute
African American Early Childhood Leadership Resource Center
1023 15th St. NW Suite 600
Washington, DC 20005
202-387-1281
Fax: 202-234-1738
http://www.nbcdi.org

Head Start Fellowships
Council for Early Childhood Professional Recognition
2460 16th Street NW
Washington, DC 20009
202-265-9090
Fax: 202-265-9161
http://www.cdacouncil.org

Convene.com
Partner: Pacific Oaks
595 Market Street, 12th Floor
San Francisco, CA 94105
415-782-0500
Fax: 415-782-0505
http://www.convene.com/partners/default.htm

About the American Business Collaboration for Quality Dependent Care

Funding for the development of this book was provided by the American Business Collaboration for Quality Dependent Care (ABC). The American Business Collaboration for Quality Dependent Care is a groundbreaking strategy intended to increase the supply and improve the quality of dependent care services in the United States. It was formed in 1992 as a corporate response to the key labor force changes brought about by the increasing number of women and dual-income families in the labor force, the growing technological skill gap in new jobs, and the increasing caregiving responsibilities of employees. Collaboration addresses the diverse needs of employees on a local community basis.

The ABC allows the business community to identify common interests, pool their resources, and invest business dollars in a range of care settings in many geographic areas. These efforts are targeted specifically at the needs of company employees but also support existing community services. During the first phase of collaboration, a total of 156 businesses and public-/private-sector organization invested a record $27.4 million in 355 dependent care projects serving 45 targeted communities. A joint statement announcing the collaboration stressed: "By working together we can do more to meet the dependent care needs of our employees than if we worked alone."

The second phase of this effort was announced on September 14, 1995. The chief executive officers of 22 champion companies signed a statement supporting the mission of collaboration. The 22 major U.S. companies are: Aetna, Allstate Insurance Co., American Express, BP Amoco, AT&T, Bank of America, Citigroup, Chevron, Deloitte & Touche, Eastman Kodak, Exxon, GE Capital Services, Hewlett-Packard, IBM, Johnson & Johnson, Lucent Technologies, Mobil, Bell Atlantic, Pricewaterhouse Coopers, Texaco, Texas Instruments, and Xerox. The second phase of the collaboration signifies a commitment of $100 million for the development of projects in more than 60 targeted communities through the year 2000. Programs funded include: the development of day-care centers, school-age programs, recruitment of family child care providers, training of early childhood and school-age providers and program administrators, and the development and enhancement of elder care programs and services. Collaboration investment dollars also fund the research and development of Championship Model programs that are national in scope and can be replicated in many diverse communities.

Boston-based WFD, formerly known as Work/Family Directions, is the national consulting firm working on behalf of the corporations to manage this effort, the largest business collaboration of its kind. For more information about WFD and the American Business Collaboration, please call 1-800-447-0543, or access the website at www.wfd.com.

About the Editor and the Contributors

Mary L. Culkin, editor, is associate professor of early childhood education at Metropolitan State College and a research professor at the University of Colorado Health Sciences Center, School of Nursing—both in Denver, Colorado. Mary worked as a practitioner in the classroom and in an administrative role for many years. She was the founder and director of a school for children with special needs in Boulder, Colorado before becoming engaged in policy research and teacher preparation activities. She served as a principal investigator on the Cost, Quality, and Child Outcomes Study of Child Care Centers, and in that study, the research team investigated the role of the administrator. She continues to investigate leadership and training issues through her work with children, early care and education administrators, and their teaching staff. Mary holds a Ph.D. in early childhood education from the Union Institute and is an active volunteer in local community education schools and agencies.

Paula Jorde Bloom is a professor of early childhood education and director of the Center for Early Childhood Leadership. She also serves as the program coordinator for the M.Ed./C.A.S. in Early Childhood Administration. As one of the country's leading experts on early childhood leadership and program management issues, Dr. Bloom is a frequent keynote speaker at national and international conferences. She also serves on several national advisory boards providing consultation on different professional development policy issues. Paula received her master's and doctoral degrees from Stanford University. She has taught preschool and kindergarten, designed and directed a child care center, and served as administrator of a campus laboratory school. Her current research interests are in the areas of organizational climate and occupational stress as they relate to indices of job satisfaction in early childhood settings. Paula is the author of numerous journal articles and several widely read books including *Avoiding Burnout: Strategies for Managing Time, Space, and People; Living and Learning with Children; A Great Place to Work: Improving Conditions for Staff in Young Children's Programs;* and *Blueprint for Action: Achieving Center-Based Change Through Staff Development.*

Sue Bredekamp is currently Director of Research at the Council for Early Childhood Professional Recognition and is a Senior Advisor to the Head Start Bureau. From 1984 to 1998, she served as Director of Professional Development of the National Association for the Education of Young Children where she developed a national accreditation system for early childhood programs. She is the primary author of NAEYC's best-selling publication *Developmentally Appropriate Practice in Early Childhood Programs*. In addition to her work on defining best practice in programs for young children, Sue coordinated NAEYC activity relevant to teacher education, developing guidelines for associate, baccalaureate, and advanced degrees. Her professional experiences include teaching and directing child care and preschool programs for children ages 2 to 6 as well as work in higher education training teachers. She holds a Ph.D. in Early Childhood Education from the University of Maryland.

Nancy H. Brown has served as teacher, administrator, and supervisor in both the public and private sector and in preschool settings, elementary and secondary schools, and higher education. Nancy holds the Ph.D. from the University of Maryland with a major in early childhood education. Currently she is an independent consultant with a primary focus on career development systems for child care personnel. She provides training to directors and other early childhood personnel. She was the founding director of the U.S. Senate Employees' Child Care Center in Washington, DC. Dr. Brown is active in professional organizations and served as President of the North Carolina Association for the Education of Young Children.

Dorothy W. Hewes is professor emeritus in the Department of Child and Family Development at San Diego State University. Her books and articles were among the first to focus on in-depth analysis of the role of the early childhood center director. Dorothy's publications focus upon management of early childhood programs and the history of educational systems. Her most recent book is *"It's the Camaraderie": A History of Parent Cooperative Preschools* published in 1998. She holds a Ph.D. in History from the Union Institute and her historical analysis has kept the history of the early childhood field alive. She paves the way for others to become historians of early care and education.

Karen Hill-Scott is president of Karen Hill-Scott and Associates, a private consulting firm, which manages projects in children's television programming, corporate work-family initiatives, and public policy analysis. Dr. Hill-Scott has served in various capacities in early care and education programs, from teaching in a Head Start classroom, to managing an agency, to giving testimony before Congress. She was co-founder and Founding Executive Director of Crystal Stairs, Inc. a nonprofit child development agency. She serves on the faculty of the UCLA School of Public Policy and Social Research and is a civic volunteer serving on the boards of local and national nonprofit organizations. In 1998 she was appointed Co-Chair of the California Universal Preschool Task Force. Dr. Hill-Scott holds a Ph.D. from UCLA.

John P. Manning, Ph.D., is the Regional Director for the Massachusetts Office of Child Care Services in Springfield, Massachusetts. He completed his doctorate at the University of Massachusetts concentrating in early childhood administration and public policy. John has taught toddlers, preschoolers, and kindergartners as well as undergraduates in education. He served as a child care licensor, a licensing supervisor and an Assistant Director for the Group Day Care Licensing Program in Massachusetts during which time he visited over 700 different child care centers. He is active in early childhood community policy and practice efforts. He currently serves as a member of the Boston Association for the Education of Young Children (BAEYC) Committee for Administrative Leadership and as the Chair of NAEYC's Licensing Caucus.

Anne Mitchell is the President of Early Childhood Policy Research (ECPR), an independent consulting firm started in 1991. ECPR specializes in evaluation research, policy analysis, and planning on child care/early education issues for government, foundations, and national nonprofit organizations. Previously she was Associate Dean of the Research Division at Bank Street College of Education in New York City. From 1986–89, she co-directed the first national study of public schools as providers of programs for children under six. In 1981, she founded the Bank Street College of Education graduate program in early childhood leadership, drawing on her previous experience directing child care centers in Massachusetts and Vermont. She received her B.S. degree (1972) in astronomy from Wellesley College and her M.S. degree (1988) in early childhood education leadership from Bank Street College of Education.

Gwen G. Morgan is a lecturer at Wheelock College, where she founded and heads up the Center for Career Development in Early Care and Education. Ms. Morgan has been instrumental in developing at Wheelock College some of the first coursework for administrators in child care programs. She is also Senior Child Care Resource Development Consultant for Work/Family Directions (W/FD) Development Corporation, which she founded in 1983 with Fran Rogers. W/FD is a management and consulting firm with large corporate clients. Ms. Morgan has served as a consultant or staff member to a number of child care policy research studies. She began her interest in child care through starting an employer-sponsored center in Cambridge, Massachusetts in 1966. From there she went to the Commonwealth of Massachusetts, where she was Senior Child Care Planner for the state.

Roger Neugebauer, and his wife Bonnie, jointly publish Child Care Information Exchange, a bimonthly management magazine for administrators of early childhood programs. The magazine was launched in 1978 and now has nearly 30,000 subscribers in the United States, Canada, and ten foreign countries. Roger and Bonnie are also the organizers of the World Forum on Early Care and Education, an annual gathering of early childhood practitioners worldwide. Mr. Neugebauer has served on the national governing boards of NAEYC, AWLP, and NACCRRA.

Marsha Poster is the Executive Director of the Cyert Center for Early Education and Program for Collaborative Learning at the Carnegie Mellon University in Pittsburgh, Pennsylvania. The Cyert center is one of the few school facilities in the United States built to support the work of children, educators, and families in dialogue with the Reggio Emilia Approach to Early Care and Education. She received her Ph.D. from the University of Pittsburgh where, in her dissertation research, she was an early investigator of the role of the director of full day early care and education (or child care) programs. Marsha serves as an active advocate and trainer in her community and is a member of the editorial review board of Early Childhood Research and Practice, an internet journal on the development, care and education of young children.

Karen VanderVen, Ph.D., is Professor and Director of the Program in Child Development and Child Care at the University of Pittsburgh. She recently served as Secretary of the National Association of Early Childhood Teacher Educators, and has been a frequent presenter at the National Association for the Education of Young Children's Institute for Professional Development and Annual Conference. Karen has written and presented extensively on career development and administration in early childhood education. She is the Guest Editor of "Making Primary Developmental Work with Children a Profession: The Example of Early Childhood Education," a special issue of the Child and Youth Care Forum Journal.

Index

Burnout
  causes and consequences of,
      190–192
  methods of combating, 191–200
Business approaches
  American Business Collaboration
      for Quality Dependent Care
      (ABC Initiative), 2–3, 164
  continuous improvement, 83
  customer service and, 110, 140
  developing ability, 107–110
  early care and education (ECE), 25–
      27, 33–37, 164
  health and safety regulations, 26–27
  organizational issues and, 82–83,
      87–88, 109
  participative management, 37
  standardization. See Standardization
  total quality management (TQM),
      37, 83
Byler, P., 3

Caffarella, R. S., 71
Cahan, E., 36
California
  Alternative Payment Programs, 215
  California Early Childhood Mentor
      Program, 193–195
  cooperative nursery schools, 30–31
  credentialing by, 13, 14, 158
  prekindergarten programs, 165, 210,
      215
  survey of licensing laws, 32
  TANF child care and, 210
Caplow, Theodore, 98, 108
Career development
  career lattice in, 111, 181–182,
      216–217
  credentialing versus, 144–145,
      147–149
  stages of, 116–120
Caring, 10–11, 24–25, 27, 36–37, 140,
      147
Cartwright, C. A., 9
Caruso, J. J., 81–82
Casper, L. M., 204, 205, 211
Cauman, Judith, 32

Celebreeze, Anthony J., 32
Center for Career Development in
      Early Care and Education
      (Wheelock College), 174, 185, 200,
      213, 218
  materials produced by, 82
  Taking the Lead Initiative, 2, 3, 13–
      17, 148, 166, 177, 201, 218
Center for Early Childhood Leader-
      ship (National Louis University),
      82, 199
Cherniss, Cary C., 190
Child Care Information Exchange (jour-
      nal), 31, 81, 82, 208
Child development
  Bronfenbrenner model of, 117
  impact of early child care on, 3–4
Child Development Associate (CDA)
      certificate, 33, 156, 158, 160, 168 n.
      2, 171–172, 173, 174, 176, 177, 179,
      180
Child Development Training Consor-
      tium, 194
Children's Bureau, 29
Child Welfare League of America, 32,
      34–35
Chira, S., 200
Chodorow, N., 71
Christian Director's Child Develop-
      ment Education Credential, 14,
      163
Citrenbaum, C., 126
Class, Norris E., 47
Clifford, R. M., 3, 195
Clinchy, M., 64, 71, 74
Cohen, D. L., 200
Cohen, N. E., 83, 153, 213, 215
Colorado
  The ART of Teaching, 195
  funding standards, 52
  Head Start parent training, 33
Communicative competence, 81, 85
Community. See also Stakeholders
  acquiring knowledge of, 90
  collaboration with, 46
  core knowledge of, 83–84, 89–91
  reputation of program in, 103